Martin Luther

Dr. Martin Luther's Church-Postil

Martin Luther

Dr. Martin Luther's Church-Postil

ISBN/EAN: 9783337127145

Printed in Europe, USA, Canada, Australia, Japan

Cover: Foto ©Lupo / pixelio.de

More available books at **www.hansebooks.com**

DR. MARTIN LUTHER'S
CHURCH-POSTIL.

SERMONS ON THE EPISTLES:

FOR THE

DIFFERENT SUNDAYS AND FESTIVALS IN THE YEAR.

Translated from the German.

NEW MARKET, VA.
NEW MARKET EVANGELICAL LUTHERAN PUBLISHING COMPANY
1869.
HENKEL & CALVERT, Printers.

Copy-right secured according to law.

PREFACE.

Dr. Martin Luther's Church-Postil, comprising Sermons on the Gospels and Epistles for the different Sundays and Festivals in the year, is, in the language of Dr. Plochmar, in his preface to the Church-Postil, designated by Luther himself as THE BEST WORK HE EVER PRODUCED. Its origin is found in the great want of sermons for the common reader. In the beginning of the Reformation, this want was deeply felt by Luther and his friends. Except the Sermons of Taular and Geiler of Keiserberg, there were no sermons extant, in print. For the most part, the Epistles and Gospels were simply read in the churches, the greater number of the clergy of that day being scarcely capable of explaining them to the people. For the purpose of supplying this want, and of placing in the hands of the ministers themselves a model for the proper explanation of those Biblical pericopes or lessons, Luther resolved upon the publication of his Church-Postil. A further inducement was held out by Frederick the Wise, Elector of Saxony, who encouraged Luther in this work, partly for the purpose of building up the pure Christian Church, and partly for the purpose of drawing this precious man away from the unhappy controversies, in which his pen had been engaged during the first years of the Reformation.

The Postil was commenced in the Latin language, and the Sermons on the four Sundays in Advent appeared in 1521, in Wittemburg. The German work was commenced at Wartburg, whither, on his return from Worms, at the instance of the Elector of Saxony, Luther was conducted under profound secrecy.

These sermons performed an important part in the great work of the Reformation. For, while the confessional and doctrinal writings enlightened the understandings of the people, these sermons reached and penetrated their hearts, inciting and exhorting them to action.

The Christian Book of Concord, or Symbolical Books of the Evangelical Lutheran Church, Luther on the Sacraments, and other works of a DOCTRINAL character, published in the English language, have exerted a wholesome and salutary influence in the Church, especially in regard to her doctrinal stand-point.

A work, emanating from the illustrious Reformer, more PRACTICAL and PASTORAL in its design, adapted to the popular reader, in the English language, will at this time, we make no doubt, be of incalculable value and interest to the Church. Dr. Luther's Sermons on the Epistles, contained in the Church-Postil, are, in our view, pre-eminently a work of this character.

The want of an orthodox, practical work, sanctioned by the great Reformer, is as deeply felt, perhaps, at this period, under the present aspect of the Church, as it was in the days of the Reformation.

St. Paul,—Rom. 12, 7, 8,—says Dr. Luther, divides the office of the minister into two parts, DOCTRINE and ADMONITION. Both these should be urged. Both are necessary in the successful up-building of the Church. The wants of the Church have been supplied to a greater or less extent, in regard to the former, by the publication of those doctrinal works, in the English language; and perhaps, her wants in reference to the latter, will be partially met by the appearance of these Sermons in an English dress.

We presume, therefore, that every zealous member of the Church, every Protestant, will hail with pleasure these venerable productions of the Reformation, in the English, especially at this time, when a healthful re-action is taking place in the Church, when her tendency is towards her authorized works, and a deeper interest is felt in them.

The Sermons on the Epistles naturally and properly succeed the publication of those works, which are more didactic in their nature, and which have been so extensively circulated. They seem to be demanded by the necessity of the times, rather than those on the Gospels.

PREFACE.

At the earnest solicitation of many zealous members of the Church, we determined to publish, in the English language, the Sermons on the Epistles, contained in the Church-Postil, in monthly numbers.

The translation was prepared under the superintendence of DR. S. G. HENKEL, who, in order to secure a faithful translation, engaged the talents of men familiar with the German and English languages, as well as with the doctrines of the Church. The translation was made from the German edition of 1827, published at Erlangan, by Dr. J. G. PLOCHMAN. In this work the Epistle Sermons appear in three volumes. The first volume, in a version purely literal, was furnished by Rev. AMBROSE HENKEL; the second volume was translated in the same manner, by Rev. J. R. MOSER, and the third, by Rev. H. WETZEL.

These translations when collected, were carefully compared with the original German, revised, transcribed, and prepared for the press, by Rev. SOCRATES HENKEL.

Although the texts of the Epistles do not appear in print, in the Erlangan edition from which the translation was made, and as it is destitute of head-lines, it was deemed proper, for the convenience of the reader, to introduce them into the English. The head-lines were translated from Walch's edition.

It was also thought necessary to retain the foot-notes as arranged by Dr. Plochman in his edition. By these notes, according to his statement in his preface, he indicates the various readings of the different editions which appeared during the life of Dr. Luther. These he arranged, he says, under three classes, and designated the various readings by the several classes, under the letters, A, B, C. Under the letter A, are included the editions from 1522 to 1540; under B, the edition of 1543, by Dr. Creutziger, under C, the issues by Spener, Bœrner, and Walch.

The introduction of a word or phrase designed to complete the sense, or required by the structure of the English language, is usually indicated by ([]) brackets.

In the preparation of this work for the press, it was deemed most compatible with its nature, to preserve as just and uniform medium as possible, between a translation strictly literal, and one that admits the freedom and elegance of English style, and to preserve as far as possible the serious tone and spirit, as well as the simplicity of the style and figures, of the pious original. The object was to present a correct and faithful translation.

These Sermons in an English dress, we trust will, in the hands of Providence, accomplish much good in building up the Redeemer's Kingdom, and we pray that they may be accompanied with the same Divine blessings, which rendered them in the original language so profitable to the Church.

THE PUBLISHERS.

NEW MARKET, SHENANDOAH CO., VA.

DR. LUTHER'S CHURCH-POSTIL.

SERMONS ON THE EPISTLES.

ROMANS XIII, 11-14.

FIRST SUNDAY IN ADVENT.

EPISTLE, ROMANS 13, 11-14.

And that, knowing the time, that now it is high time to awake out of sleep: for now is our salvation nearer than when we believed.

The night is far spent, the day is at hand: let us therefore cast off the works of darkness, and let us put on the armor of light.

Let us walk honestly, as in the day; not in rioting and drunkenness, not in chambering and wantonness, not in strife and envying.

But put ye on the Lord Jesus Christ, and make not provision for the flesh, to fulfil the lusts thereof.

THIS EPISTLE does not treat of faith, but of the works and fruits of faith, showing how a Christian should live externally among men on earth, in regard to his body. For, how we should walk in the spirit and before God, faith teaches; of which St. Paul writes and treats in a very copious and apostolic manner in the language preceding this Epistle. If we examine this Epistle properly, we find that it is not occupied in teaching, but in inciting, exhorting, urging, and awakening those who already know what they should do. For St. Paul, Rom. 12, 7, 8, divides the office of the minister into two parts, *doctrinam et exhortationem*, doctrine and exhortation. Doctrine consists in preaching that which is not generally known, instructing or enlightening the people; *exhortation*, in inciting and urging persons to that which they already well understand. Both parts necessarily claim the attention of a minister, and hence, both are employed by St. Paul.

In order, therefore, that this admonition may be the more pleasing and impressive, he employs many beautiful, figurative terms, making an elegant, flowery address. He introduces the words *sleep, darkness, light, awake, armor, work, day,* and *night*; these are purely figurative words, through which something different from their literal and natural import is conveyed. For he speaks not, indeed, of natural night, day, darkness, light, awakening, sleep, armor, and works; but he portrays for us through these natural media a simile, by which he incites and leads us into our spiritual element. As if he should say: you see that, on account of temporal advantages, persons rise from sleep, lay aside the work of darkness, and assume the work of day, when the night has passed by, and the day appeared; how much more, then, should we awake from our sleep, cast off the works of our darkness, and enter upon the works of our light, since our night has passed away, and our day has broken forth.

By *sleep*, he means the works of wickedness and unbelief. For sleep is a work which properly takes place in the night, and he thus explains himself, when he says: "Let us cast off the works of darkness." Thus again, *awakening* and *rising up* denote the works of faith and piety. For *rising* is properly a work of the morning and day, concerning which he also says, 1 Thess. 5, 4–10: "But ye, brethren, are not in darkness. * * Ye are all children of light, and the children of the day: we are not of the night, nor of darkness. Therefore let us not sleep, as do others; but let us watch and be sober. For they that sleep, sleep in the night; and they that be drunken, are drunken in the night. But let us, who are of the day, be sober, putting on the breast-plate of faith and love; and for an helmet, the hope of salvation. For God hath not appointed us to wrath, but to obtain salvation by our Lord Jesus Christ, who died for us, that whether we wake or sleep, we should live together with him."

Here it is evident that he does not forbid natural sleep, and yet he employs the comparison between natural sleep and wakefulness in elucidation of spiritual sleep and wakefulness; that is, pious and impious life. In short, *rising up from sleep* is equivalent to his declaration, Tit. 2, 11–13: "For the grace of God that bringeth salvation, hath appeared to all men. Teaching us, that denying ungodliness and worldly lusts, we should live soberly, righteously, and godly, in this present world; looking for that blessed hope, and the glorious appearing of the great God and our Saviour Jesus Christ." The denying of ungodliness and worldly lusts, he calls here, rising from sleep; and the sober, righteous, godly life, he calls here, waking and putting on the armor of light. The appearing of grace is the day and the light; as we shall hear.

Now observe the comparison between natural and spiritual sleep. He who sleeps, neither sees nor feels any of the things or realities, which are upon the earth, and round about him. He lies in the midst of these things as a dead, useless person, who has neither use nor care for any thing; and although he lives in himself, yet he is, as it were, dead to all things. Instead, moreover, of real things, he is occupied in his dreams with mere images and useless forms of realities, and he is so foolish as to think they are truly realities; but when he awakes, these dreamy illusions fall away and vanish. He then begins to be occupied with real things, excluding all images.

Thus, too, spiritually. The individual who lives in ungodliness, sleeps, and is, as it were, dead before God, neither seeing nor feeling the real spiritual blessings, offered and promised to him through the Gospel, regarding them as vain and useless. For these blessings can be seen only by faith in the heart, being yet concealed. Still, however, he mingles in temporal, transitory things, luxuries and honors, which, in contrast with eternal life, joy, and happiness, are to be regarded as dreamy images compared to natural, physical creatures.

When he awakes, and obtains faith, all these transitory things will vanish, and show how futile they are; concerning which it is said* :—Ps. 73, 20: "As a dream when one awaketh; so, O Lord, when thou awakest, thou shalt despise their image;" and Isa. 29, 8: "It shall even be as when an hungry man dreameth, and, behold he eateth; but he awaketh, and his soul is empty; or as when a thirsty man dreameth, and, behold, he drinketh; but he awaketh, and, behold, he is faint, and his soul hath appetite: so shall the multitude of all the nations be, that fight against mount Zion."

Behold, now is it not entirely too contemptuous, to compare this world's highest power, riches, pleasure, and honor, to a dream and dreamy images. Who dares to say that kings, princes, wealth, possessions, pleasure, and power, are the creatures of a dream, when there is so much raging and raving after them on earth? It is because men sleep, and do not rise up and see this light in faith.

"For now is our salvation nearer than when we believed."

What is implied by this? Did we believe before, or do we not believe now? Here it is necessary to know, as St. Paul, Rom. 1, 2, 3, says, that through his prophets God promised in the Holy Scripture, the Gospel of his Son Jesus Christ, our Lord, that through him all the world should be saved, as the words, Gen. 22, 18, to Abraham, read: "In thy seed shall

---

* A. Ps. 76, 5: "The stout-hearted are spoiled, they have slept their sleep; and none of the men of might have found their hands."

all the nations of the earth be blessed." This blessing promised here to Abraham in his seed, is nothing else but the grace and salvation in Christ, presented through the Gospel to all the world, as St. Paul, Rom. 4 and Gal. 4, also declares. For Christ is the seed of Abraham, that is, his natural flesh and blood, in whom all, who believe and call on him, will be blessed.

This promise of God was afterwards more carefully set forth and widely circulated by the prophets, and all of them wrote concerning the advent of Christ, his grace and Gospel, as St. Peter, Acts 3, 18–24, says. This same divine promise was believed by all the saints before the birth of Christ, and thus in and through the Christ yet to come, they were preserved and saved by this faith; so that even Christ, Luke 16, 22, calls this promise Abraham's bosom, into which all the saints from Abraham to Christ were gathered. Now, this is what St. Paul means, when he says: "Our salvation is nearer than when we believed." As if he should say: The promise of God, made to Abraham, is now no more to be awaited in the future; it is fulfilled; Christ is come; the Gospel has arisen, and the blessing is distributed through all the world; and now all that we waited for and believed in the promise, is here. By this the apostle has described the *spiritual day*, concerning which he afterwards speaks, and which is properly the *rising* and the *light* of the *Gospel*; as we shall hear.

But faith is not, therefore, abolished, but rather established. For even as men formerly believed in the promise of God, that it would be fulfilled; so we believe on the same promise of God, that it is now fulfilled; one faith is like the other, in itself, except that one succeeds the other, like the promise and the fulfillment succeed each other; For they are both based on the seed of Abraham, that is, on Christ, the one preceding and the other succeeding his advent. For he who would now believe, like the Jews, that Christ is yet to come, as if the promise were not yet fulfilled, would be condemned, because he would make God a liar, pretending that he has not yet fulfilled his promise, which, however, he has fulfilled. Thus our salvation would still be far from us, and we would have to wait for it yet in the future.

Concerning these two faiths Paul, Rom. 1, 17, says: "In the Gospel is the righteousness of God revealed from faith to faith." What is meant by the expression: "From faith to faith?" Nothing else but,—although the faith of the fathers and our faith are one and the same, trusting in Christ yet to come, and in Christ who has already come, still the Gospel leads us from that faith to this faith,—that now it is necessary to believe, not only the promise, but also the fulfillment already made, which Abraham and the ancients had not then to believe, although they had the same Christ that we have. One faith, one spirit, one Christ, one community of all saints, except that they preceded, and we succeed Christ.

Thus we, (that is, the fathers with us,) have, in the same common faith, believed in one Christ, and still believe in him, but in a different condition. And as, for the sake of the common faith and of Christ, we say, when the fathers believed, that we have believed, although we did not live in their time; so, on the other hand, they say, when we hear, see, and believe Christ, that they hear, see, and believe him, although they do not live in our day. For David thus speaks, Ps. 8, 3: "When I consider thy heavens, the work of thy fingers*;" again, Ps. 9, 2: "I will be glad, and rejoice in thee: I will sing praise to thy name, O thou Most High;" and in many other similar passages; so that one person is taken for, or assumes another, in consequence of the common faith, through which they have Christ in the midst of them and become one body.

His declaration, "Our salvation is nearer than when we believed," can not be understood of nearness of possession or occupancy. For the fathers had the same faith, and even the same Christ, that we have, and he

---

* A. That is, the Apostles, (B.) and yet he did not live to do it.

was equally as near to them as he is to us; as Heb. 13, 8, says: "Jesus Christ the same yesterday, and to-day, and for ever;" that is, Christ has been from the beginning of the world to the end, and through and in him all are preserved. To him that believes most, he is nearest, and from him that believes least, salvation is farthest, so far as possession and occupancy are concerned. But St. Paul has reference here to the nearness of the manifestation [of this salvation.] Since, in the days of Christ, the promise was fulfilled, and the Gospel arose in all the world, and appeared, and was publicly preached through him to all men, the Apostle says "our salvation is nearer" than when it lay concealed in the promise and was not developed. Thus it is said, Tit. 2, 11: "For the grace of God, that bringeth salvation, hath appeared;" that is, it has arisen and is publicly preached; although all the saints who lived previous to this appearing of that grace, were likewise in possession of it.

The Scripture teaches, therefore, that Christ shall come, notwithstanding he has already been in all the fathers. He did not come to all, however, through public preaching, until after his resurrection from the dead. Of this coming, or advent the Scripture mostly speaks, in consequence of which he also came bodily in the human nature. For his becoming man would have benefited no one if a gospel had not resulted from it, through which he might be presented to all the world, and through which it might be made known why he became man; so that the promised blessing might be imparted to all who through the Gospel believe in him. Hence St. Paul, Rom. 1, 2, says; that the Gospel was promised of God. As if he would say: God was more concerned about the Gospel and this public coming or advent through the word, than about the bodily birth or advent in the human nature. He was occupied with the Gospel and our faith; he therefore permitted his son to become man, so that the Gospel might be preached concerning him, and thus, through the revealed word, his salvation might draw near and come to all the world.

Some have presented four different advents of Christ, according to the four Sundays in Advent. But the one, which is the most useful, upon which all the efficacy depends, and concerning which St. Paul here speaks, they did not perceive. For they do not know what gospel is, or why and for what purpose it was given. They talk much about the advent of Christ, and yet they drive him farther from us than heaven is from earth. Of what use is Christ, if he is not embraced by faith? But how can he be embraced by faith where the Gospel is not preached?

"The night is far spent, the day is at hand."

This is equivalent to saying our salvation is near. For by the word *day* Paul means the *Gospel*, which is a day that enlightens the hearts or souls; therefore, since the day has broken forth, our salvation is near to us; that is, Christ and his grace promised to Abraham, have now arisen; are preached in all the world; they enlighten all men; they awaken us all from sleep, and show us the true, eternal blessings; so that we may be occupied with them, and walk honorably in the day. By the word *night*, however, we must understand all *doctrines which are not the Gospel*; for there is no saving doctrine but that of the Gospel; all else is night and darkness.

Observe the words of Paul. He describes the most lovely and cheerful part of the day; namely, the lovely, joyful dawn, and rising of the sun. For the dawn is the time, at which the night has passed away and disappeared, and the day has broken forth. Then we see, in consequence of the dawn, all the birds singing, all the beasts moving, and all human beings lifting themselves up; so that when the day breaks and the redness of the sky appears, it seems as if the world were new and all things were re-animated. Therefore, in many portions of the Scripture, the consolatory, vivifying preaching of the Gospel, is compared to the dawn, and to the rising of the sun, sometimes under figures, sometimes in plain language; as, here, Paul in plain terms styles the Gospel the breaking day.*

This day, the most lovely sun, Jesus Christ, produces. Hence Malachi calls him Sun of righteousness, saying, ch. 4, v. 2: "But unto you that fear my name shall the Sun of righteousness arise with healing in his wings." For all who believe in Christ, receive from him the brightness of his grace, and righteousness, and shall be happy under his wings. In the 118th Ps. v. 24, it is also said: "This is the day which the Lord hath made; we will rejoice and be glad in it." As if he should say: the natural sun makes the natural day, but the Lord himself, this day. He is the sun himself, from whom the brightness and the day, that is, the Gospel, proceed, and shine in all the world. John 9, 5: "I am the light of the world."

Ps. 19, 1, both, the sun and the day, Christ and the Gospel, are described in the most lovely manner: "The heavens declare the glory of God;" that is, like the natural heavens show forth the sun and the day, and as the sun is in the heavens; so in their preaching, the Apostles present and introduce the real Sun, Christ; and then follows: "In them hath he set a tabernacle for the sun; which is as a bridegroom coming out of his chamber, and rejoiceth as a strong man to run a race. His going forth is from the end of the heaven, and his circuit unto the ends of it; and there is nothing hid from the heat thereof." All this is spoken of this lovely breaking of the day, that is, of the Gospel, which the Scripture extols in a high and lovely manner; for it produces life, joy, pleasure, energy, and brings with itself all that is good; it is therefore also called Gospel, that is, joyful news.

Who can enumerate, however, what this *day* reveals to us? It teaches us all things,—what God is, what we are, what has passed, what is to come, in regard to heaven, to hell, earth, angels, devils. Here we see how we should demean ourselves in regard to all these things,—whence we are, and whither we are going. Yet the devil has so deceived us that we forsake the day, and seek truth from philosophers and heathens who never knew a solitary thing about all this, and, permitting ourselves to be blinded by human doctrines, we return to the night. Whatever is not this day, cannot indeed be light. Otherwise St. Paul and all the Scripture would not urge this day alone and pronounce all else night.

Our disposition to seek, in opposition to declarations of Scripture so clear and express, secondary lights. when the Lord himself declares that he is the light and sun of the world, must result from the displeasure of Providence, which we have incurred; and were there no other indications, by which we might know that the high schools of the Pope are the most abominable harlotries and knaveries of the devil, the fact alone indeed would be abundantly sufficient, that they so shamelessly introduce and extol Aristotle as a secondary light, and that they exercise themselves more in him than in Christ; nay, they exercise themselves, not in Christ, but wholly in Aristotle.

"Let us therefore cast off the works of darkness, and let us put on the armor of light."

Precisely as Christ is the sun, and the Gospel is the day, so faith is the light or medium of sight and wakefulness on this day. For it profits us nothing for the sun to shine, and make the day, if our eyes do not perceive the light. Therefore, although the Gospel has arisen, and preaches Christ in all the world, none are enlightened by it, except those who receive it, and have risen from sleep through the light of faith. But to the sleeping the sun and the day are useless; for from these they receive no light, and see as little as if there were neither sun nor day. Now is the time and the hour, of which he says: "Beloved breth-

---

* A Again, Ps. 110, 3: "Thy people shall be willing in the day of thy power, in the beauties of holiness from the womb of the morning, thou hast the dew of thy youth." Here the Gospel is clearly called womb of the morning, and day of the power of Christ, in which, like the dew, we are conceived and born children of Christ, without the works of man, from heaven and through the grace of the Holy Spirit.

ren, that knowing the time, that now it is high time to awake out of sleep," &c. Although it is a spiritual time and hour, it has arisen in natural time, and still daily arises; in which we must rise up from sleep and lay aside the works of darkness, &c. Thus St. Paul shows that he is not speaking to those who are yet in unbelief. For, as already said, he does not teach the doctrine of faith here, but the works and fruits of faith. He says they know that the time is here, the night is past, and the day has broken forth.

But if you ask, what need have these of such an epistle? It has been already stated that there are two kinds of preaching: one, which teaches; the other which incites and exhorts. Now, no one ever knows so much as to make it unnecessary to admonish him, and continually to urge him to fresh meditations on that which he already knows, in order that the devil, the world, and the flesh, his unceasing enemies, may not render him weary and negligent, and ultimately careless, and thus lull him to sleep. For St. Peter, 1 Epist. 5, 8, says:— "Your adversary, the devil, as a roaring lion walketh about, seeking whom he may devour;" therefore says he: "Be sober, be vigilant." Here too the design of St. Paul, is that, since the devil, the world, and the flesh cease not to assail us, there should be no cessation in exhorting, inciting and impelling to vigilance and activity.*

For this reason St. Paul likewise arranges his language so appropriately. He calls, not the works of darkness, but the works of light, *armor*, and not *works*. Why this? Without doubt, to show that in maintaining proper vigilance and a pious life, conflicts, pains, labor, and danger will be incurred, since these three powerful enemies, the devil, the world, and the flesh, incessantly oppose us day and night. Hence Job, ch. 7, v. 1, says, that the life of man on earth is strife and contention.

Now, it is by no means a light matter, to stand continually in battle-array during our whole life. Hence it is necessary, indeed, to have good trumpets and bugles; that is, such preaching and exhortation as will enable us valiantly to maintain our position in the battle. Good works are armors; evil works are not; unless we conform to them, and allow them to control us. If so, they likewise become armors; as St. Paul, Rom. 6, 13, says: "Yield not your members as instruments of unrighteousness unto sin." As if he should say: Let not the works of darkness so overcome you as to render your members instruments of unrighteousness.

Now, it has already been sufficiently stated that here by the word *light faith* is implied, which shines from the day of the Gospel, out of the sun, Christ, into our hearts; hence the *armors* of *light* are nothing else but the *works of faith*. *Darkness*, on the other hand, is *unbelief*, reigning in the absence of the Gospel and of Christ, through the doctrines of men and their own reason, instigated by the devil. The *works of darkness* are, therefore, the *works of unbelief*; for even as Christ is a Lord and Ruler of that brilliant faith, so, as St. Paul, Eph. 6, 12, says, the devil is a ruler of this darkness; that is, over unbelievers; as 2 Cor. 4, 3, 4, he also says: "But if our gospel be hid, it is hid to them that are lost: in whom the God of this world," (that is, the devil,) "hath blinded the minds of them which believe not, lest the light of the glorious gospel of Christ * * should shine unto them." The character of these two different works, however, will hereafter appear.

"Let us walk honestly, as in the day."

In the day, the works of darkness are not performed; one is ashamed of another, and conducts himself honorably. The expression, the night is shameless, is proverbial; and it is true. Therefore, the works of which we would be ashamed in the day, are performed in the night. But the day is shame-faced, and constrains us to an honorable walk. A Christian should, therefore, so live and conduct himself that all his works may be of

---

* A Hence the Holy Spirit is called *Paracletus*, a comforter, who incites and urges on to good.

such a character as never to cause him to be ashamed of them, although all the world should see them. For he that so lives and acts as to be unwilling for his deeds to be seen or heard, openly before every one, lives certainly not in a Christian manner. Of this, John 3, 20, Christ speaks: "For every one that doeth evil, hateth the light, neither cometh to the light, lest his deeds should be reproved. But he that doeth truth cometh to the light, that his deeds may be manifest that they are wrought in God."

Hence you perceive the great necessity of this incitation and exhortation to be vigilant and to put on the armor of light. How many Christians are there at the present time, who could bear for all their works to come to the day? But what kind of a Christian life do we hypocrites lead, that we cannot bear for our conduct to be exposed to men, which, however, is already exposed to God, his angels, and all his creatures, and, on the last day, shall be exposed to every one? A Christian should, therefore, live as he would be found in the last day and before all men; Eph. 5, 9: "Walk as children of light; for the fruit of the Spirit is in all goodness and righteousness and truth;" and Rom. 12, 17: "Provide things honest," not only in the sight of God, but also, "in the sight of all men." Again, 2 Cor. 1, 12: "For our rejoicing is this, the testimony of our conscience, that in simplicity and godly sincerity, not with fleshly wisdom, * * we have had our conversation in the world."

But such a life indeed cannot be perpetuated where faith does not exist, since this vigilant, active, valiant faith has enough to do to continue in such a life, without falling asleep or growing weary. As necessary, therefore, as it is to preach doctrine to the illiterate, so necessary is it to exhort the literate, so that they may not fall off from their incipient good life, through the assaults of the raging flesh, the subtle world, and the treacherous devil.

"Not in rioting and drunkenness, not in chambering and wantonness, not in strife and envying."

Here he enumerates the works of darkness by name, one of which he calls *sleep*, in the commencement of this discourse; as, 1 Thess. 5, 6, it is written: "Let us not sleep as do others; but let us watch and be sober." Not that he forbids natural sleep, but spiritual, which consists in unbelief, from which the works of darkness result; although natural sleep is a work, too, of darkness, if indulged in through lust and inebriety,* to the obstruction of the light and its armor. *These six works of darkness* include all others; such as are enumerated in Gal. 5, 19, 20, 21, and Col. 3, 5, 8. We shall briefly divide them into two classes, the one upon the right, the other upon the left. Upon the right side, these four, *rioting, drunkenness, chambering, and wantonness,*† are arrayed; on the left, *strife* and *envying*. For in the Scripture the left side signifies adversity, and all that results from adversity; as, *wrath, envying*, &c. The right side means prosperity, and all that results from prosperity; as *rioting, drunkenness, lust, indolence*.

It is certain, therefore, that St. Paul wishes to include under these two works of darkness, *strife* and *envying*, all others of similar character; as those enumerated in Eph. 4, 31: "Let all bitterness, and wrath, and anger, and clamor, and evil-speaking be put away from you, with all malice;" and in Gal. 5, 20: "Now the works of the flesh are hatred, variance, emulation, wrath, strife, seditions, heresies, envyings, murder," &c., and, in a word, all the evils so innumerable, which may result from wrath, in words and actions.

Thus, too, under these four vices, *rioting, drunkenness, indolence,* and *lewdness*, he includes all the vices of unchastity in words and actions, which no one would desire to enumerate; so that by these six enumerated works it is briefly understood that the individual who lives, under darkness, in unbelief, does not keep himself pure before his neighbor, but is inordinate in all his actions in regard to himself

---

* B. Through indolence and excessive inebriety, and † (A) drunkenness and unchastity.

and his fellow-man. Further comments, these words, indeed, need not; every one knows well what rioting and drunkenness, or excessive eating and drinking, more for the gratification of the appetite, than for the nourishment of the body, mean. Again, there is no difficulty in understanding what is meant by idleness in beds and chambers, by lewdness and unchastity; that is, the indulgence of the lusts and appetites of the flesh, by excessive sleeping and indolence, by every species of unchastity and carnality, committed in beds, by the satiated, indolent, drowsy, and lazy, whether in the day or night, in bed or elsewhere, alone or in company,—vices, all of which also seek natural darkness and secret places, and which St. Paul expresses by the words chambering and wantonness; and so, too, strife, envying, &c., are generally understood.

"But put ye on the Lord Jesus Christ."

Here he embraces and exhibits in a few words all the *armors of light*, when he admonishes us *to put on Christ*. Christ is put on in two ways. *First*, when we clothe ourselves with his own virtues; this is effected through the faith which relies on the fact that Christ died and accomplished all things for us. For, not our righteousness, but the righteousness of Christ, reconciled us to God, and redeemed us from sin. This mode of putting on Christ belongs to the doctrine which teaches faith; and in this way Christ is given to us as a gift and a pledge.*

Secondly, he is our *example* and *pattern*, which we should follow and like which we should become, clothing ourselves even in the virtuous garment, in which he walked. Hence St. Paul says we should put on Christ. Again, 1 Cor. 15, 49: "As we have borne the image of the earthly, we shall also bear the image of the heavenly;" and Eph. 4, 22, 23, 24: "That ye put off concerning the former conversation the old man, which is corrupt according to the deceitful lusts; and be renewed in the spirit of your mind; and that ye put on the new man, which after God is created in righteousness and true holiness."

Now, *in Christ* we perceive nothing but pure *armors of light*. Here there is no gormandizing, or drunkenness, but fasting, moderation, and restraint of the flesh, through labor, active exertion, preaching, praying, and doing good for mankind; here there is no indolence, apathy, or unchastity, but true discipline, purity, chastity, vigilance, wakefulness, sleeping in fields, having neither house, nor chamber, nor bed; here there is no wrath, strife, or envying, but pure goodness, sweetness, love, mercy, patience, &c. In order, therefore, to present Christ in a few words, as an example, St. Paul says in the words, Col. 3, 12, 15: "Put on therefore, as the elect of God, holy and beloved, bowels of mercies, kindness, humbleness of mind, meekness, long-suffering; forbearing one another, and forgiving one another, if any man have a quarrel against any: even as Christ forgave you, so also do ye. And above all these things put on charity, which is the bond of perfectness."* Again, in Phil. 2, 2, after commanding them to love one another, and serve, and be the servants of one another, he also presents as an example, this same Christ who became a servant for us, saying: "Let this mind be in you, which was also in Christ Jesus: who being in the form of God, thought it not robbery to be equal with God; but made himself of no reputation, and took upon him the form of a servant, and was made in the likeness of men: and being found in fashion as a man."

Now, in short, the *armors of light* are *good works* in opposition to rioting, drunkenness, lechery, and indolence, strife and envying; such as, fasting, watchfulness, prayer, labor, chastity, modesty, temperance, goodness, endurance of hunger, thirst, cold, heat; and not to employ my own words, let us hear St. Paul himself in

---

* B. In regard to this, more will be said in the Epistle for New Year's day, Gal. 3, 27:— "For as many of you as have been baptized into Christ, have put on Christ."

* A. And let the peace of God rule in your hearts, to the which also ye are called in one body; and be ye thankful."

his own enumeration of them, Gal. 5, 22: "The fruit of the Spirit is love, joy, peace, long-suffering, gentleness, goodness, faith, meekness," &c. But still more abundantly does he enumerate them, in 2 Cor. 6, 1–10: "We * * beseech you also that you receive not the grace of God in vain. (For he saith, I have heard thee in a time accepted, and in the day of salvation have I succored thee; behold, now is the accepted time; behold, now is the day of salvation,") as if he should say: For now is our salvation nearer than when we believed, and now is the time to awake out of sleep; " Giving no offence in any thing, that the ministry be not blamed: but in all things approving ourselves as the ministers of God, in much patience, in affliction, in necessities, in distresses, in stripes, in imprisonments, in tumults, in labors, in watchings, in fastings, by pureness, by knowledge, by longsuffering, by kindness, by the Holy Ghost, by love unfeigned, by the word of truth, by the power of God, by the armor of righteousness on the right hand and on the left, by honor and dishonor, by evil report and good report; as deceivers, and yet true; as unknown and yet well known; as dying, and, behold, we live; as chastened, and not killed; as sorrowful, yet always rejoicing; as poor, yet making many rich; as having nothing, and yet possessing all things." Behold, what a fertile stream flows from the lips of St. Paul. Here you perceive abundantly enough which are the armors of light, on the left hand and on the right. *This is truly putting on Jesus Christ.*

It is, however, a very important circumstance that in this epistle the highest example, the Lord himself, is presented, when it is said: "Put on the Lord." This is a strong incentive. For the individual that can see his master fasting, and enduring hunger, labor, watchfulness, and fatigue, and at the same time be feasting and regaling himself, lolling and sleeping, and living in luxury, must be a scoundrel. What master could allow such conduct in his servant? Or what servant would dare to undertake it? It cannot be otherwise, we must blush when we behold Christ, and see that we are so very unlike him.

Who will incite and impel to action him who will not be warmed, exhorted, and incited by Christ's own example? What shall the leaves and words accomplish by their rustling, when this thunder-clap of Christ's example does not move us? Therefore St. Paul added especially the word, *Lord*, and said: " Put on the Lord Jesus Christ;" as if he should say; ye who are servants, think not yourselves great and exalted; look upon your Lord who himself, though under no obligation, thus acted.

"And make not provision for the flesh,* to fulfill the lusts thereof."

Here in a few words St. Paul mentions *two different cares* or *provisions for the flesh*. *The one* is *natural*, providing for the body food and raiment necessary to sustain life and vigor, so that the body may not by too many deprivations be enfeebled and unfitted for labor.

The other is sinful, gratifying the lusts and excessive appetites. This one St. Paul here forbids. For from it works of darkness result. For the flesh must be so constrained as to serve, and to be subservient to the spirit, and not to dismount its master, but to go on and carry him if necessary. Sirach, ch. 33, 25, says: "A sack of food and a rod are necessary for the ass, and food, a scourge, and labor for the servant." He does not say that you should mistreat or maim the ass; nor does he say that you should abuse or imprison the servant. Thus, to the body belong, subjection, labor, and all that is essential to its proper subsistence; and St. Paul himself says: "I keep under my body, and bring it into subjection." He does not say: I bring it into sickness or death, but to serve in submission to the spirit.

This addition St. Paul made on account of two classes of people. The one are those who, under the appearance of natural necessity, indulge and gratify their lusts and fancies; and this misconception is so easy to fall in.

* H. So that it becomes lewd.

to, that many saints have complained of it, and, in opposition to it, have often too much restrained their bodies. Nature is so subtle and deceptive in regard to its demands and lusts, that no one can sufficiently secure it, but must live here amidst cares and insecurity. The others are blinded saints who imagine that the kingdom of God and his righteousness consist in meats and drinks, garments and couches, which they choose; they look no further than at the work, and imagine that, if they so fast that their heads become frantic, or their stomachs disordered, or their bodies emaciated, they have done well. Concerning this, Paul, 1 Cor. 8, 8, says: "Meat commendeth us not to God: for neither, if we eat, are we the better; neither, if we eat not, are we the worse;" again, Col. 2, 18, 23: "Let no man beguile you of your reward, in a voluntary humility and worshipping of angels, * * * which things have indeed a show of wisdom in will-worship, and humility, and neglecting of the body; not in any honor to the satisfying of the flesh."

Gerson commends the Carthusians for not eating meat, even when debility renders it necessary, although they should die for the want of it. Thus this great man was deceived by this superstitious, angelic spirituality. How, if God judges them as murderers of their own bodies? Indeed, no orders, statutes, or vows contrary to the command of God, can be made; and if they should be, they avail nothing, as little as if you would vow to break your marriage contract. Now, indeed, here through St. Paul, God has forbidden such murder of our own bodies; and it is our duty to allow the body whatever is necessary for it, whether wine, meat, eggs, or any thing else, whether it be on Friday or Sunday, in Lent, or after the feast of Easter, regardless of all orders, traditions, and vows.* No prohibition contrary to the command of God can avail, though all the angels should make it.

This wretched folly arises, however, from darkness and blindness, when they look upon works themselves, as if they would be saved by the magnitude and multiplicity of them. St. Paul wishes to make *armors* of *light* out of them, and to use them so as to overcome the works of darkness; so far, then, and no further, should fasting, vigilance, and labor be employed. Therefore, in the sight of God, nothing at all depends on the fact that you eat fish or meat, drink water or wine, wear red or green, or do this or that. They are all good creations of God, created to be used. You should only be careful, then, to be temperate in them, and to abstain from them so far as it is necessary for you to overcome the works of darkness. Hence, it is impossible to give a common rule for this abstinence; for all bodies are not alike constituted: one needs more, another less; every one must judge for himself, and regulate his body according to the declaration of Paul:— "Make not provision for the flesh, to fulfil the lusts thereof." If there had been any other rule to give, St. Paul would not have omitted it here.

Hence you see that these ecclesiastical traditions which flatly forbid the eating of meat, are contrary to the Gospel, and predicted by Paul, 1 Tim. 4, 1, 2, 3, where he says: "Now the Spirit speaketh expressly, that in the latter times some shall depart from the faith, giving heed to seducing spirits, and doctrines of devils; speaking lies in hypocrisy; having their own conscience seared with a hot iron: forbidding to marry, and commanding to abstain from meats, which God hath created, to be received with thanksgiving." That these words have a reference to the orders of the ecclesiastics and the whole papacy, no one can deny; they are clear; hence their works are manifest.

In like manner, you perceive here, that St. Paul does not teach* the fanatical devotion of certain effeminate saints who set apart for themselves particular days for fasting, as a special service to God.† Regardless of any distinction of days and meats, our

---

* A. Even of the Pope.

* B. Wish the frantic devotion, &c., &c.
† A. One for this saint, another for that saint; these are all blind paths leading us to base our blessings on works.

whole life should be temperate and sober. For if these things are to be armors of light, and if our whole life is to be pure and chaste, we must *never lay off these armors*, but be always found sober, temperate, vigilant, energetic, &c. But these fanatic saints fast one day on bread and water, and afterwards eat and drink to excess every day for a quarter of a year. Some likewise fast by abstaining from food in the evening, but drink to excess;— and who can enumerate all the folly and works of this darkness? all of which have originated from the fact that merely the work, and not the use of the work, is regarded by them, converting the armor into a mirror, and not knowing why they fast or abstain; precisely as one who bears a sword merely to look at, and when assailed, does not use it. Let this suffice on this Epistle.

SECOND SUNDAY IN ADVENT.

EPISTLE, ROMANS 15, 4-13.

For whatsoever things were written aforetime, were written for our learning, that we through patience and comfort of the scriptures might have hope.
Now the God of patience and consolation grant you to be like-minded one toward another according to Christ Jesus.
That ye may with one mind and one mouth glorify God, even the Father of our Lord Jesus Christ.
Wherefore receive ye one another, as Christ also received us, to the glory of God.
Now I say that Jesus Christ was a minister of the circumcision for the truth of God, to confirm the promises made unto the fathers:
And that the Gentiles might glorify God for his mercy; as it is written, For this cause I will confess to thee among the Gentiles, and sing unto thy name.
And again he saith, Rejoice, ye Gentiles, with his people.
And again, Praise the Lord, all ye Gentiles; and laud him, all ye people.
And again Esaias saith, There shall be a root of Jesse, and he that shall rise to reign over the Gentiles; in him shall the Gentiles trust.
Now the God of hope fill you with all joy and peace in believing, that ye may abound in hope, through the power of the Holy Ghost.

It is quite probable that the individual who arranged this Epistle, knew but little about Paul. He includes in it more than really belongs to it. The first part, which says,— "Whatsoever is written," &c., belongs to the foregoing text. He should have commenced with the words:— "Now the God of patience," &c. In order, then, that we may understand this Epistle clearly and methodically, it will be necessary for us to observe that the Romans, to whom the Apostle writes, were partly Jews and partly Gentiles, converted to Christ. For at that period, there were in all countries, and especially at Rome, many Jews residing; as the Acts of the Apostles, ch. 17, show. Now, having properly inculcated the doctrines of *faith* and of *good works* throughout this Epistle, the Apostle introduces in the conclusion several exhortations to preserve among them a unanimity in faith and good works, removing the causes which might be productive of discord, and subversive to the unity of the Spirit; and of these, there are *two*, which still, even at this day as well as at all times, very much militate against the unity of the spirit, against faith, and good works. Hence they must be carefully marked and described.

The first is this: Some converted from among the Jews, entertained fears that if they should deviate in their conduct from their previous customs, they would commit sin; although they had been informed that, in the New Testament, all kinds of meats, days, clothing, vessels, persons, conditions, and fashions, were left optional, that faith alone renders us pious before God, and that the law in regard to the eating of flesh and fish, to holidays and apparel, to conditions and vessels, was entirely abolished; yet their weak consciences and imperfect faith were so completely fettered by old customs, that they could not take such liberties. Like these, both Gentiles and Jews, in consequence of this same sickly impression could not venture to eat of the bread and meat offered to idols, by the unbelieving, though they were publicly offered for sale, and sold in the market. They imagined that if they would eat of these, they would in this way honor the idols, and deny Christ, when in truth, however, it was nothing. For all kinds of food are clean and good creatures of God, whether Heathens or Christians have them, whether offered to God or to the devil.

The second is this: Those, on the other hand, who were already better informed in reference to these things, and possessed a stronger faith, had not sufficient regard for the weak, but exercised their liberty rather indiscreetly, and to the offence of the weak, ate and drank indiscriminately whatever was set before them. Nor was there any thing wrong in this. But the wrong consisted in their indiscretion in regard to the weak, and in thus causing them to err. For the weak, seeing them act so indiscreetly, could neither coincide with them, nor dissent from them. Had they coincided, their weak conscience would have stood in the way, and said: It is sinful, do it not. Had they dissented, their conscience would again have stood in the way, and said: You are not Christians; for you do not act like other Christians; your faith must be wrong. Behold, thus they could go neither backward nor forward; in either case they would have acted contrary to their conscience. Now, to act contrary to conscience is equivalent to acting contrary to faith, and it is a grievous sin.

Now, Paul teaches us here to have *patience* and to *bear with the weak*, and not to demean ourselves so incautiously in regard to them; but to coincide with them and become weak with them until they also become stronger in faith, and perceive their liberty, so as not to create discord in faith, in consequence of meats and drinks, or of any other temporal thing. The Apostle, however, makes a distinction in matters of this kind, and teaches that there are two classes of persons to be kept in view in regard to this matter: Some, who are weak in faith, of whom we have already spoken, and of whom alone St. Paul here speaks. These are good, pious, plain people who would freely do better, if they had the knowledge or power; they are not tenacious in their opinions; their defect consists wholly in the weakness of their consciences and faith; they cannot extricate themselves from the prevalent doctrines and customs.— The others are obstinate; they are not satisfied to use such liberties themselves in the course of their conduct, but insist upon their use, and teach others and lead them into the same course of conduct, pretending that so it is right, and thus it must be; nor will they listen to the real truth of Christian liberty, but strive against it. These are a cause why the former are weak. For in these, their doctrines, they disregard the weak consciences, and so ensnare them, that they imagine that they must thus act; they delight in thus subduing and bringing into subjection to them the simple consciences. Here St. Paul does not speak of these; no, but he teaches elsewhere that we should oppose them with all diligence, and always act in opposition to them, Tit. 1.

The best rule, therefore, in matters of this kind, is that of *love*, and, in regard to these two classes of persons, you should act, as you would in regard to a wolf and a sheep. If a wolf should almost fatally wound a sheep, and you would go on, enraged at the sheep, saying it is wrong for it to be thus wounded, it should be whole, and you should compel it with violence to follow the other sheep to the pasture and to the cote, without giving it special care; who would not say that you are inconsiderate? The sheep might with propriety say: Certainly it is wrong for me to be thus wounded, and I should, undoubtedly, be whole; but be angry with the one that inflicted the wounds, and assist in my recovery. Behold, thus, too, should these Romans have acted, and repelled with all diligence these teachers and wolves. But the consciences enfeebled and depressed by such doctrines, they should have taken into consideration; they should not have repelled or disregarded them, but have leisurely healed them, and ultimately eradicated these doctrines, being patient and bearing with their weak brethren, so as not to cause them to err.

Now, although this matter, about which St. Paul here speaks, has long since passed away, and the law of Moses concerning meats, drinks, apparel, places, &c., is no longer in use; yet, instead of it, a worse one has been introduced, so that this doctrine of Paul is more necessary now than it was at that time. For there is such a system, established now throughout the world, by the Pope and the Clergy, with human devices, in regard to meats and drinks, apparel and places, days and seasons, persons and orders, fashions and performances, that scarcely any one can eat a morsel, drink a drop, yea, open his eyes, but that there is a law concerning it, and thus our liberty is usurped, especially in convents and cloisters. They unanimously contend that we must thus be clothed and shorn, that we must thus demean ourselves, and that we must not eat this meat, drink that drink, &c., lest we commit sin and an act of disobedience. They have so elevated obedience to human doctrines, that nothing is esteemed more highly than this obedience; and the monks and nuns regard this obedience as the foundation and corner stone of their religion, and build upon it their soul's salvation.

Here no one will lift up his eyes and see that it is nothing but human devices and doctrines that here ensnare the souls, enfeeble the conscience, dissipate Christian liberty and faith, and replenish hell. O wolves! O wolves! How abominably, terribly murderous, worrying, and destructive are these things in all the world! As to this matter, it has never been agitated to such an extent as to enable persons to discover the weak consciences; for no one preached or acted in opposition to these things, by which the weak consciences might be offended; but whoever deviated from them was condemned, and denounced as an apostate, a roving monk, an abandoned Christian, and thus by force, the sheep were not only enfeebled, but driven into the jaws of the wolf. O, the wrath, the indignation, the displeasure of Divine Majesty!

Behold, now if God would so grant his grace that all these things would be recognized as a mere human device, assumption, and wrong, in regard to which God has commanded nothing, and that some would begin to use the masses, prayers, apparel. and meats, in a manner different from that heretofore customary, and to maintain their Christian liberty according to the Gospel, these two classes of persons would be offended. The first, the Papists would rant and rage, cry out and bawl: These things must be observed; he that does not observe them, is a heretic, a heathen, a Jew, and disobedient to the Church, and thus proceed still to cry out obedience to the church wholly to retain in fetters and death, the consciences which regard, as they pretend, these things as obedience to the church. when, at the same time, they are nothing but their own knavery and satanic devices, by which many saints even have been misled and deceived; as, St. Francis and others.

The second, the weak, listening to this bawling, and thus hitherto accustomed, would err, not knowing with whom to coincide, although implicitly desirous from their hearts to follow the right way. But in whatever direction they would go, their consciences would oppose them. Should they coincide with you, their custom and this papistical bawling would stand in the way, and, their consciences captivated by these, they would not dare to deviate, fearing they would act against their God. If, on the other hand, they should not coincide with you, they would again be fearful that they would act against that God whom you hold forth and preach. Whither, then, shall such a poor, weak conscience flee, about which Christ and the devil are thus contending?

Here, then, this doctrine of St. Paul comes in very appropriately. The doctrine of the devil and his Papists is destitute of all mercy and compassion; with rage and violence it compels and forces an immediate retraction from this doctrine; it excommunicates and execrates you, and casts you down four thousand miles below hell, if you do not recant in the twinkling of an eye, and renounce every letter and tittle. From this rage, as from the fruit, we perceive who is the author of such doctrine. The doctrine of Christ, however, does not proceed in this manner; it does not reject you so suddenly, although you do not retract so quickly, and desist so readily; notwithstanding, it would have much more reason so to do; but it sees that you are weak and wounded; it approaches you in a friendly manner; it teaches you the real truth and liberty in regard to all human laws; it is patient, however, and bears with you, if you do not so immediately abandon and forsake your ways; it gives you time to learn to forsake them; it allows you to act as you can or are accustomed till you are made whole, and purely and clearly perceive the truth.

A Christian should, therefore, in regard to this matter, discriminate also between these two classes of persons. The weak he should instruct in a friendly manner, and mildly bear with them; but the raving and ranting, he should oppose with earnestness; he should do and teach all that is grievous and opposed to them, silently pass and omit all that they love, and place upon their ban, as an honor, a great easel-box. All this is very appropriately suggested by Christian love; every one indeed desires to be treated thus himself. For any of us, who may be misled by such weakness of conscience, would desire to have time granted him, and not to be so precipitately cut off; but to be kindly instructed, to be borne with for a while, and to have the wolves resisted.— Hence Christ also acts thus towards us, and desires that one should thus act towards another.

The other cause of discord, which St. Paul removes, is this: There is also and will remain, at all times, among the people of Christ, another kind of persons who are *weak* and *sick in good works*, even as the first were *weak and defective in faith;* so that among Christians two kinds of invalids are found, internally in faith and conscience, externally in works and deportment. None of whom Christ desires to be rejected, but to have all received, so that Christian love may have an abundance, in which to exercise itself, to do good, and heal and bear with its neighbors, internally and externally, in faith and conduct. *These* weak ones, however, are those who sometimes fall into open sin; again, they are those who are called in German, *wunderliche Kœpfe und Seltsame*, who are easily irritated, or are in other respects defective, in consequence of which it is difficult to get along with them; as, this is especially the case between husband and wife, master and servant, ruler and subject.

Now, where this Christian doctrine of St. Paul does not exist, the natural consequence is, that each one forgets the beam in his own eye, and perceives only the mote in his neighbor's eye; one will not bear with the imperfections of another, but each one requires perfection in the other; hence they reflect upon each other; one resorts to this subterfuge, the other to that, in order to evade the harassing censures and displeasures of each other. Whoever is able, however, takes his leave from the other, discards him, and afterwards justifies himself by saying he did it from a love of righteousness, being unwilling to associate with wicked persons, but desiring to be in the company of good and pious persons only, like himself.

This evil reigns mostly in those who are somewhat important in the estimation of others, and who lead an honorable life, and are more highly favored than others. These puff themselves up and put on airs. Whoever is not like them, must be held in disgrace, disparagement, and contempt, and they alone must be the beautiful and admirable. Again, whoever is like them, and also leads an honorable life, ah! he is so pious, he is so good a friend, with him they can associate, fully satisfied in their conceits, as those who love nothing but piety and the pious, and as those who hate nothing but wickedness and the wicked.

They do not see, however, the satanical pride which lies concealed in the inmost recesses of their hearts, in consequence of which they so haughtily and miserably contemn their neighbors, on account of their imperfections.

Now, the love of virtue, and the hatred of vice, are of two kinds: The one is Heathenish, the other Christian; for Christ, too, is an enemy to sin, and a friend to righteousness; as Ps. 45, 7, says in reference to him:—"Thou lovest righteousness and hatest wickedness;" yet in such a way, however, as to accord with the declaration which Moses makes in regard to him, Deut. 33, 3: *Dilexit populos,* "yea, he loved the people." But the Heathen love and hatred is an unreasonable sow, rooting up and raffling together indiscriminately persons and their vices and virtues; yes, indeed, a friend to no one but herself. This we may perceive from the fact that so far and so long as a person is decorated with virtues, so far she loves him, and feels an interest in him; but where there is no virtue, or where it has failed, she rejects the person also.

Now, this is the character of a *Christian hatred of sin*: It discriminates between vices and persons; it endeavors to exterminate the vices only, and to preserve the persons themselves.— Therefore, it neither flees from, nor evades, nor rejects, nor contemns any one, but it much rather receives, freely interests itself in him, and treats him in such a manner as to relieve him from his vices, admonishing him, instructing him, praying for him, being patient, and bearing with him; it does nothing but what it would desire others to do to it, were it in similar circumstances of imperfection.

For a Christian lives wholly for the purpose of being useful to mankind, and of exterminating, not the persons, but their vices; a thing which he cannot do, if he will neither endure any one, nor have anything to do with any one who is defective. It were a very inconsistent act of charity, if you would desire to feed the hungry, satiate the thirsty, clothe the naked, visit the sick, and you would, nevertheless, not allow the hungry, thirsty, naked, and sick to approach or be about you. Thus, too, your unwillingness to allow a wicked or defective person in your presence, is equivalent to your unwillingness to be useful to any one, or to assist him in becoming pious.

Let us, therefore, learn from this Epistle that a Christian walk and love do not consist in seeking pious, upright and holy people, but in making people pious, upright, and holy; and let it be the labor and exercise of a Christian on earth to make such people, whether by admonition, prayer, patience, or otherwise. Even as a Christian does not live to seek wealthy, strong, hale persons, but to make such out of the poor, weak, and infirm.

Hence, then, this Epistle admonishes us to Christian love, and to a noble, good work, not only to bear with our neighbor's spiritual imperfections, both as to his faith and conduct, but also to receive him, and to heal him, removing his infirmities. For those who do not this, create seditions, sects, and divisions; as, in former times, the heretics, Donatists, and Novatians, and many others, separated themselves from the church, being unwilling to tolerate sinners and defective persons among them; it cannot be otherwise, there must be heretics and sects where this doctrine is not observed.

Therefore, St. Augustine also says, on Gal. 6: "Nothing exhibits the religious character of a person so well as if, in approaching the sins of another, he insists rather on his redemption than on reproach, rather on his welfare than on his reproof." In regard to this, St. Paul also says, Gal. 6, 1, 2: "Brethren, if a man be overtaken in a fault, ye which are spiritual, restore such an one in the spirit of meekness; considering thyself, lest thou also be tempted. Bear ye one another's burdens, and so fulfil the law of Christ." As if he should say: Burdens, and whatever is grievous to be borne by your neighbor, you should take to yourselves, and not neglect. You should not seek advantages from him, but *bear his burdens;* for to have an advantage is not to bear, but to be borne; this belongs to the angels in yonder life. Yet, in this respect, we should maintain a difference between the two classes of persons before mentioned, so as to avoid as heathens, those who obstinately attempt to justify their sins and are unwilling to reform; as Christ, Matt. 18, 17, teaches. This doctrine, however, has reference only to such persons as perceive the wrong, and yet, through their weakness or imperfection, stumble. Let us then examine this Epistle.*

The Apostle begins with the fifteenth chapter to teach the aforesaid principle of love, which is to be exercised in regard to the defective walk of our neighbor,—even as, in the fourteenth chapter, he had taught love to be manifested in reference to the imperfect faith of our neighbor,—saying: "We then that are strong ought to bear the infirmities of the weak, and not to please ourselves. Let every one of us please his neighbor for his good to edification. For even Christ pleased not himself; but as it is written, The reproaches of them that reproached thee fell on me. For whatsoever things were written aforetime were written for our learning, that we through patience and comfort of the scriptures might have hope." In these words, so forcible indeed, Paul teaches that principle of love, through which we are to bear with the defective conduct of our neighbor.

First, he says, we are under *obligation to do it.* Whence arises this obligation? Undoubtedly from love and the law, Matt. 7, 12: "All things whatsoever ye would that men should do to you, do ye even so to them; for this is the law and the prophets." Now there is no one among us who would not that others should bear with him in his infirmities, and aid him in ameliorating his condition;—hence, in return, we are under obligation to act in a similar manner towards others, and those who are able should bear with those who are feeble, and assist them in their amelioration.

Secondly, he says, *we should not delight in ourselves*; that is, we should not consider ourselves good, because we have abilities superior to those of our neighbors; for this is nothing but to delight in seeing others lying in sin and depravity, lest they might indeed be equal to us or superior; and to rejoice at their misfortunes, lest they should gain the ascendancy. This is diametrically and fundamentally, indeed, opposed to love. Even as the Pharisee in the Gospel, Luke 18, 11, "Thanks God that he is not like other men," esteeming himself so good, and delighting in himself so much, that it would have been painful, indeed, to him, if any one besides himself had been without sin.

Now, behold, are not those persons detestable, who begrudge grace and salvation to others, and delight and rejoice to see them in their sins and ruin, and yet desire to be regarded as pious and holy, as great enemies to sin, and friends to piety. But what does St. Paul teach us? Not, not thus! No one should too highly approve of himself, and regard himself as good. What then? He should secure the approbation of others, and each one should so conduct himself as to gain the approval of his neighbor, so that he may bear his infirmities with patience and moderation, and act towards him in such a manner as to gain his love and confidence; not treating him so rashly and severely as to give him reason to fear him, and to drive him further away so as never to expect any favors, and to grow worse.

Yes, you will say, if I am to act so as to please him, I shall have to grant him his will to continue as he is. Not so, says St. Paul, and therefore he adds the expression, *for his good;* so that every one should act in such a manner as to please his neighbor, yet in that only which contributes to his amelioration. Our conduct towards him can indeed be of such a nature as not to allow him his will, and still not

---

* A. "Beloved brethren, for whatsoever things were written aforetime, were written for our learning, that we, through patience and comfort of the scriptures, might have hope."

The person who arranged this Epistle should not have commenced it with these words; as they belong to the foregoing part of the chapter. We shall therefore present it in its order.

incur his displeasure. But if he is so dissolute that he will profit by nothing that we do, let him go; yet we have done so much, however, as to have made a reasonable effort to gratify him in whatever would contribute to his amelioration. We cannot force him to approve what we have done to please him. Nor does St. Paul require any more from us than to please him only in those things which contribute to his amendment. The world does not delight even in the fact that God gave his own Son into death to please it.

Therefore, when Paul says: Every one should please his neighbor in regard to that which is good, he does not design that we should make an effort merely to please our neighbors; for this is not required of us: but, in accordance with the principles of love, we should conduct ourselves in such a manner that it would be reasonable for them to be pleased with it, and so that it is not our fault, if they are not. Thus, too, says Paul, 1 Cor. 10, 33: "Even as I please all men in all things;" so should you please all men in all things. How did Paul please all men, when the Jews and Gentiles were his deadly enemies? He did all that was good and profitable for them, and all that should reasonably have pleased them.

Now,* in order that this doctrine may be the more effectually impressed, he introduces the example of Christ, saying: Christ did not please himself. How so? Why! although he was holy and full of grace, yet he did not despise us; nor did he pride in himself, like the Pharisee, because he possessed something that we do not; nor was he delighted because we had nothing, and he possessed and could do all things: but, on the other hand, it was painful to him because we had nothing; he proceeds, and devises a plan by which we become like he is, have what he has, and are liberated from our sins. As this could be accomplished in no other way, he put forth all that he was and had; he assumed our sins and exterminated them. He thus acted towards us, for

the purpose of pleasing us, and of winning our affection; and thus, the passage, Ps. 69, 9, is fulfilled: "The reproaches of them that reproach thee are fallen upon me." Our sins reproach and dishonor God, as our good conduct contributes to his honor and praise. Therefore the prophet calls them God's reproach and dishonor. All these are fallen upon Christ, so that they are removed from us. Now, if he had treated us, like the Pharisee did the publican, and the haughty saints do poor, defective sinners, who then would have been redeemed? He also introduces even this example in Phil. 2, 5, 6, 7, where he says: "Let this mind be in you, which was also in Christ Jesus: who being in the form of God, thought it not robbery to be equal with God; but made himself of no reputation, and took upon him the form of a servant, and was made in the likeness of men; and being found in fashion as a man, he humbled himself, and became obedient unto death, even the death of the cross."

Thus, too, should we act in regard to the sins of our neighbor. We should not judge, backbite, or contemn him; but keep an undesigning eye upon him, wholly for the purpose of extricating him, at the hazard of our bodies, lives, fortunes, and honors. Whoever acts otherwise, should know that he has already lost Christ, and is a heathen saint.

Here, then, follows this Epistle:— "For whatsoever things were written aforetime," &c. This declaration St. Paul makes, because he introduces from the Psalms a passage concerning Christ. Now, in order that no one may wonder how this passage accords here, and what it concerns us, since it was spoken in regard to Christ and is fulfilled in him, he proceeds to give us a general rule to read the Scripture, saying that not only this passage, but also the entire Scripture is written for us as doctrine. It is true, indeed, in it much is written concerning Christ and many saints; as, Adam, Abel, Noe, Abraham, Isaac, Jacob; but it was not written on their account; for it was written long after their time, and they have never

* B. In the third place.

seen it. Thus, although much is written concerning Christ, yet it is not written for his sake; for he had no need of it; but it is written for us, as doctrine. In regard to Christ, his work and deeds are written, but for our edification, so that we may also thus act.

To the same effect, too, he speaks, 1 Cor. 9, 9, 10, where he says: "For it is written in the law, Thou shalt not muzzle the mouth of the ox that treadeth out the corn." Do you suppose that God takes care for oxen?— Or is it not written altogether for our sakes?* As if he should say: God cares not for oxen, but for us. Not that he does not regulate and provide for all things; but that in writing and speaking he does not regard them. What should he write and speak to oxen? For persons only does he write and speak. So, too, here, although it is spoken concerning Christ, yet it is not spoken to Christ, but to us for doctrine; so that we, too, should do as we hear it stated in the Scripture, that Christ and all saints have done.

But mark here what kind of a book the Apostle presents to Christians to read and study; namely, the *Holy Scripture* alone, and says that in it is our doctrine. If, then, our doctrine is in the Scripture, we should, undoubtedly, not seek it elsewhere, but all Christians should daily use this book.

Observe, however, what the devil has accomplished through the Papists. It was not enough for them to throw this book under the table, and to make it so rare, that few doctors of the Holy Scripture possess it, much less read it; but lest some one should bring it to notice, they have branded it with infamy, blaspheming God, and saying it is obscure; we must follow the glosses of men, and not the pure Scripture. What else is this but giving Paul the lie here, who says it is our manual? And they say it is obscure, and calculated to mislead us.

What kind of reward should God confer upon such blasphemers and murderers of the Scripture? Had he consulted with me, I would have entreated him, since they reproach his lucid Scripture as obscure and dangerous, and exclude it from the hearts and eyes of all persons, by throwing it under the table, to give them instead of it Aristotle and Averrois together with the endless statutes and glosses of the Pope, and to let them become raving mad after these, to study all the days of their lives in Aristotle, and yet to learn nothing, and still to let the dolts be crowned and made masters of the Liberal Arts and doctors of the Holy Scriptures.*

Now, let us return to Paul who shows us here what we should read and where we should seek our doctrine. Were there another book for us to read, he would have pointed it out too. Besides, he shows us what kind of fruit this reading bears, and he says: "That we through patience and comfort of the Scriptures might have hope." Here let all doctrine stand forth, let all books be introduced, and see if they have so much virtue or power as to comfort one soul in the least tribulation; it is not possible indeed to comfort a soul, unless it hear the Word of God. But where is the Word of God in any book, except the Scripture? What, then, do we accomplish by reading other books, and omitting this one? They may

---

* A. "For our sakes, no doubt, this is written," &c.

* A. Although up to this time, none of them have yet understood a single line in Aristotle, and if they did understand him, yet they learned no more in him than a child of five years old, and the most depraved dolt, knows; for Aristotle is a hundred times more obscure than the Holy Scripture; and if you wish to know what he teaches, I will tell you in a few words: "A potter can make a pot out of clay; this a blacksmith cannot do, unless he learns it." If there is anything in Aristotle more exalted than this, believe not a word of what I say, and demand of me to prove it, and so I will.

This I say in order that we may perceive how richly Christ has rewarded the Papists for reproaching his Scripture as obscure and dangerous, and perverting its design, by letting them read a dead Heathen who abounds, not with real science, but in nothing except darkness; and what I have said is the very best in Aristotle. I shall say nothing about his virulent and fatal positions. The universities deserve to be ground into powder. Nothing more pernicious and satanic than they are, ever has or ever will come on earth.

ADMONITION TO BEAR THE IMPERFECTIONS OF OUR NEIGHBORS. 23

murder and slay us, indeed, but no book, except the Holy Scripture, can comfort us; it alone has the title which St. Paul here gives it, namely, *Book of comfort*, which can support the soul in all tribulations, so as not to despair, but to maintain hope; for it apprehends the Word of God, in which it learns his gracious will, to which it cleaves, and continues firm in life and death. But he that knows not the will of God, must doubt; for he knows not what relation he sustains to God.

But what shall I say? The calamity is so great that it cannot be reached by words or thoughts. The evil spirit has accomplished his will, and suppressed this book, and has introduced in its stead so many books of human doctrine, that it may be well said, there is a deluge of books, and yet they contain nothing but errors, falsehoods, darkness, venom, death, destruction, hell, and the devil. This our abominable ingratitude has deserved.

Observe, however, how appropriately St. Paul proceeds; he connects both, patience and comfort of the Scriptures. The Scripture does not take away adversity, suffering, and death; no, it reveals nothing but the holy cross, so that St. Paul calls it a word of the cross; therefore patience is required. In the midst of sufferings, however, it consoles and strengthens, so that our patience may not fail, but press forward and conquer. It fills the soul with so much comfort when it hears the solacing declaration from its God, that he is with it, and presides over it, that it bears up with courage and joy beneath its sufferings.

Now, since this life is nothing else but a mortification of the old Adamic nature which must die, patience is required. Again, since the life which is to come, cannot be felt, it is necessary for the soul to have something, to which it may cleave in patience, with which it can somewhat comprehend that life, and upon which it can rest; that is, God's Word; to this it cleaves, in this it abides, and in this it is conveyed from this life to that which is to come, as in a safe ship, and thus its hope continues steadfast.

Behold, *the proper object of the Scripture is, to console the suffering, distressed, and dying.* Hence it follows that he who has not experienced suffering or death, can know nothing about the comfort of the Scripture. This comfort can be tasted and perceived, not by words, but by experience. For St. Paul mentions patience first, and then comfort of the Scripture; so that we might know that he who is unwilling to endure suffering, and seeks consolation elsewhere, cannot taste this comfort. It is the province of the Scripture alone to comfort. It must therefore meet with patience first. It is jealous; it will not allow human comfort and aid to be placed upon a level with it; for in that way patience and suffering would be hindered.

Now, it is no small portion of patience and crosses, however, to bear the imperfections and sins of our neighbors; for these are so oppressive to some, that in consequence of them, they are induced to desire death for themselves, or to wish it for others. In order, therefore, that this patience may be maintained in this life, they must comfort themselves with those portions of the Scripture, which exhibit the example of Christ, so that they may continue firm and submissive in their suffering, when they perceive that for their sakes Christ has submitted to much greater suffering, and has taken upon himself much heavier burdens of their sins in order to redeem them.

Comfort in this patience is productive of a firm hope in Christ, that we shall be like him; by this we are assured that for our sakes he has submitted and will still submit to these things. But whoever allows that example and those portions of the Scripture to escape his memory, will retain very poor hope and patience, even if the very best effort is made to console him, by things in nature. This effort must be ineffectual; it cannot penetrate into the recesses of the heart; it can afford nothing but imaginary patience and comfort.

"Now, the God of patience and consolation grant you to be like minded one toward another according to Christ Jesus."*

This has reference to the imperfections, both of our faith and conduct, but mostly to those of our faith, as we shall see: and it is a prayer, with which, after preaching and teaching, St. Paul concluded his Epistle. But in order that no one may presume to have patience and comfort of the Scripture, from his own powers, he indicates by this prayer that they are gifts of God, obtained through prayer. Much less does it lie within our own power to bear the imperfections of others and to accord with them in faith.

He says, therefore, "God of patience and consolation;" that is, he is a Lord, and grants this patience and consolation. Even as he is a God of heaven and earth, so too is he a God of patience and consolation—all things are his gifts and creatures. *He grants them to you*, says he, because you do not possess them of yourselves. If he grants them, then they are not a result of nature, but of grace, and a gift. For if he does not direct a declaration of his word to the heart, appropriate to the case, the heart will never perceive it. Yes, where he does not grant it, there the Scripture is neglected, and human doctrines are sought, as was the case with condemned popery. But, where he grants grace to search the Scriptures, there he also grants patience and consolation. There is no greater manifestation of God's wrath, therefore, than for him to permit his Word and Scripture to go down. Hence, it is not without reason that the Apostle thus prays. On the other hand, there is no greater blessing than for him to present and permit his Word to be read; so that all, should repeat, indeed, with the Apostle, this prayer.

"To be like-minded one towards another." What does this imply? How can the weak be minded like the strong? *To be like-minded*, implies that one should tolerate the prejudices of another, and be satisfied with what he thinks proper. For prejudice is the cause of all parties, sects, discord, and heresy; as the proverb says:—"His own way pleases every one; hence the land with fools is over-run." This self-prejudice and pleasure Paul desires to arrest here. For nothing is more intolerable and pernicious to the Christian faith and church than such prejudice. The person possessed with it, cannot forsake it; he must take his own way, and deviate from the common course, so as to establish one of his own, which will please himself. Hence so many parties, customs, and fashions in the institutions and cloisters in the world; none of which accord: but every one is pleased best with his own, and condemns the others.

Now, here the Apostle desires *them to be of one mind, of one opinion*, and to be satisfied with each other; namely thus: Those whose consciences are weak should regard that as good and proper, which those of strong faith and healthful consciences observe; so that their *faith, consciences, and views*, may be alike, and that they may not wrangle with one another in consequence of thoughts arising from the fact that one regards this as right and proper, and another that; so as to chime in with the declaration,* Ps. 133, 1: "Behold how good and how pleasant it is for brethren to dwell together in unity." For instance, if one of a weak faith sees one whose faith is strong eat meat, or drink, or do something, which he conceives to be wrong or sinful, he should suppress his thoughts in regard to the eating, drinking, or actions of him whose faith is strong, even if he neither would nor could thus act; he should think, as St. Paul says, concerning this matter, Rom. 14, 5: "Let every one be fully persuaded in his own mind;" so that malice, contention, and wrangling may be avoided, and unanimity of heart and disposition maintained. On the other hand, if he whose faith is weak cannot coincide with those things, those who

---

* A. Here this Epistle should have commenced. For

* A. Made in regard to him, Ps. 68: *God causes unanimity to dwell in the house;* and

are strong in faith should not force him to do so, or contemn him, but be satisfied with him as to what he eats, drinks, or does, until he also shall become strong; as Paul, Rom. 14, 1, says: "Him that is weak in the faith, receive ye, but not to doubtful disputation;" that is, ye shall not press him and say: This is right, and that is wrong; but kindly treat and instruct him, until he, too, shall become strong.

It is not necessary, however, that we all should have the same occupation. One may be a smith, another a tailor, without impairing the unity of the faith and of the heart; the one tolerating the external occupation or work of the other. But if a fool were to interfere, and teach that the occupation of a smith is an impious trade, he would cause his conscience to err, and weaken his faith. Thus, too, it is here: all kinds of external things in regard to meats, apparel, and situations, we are at liberty to use or not to use, in whatever manner and at whatever time it suits us. Whoever, then, comes and teaches you that you must not use such and such things, as the Pope and the Clergy teach, causes you to err. On the other hand, if some one else should come, and say you must use them, he also causes you to fall into error. But he that pursues a medium course, and teaches you that you are at liberty to use or not to use them, not condemning you, but allowing you still to pursue your own custom, until you extricate yourself, pressing hard, however, the wolves that force you into that custom, as if it were not optional, but must be observed, gives you the proper instruction.*

He deserves censure, however, who goes on precipitately and determines to be judge in these matters according to his own doctrine, and severs such unanimity, saying: "You do right, and you should do so; that one does wrong, and he should not do so." He is the apostle of the devil, and his teaching, the doctrine of Satan. That the Pope and the Papists do; it belongs not to shepherds, but to wolves, to preach such a doctrine. Under this aspect of things a dissolution of this Christian unanimity must follow. Here different opinions must present themselves: You are a heretic, you are disobedient to the church, you do wrong, &c. This is what the devil desires.*

But this I say in regard to those things only, which we are at liberty to hold in this light, and we should resist the Pope with his wicked and foolish laws, as we would a wolf, and yet we should allow those who are weak in faith to continue in their ways for a while, until we are able ultimately to extricate them; so that they may not be too hastily and precipitately cast off, and dashed to pieces in their consciences.

But, in those things which are not optional with us, but are forbidden or commanded by Christ, there is little room for disputation: whether it concerns those who are weak or those who are strong in their consciences. Here every one, the least as well as the greatest, is under obligation to withstand the Pope; as for instance, when he and all his adherents teach that the Mass must be observed as a sacrifice and a good work. This is the most enormous abomination which has ever arisen on earth, and on which his government with all his institutions and cloisters is founded; here no one is excusable, whether weak

---

* A. Now, if you should fast in honor of an Apostle, or confess during Lent, you do nothing wrong by it; neither does any one else, on the other hand, who omits these things, perpetrate any evil by his omission. Let him that wishes to fast and make confession, do so; but let one not censure, judge, condemn, or wrangle with, another on account of such things; but let one be minded like another, being satisfied with what he does, and regarding it as good, because it is good in itself.

* A. Having severed this unity, taken captive your consciences, and destroyed your liberty, the Pope proceeds and takes your money, and then gives you a bill of exchange, permitting you to eat butter, eggs, and meat,—a privilege which Christ gave you in the Gospel, of which the Pope robbed you, and which he, the pious shepherd, sells you again. This gives offence to others again; and in a word, the government of the Pope abounds with such grasping and re-grasping, offences and re-offences, exchanges and re-exchanges, that it may be easily perceived that it is nothing but a mere government of the designing devil who brings about such a confusion and medley of consciences that no one can sufficiently comprehend it.

or strong; for Christ instituted the Mass as a sacrament and testament, which no one can sell, transfer or give away, but, like Baptism, each one must receive it for himself. There are many more abominations like this in his canons; and indeed where such a foundation exists, it is easy to perceive the character of the building; all that exists in popedom is the wantonness of the devil, from the crown of the head to the sole of the foot.*

The Apostle adds that "we should be like-minded according to Christ Jesus;" that is, in a Christian point of view. For unbelievers too are of one mind, not in regard to Christ, but in regard to the flesh and the world and the devil. The Jews also were of one mind against God and his Christ, as Ps. 2, 2, says. A unanimity of mind among Christians strives against sin and all that is contrary to Christianity, without perpetrating or designing any sin. Its character, therefore, is to effect a union among all Christians, first, in regard to their faith, and then in reference to their walk and conduct.

If, however, any one is weak in faith and defective in his conduct, it is unwilling that he should continue in this condition; neither does it forsake, and much less disparage him or reject and condemn him: but it enlists in his behalf, and acts towards him as it would that others should do to it, and as Christ acted towards it in similar and more important matters. In this way a principle is perpetuated, according to which every one will do that which meets the approbation of others, conform to their views, and continue to be of the same mind. But a contrary course is pursued by the obstinate, when one forsakes, rejects, judges, and discards another, and follows his own ways, according to his own opinions, like, the orders of the Pope and all other sects now do.

"That ye may with one mind and one mouth glorify God, even the Father of our Lord Jesus Christ."

All the good that we can do towards God, is to praise and to thank him; and this too is the only right service which we can render to him as he says himself, Ps. 50, 23: "Whoso offereth praise glorifieth me: and to him that ordereth his conversation aright, will I show the salvation of God." All other blessings we receive from him, so that in return we should make him such offering of praise; and if any other service to God is offered for your consideration, rest assured it is erroneous and delusive; as for instance, the distracted world sets apart as services to God, houses, churches, cloisters, gilded, silken, and all kinds of vestments, silver vessels and images, bells and organs, candles and lamps, —an expense which should have been appropriated to the poor, if the object was to give it to God,—keeping up a murmuring and whining in the churches day and night, whilst the proper praise and honor of God, which cannot be confined to places and persons, are passed over in silence in all the world. These pretences of the priests and monks, that their system of exercises is a service to God, are false, delusive, and deceptive.

Service to God is praise to God, which must be free and voluntary, at table, in the chamber, in the cellar, in the garret, in the house, on the field, in all places, with all persons, at all times. Whoever teaches you otherwise, is no less guilty of falsehood than the Pope and the devil himself.

But how shall the honor and praise of God, the right service of God, exist among us, when we neither love him nor receive his blessings? But how shall we love him, when we know neither him nor his blessings? But how shall we know him and his blessings, when nothing is preached concerning them, and the Gospel is left lying under the table? For where the Gospel does not exist, there it is impossible to known God. There too, it must be impossible to love and praise him. Consequently it must also be impossible for a divine service to exist there.*

---

* A. He that believes it not, will experience it.

* A. Even if all the choristers were one chorister, all the priests, one priest, all the monks, one monk, all the churches, one church, all the bells, one bell, and in a word, if all the foolish services offered to God in the institutions,

This divine service, however, will not admit of being established with revenues, nor of being circumscribed by laws and statutes. It knows nothing about high and low festivals. It emanates from the Gospel, and arises as readily indeed in a poor, rustic servant as in a great bishop.

Hence, too, you may perceive who it is that has destroyed this divine service, and still daily suppresses it. It is no one else but the hopeless rabble, the Pope with his blockheads, bishops, priests, monks, and nuns, who boast, for the most part, of their divine services, and delight in suffering themselves to be called ecclesiastics, grasping by means of their juggling the advantages and honors of all the world, and living in riotousness; and yet they pretend to help other persons to heaven by their foolish works, saying nothing about the Gospel; yes, persecuting and condemning it; so that St. Peter may well term them children of condemnation.

Now, Paul says that this *divine service must be rendered with one mind and with one mouth*. This is effected when we are of one mind, and perceive that we are all equal, and have received alike blessings in Christ; so that one cannot exalt himself above another, nor assume special advantages.

If you ask, how can this be effected? I answer thus: All that are not in Christ, are condemned, one like another. One needs Christ just as well as the other. But when we are converted, one receives the same Baptism, the same Sacrament, the same Faith, the same Christ, the same Spirit, the same Gospel, in a word, the same God, that the other one receives, and here in this wilderness the *heavenly bread is equally distributed*. How then can it possibly be right for one to set himself up spiritually above another as priest above another?— What can he have that is better than Christ? Now, each one has the same Christ, and Christ also receives each one wholly and entirely.

One, indeed, may embrace Christ more firmly than another, as he may love him more, and believe in him more steadfastly; but he has not, for this reason, more than the other one has. Christ is one and the same Christ, and, in those things which pertain to salvation, alike to all. Therefore, too, is he properly Christ. Since, then, there is one common blessing for those who are weak, and for those who are firm, in faith, for those who are vigorous and for those who are defective in their walk, one should not esteem another more lightly than himself, nor reject him; but should recognize him as an equal, so that the praise of God may arise harmoniously, and go forth as if it emanated from one heart and one mind; as, in this way, each one praises God, and has treasured up in his heart and mouth even what the other one has. For all perceive Christ, and thank him for what they receive through him; as is already revealed, Ps. 72, 15: "Prayer also shall be made for him continually; and daily shall he be praised." But if any one praise God [simply] in consequence of his own advantages or possessions, he destroys that unanimity of heart and mouth, and belongs not to the community of saints; as the Papists and sects do, from whom we never hear any praise concerning Christ, but concerning their own works.

It is well for us, however, to observe* the fact, too, that he tells us to

---

churches, and cloisters, were a hundred times greater and more numerous than they are, what would God inquire after such carnivals, festivals, and impostures? Wherefore, God complains, for the most part of the Jews, Mich. 2, because they have silenced his praise, when at the same time, they piped, blared, and moaned, like we do.

* A. Especially should it be observed in our day, when we extol the honor of the saints so high that we generally hang upon the saints, and do not press forward to God. Here we find one who is satisfied if he has the favor of St. Barbara and has invoked her, whilst no one knows with certainty whether she was a saint or not. Another one has Christofel, and is satisfied with him; this, without doubt, is one of the greatest of fictions and fallacies. But there is scarcely any one who is satisfied to honor the mother of God, and to have her favor.

I fear *that abominable idolatry will insinuate itself in this way*, so that the *trust and confidence will be reposed in the saints*, which are due praise the *Father of Jesus Christ*, and that he does not leave this resting upon Christ, especially in opposition to the abominable idolatry which we practiced in regard to departed saints, placing our trust in them, and awaiting from them that which is to be expected from God alone; when at the same time even Christ himself refers us throughout the Gospel to the Father, and even came, that through him we should come to the Father.

Now, *to come to the Father* is, not to walk to Rome upon our feet, to fly to heaven on wings, but *to rely upon him with sincere confidence*, as upon a gracious father; as the Lord's Prayer commences. The more such confidence increases in the heart, the more we come to the Father.* Therefore St. Peter too, 1 Pet. 1, 18, 19, says: "Ye know that ye were not redeemed with corruptible things, as silver and gold, * * but with the precious blood of Christ, as of a lamb without blemish and without spot, * * that your faith and hope might be in God;" and St. Paul, Rom. 5, 2: "By whom (Christ) also we have access by faith into his grace," &c.†

Now, even as Christ is the common blessing of us all, as we have already heard; so, too, should we ascribe this blessing to no one but the Father alone; who, in this way, has shown in the most gracious manner, that he has drawn our hearts to him. We should, therefore love and praise him with all confidence, on account of those superabundant blessings; so that our hearts may become accustomed to console themselves in him, and to await every blessing from him, in life and in death, through Christ however, and not through ourselves. For he was given, in order that we might and should come to the Father, with such confidence, through him; as, John 14, 9, he says: "No man cometh to the Father, but by me."

Now, although Christ himself is truly God, and it were enough, if any one should place his confidence in him, yet he continually refers to the Father; so that no one may continue to hang upon the humanity, like the Disciples did before his suffering, and not raise his thoughts above the humanity up to the divinity. For according to the humanity, we must regard Christ as a way, an evidence, a work of God, through which we come to God, and place all our confidence in him entirely, and be careful indeed not to place a portion of our confidence to the mother of God, and establish an idol in our hearts.

"Wherefore receive ye one another, as Christ also received us, to the glory of God.'

Wherefore? Or what kind of a *therefore* is this? There are *two reasons*, (says he,) *why ye should receive one*

---

to God alone, and that that will be expected from the saints, which is to be expected from God alone: and if there were no other evil connected with it, yet it is suspicious whether such services and honor rendered to the saints, have any declaration or example in the Scripture to favor them, whether they are not at once opposed to this declaration of Paul, and whether they do not militate against similar declarations which teach us to press forward to God, to repose all confidence in him alone, and expect from him alone every blessing. For even Christ, &c.—*Luther's Works* 7r Bd.

* A. Now reason and experience must acknowledge that where confidence reposed in God is in the heart, there all confidence in all creatures, whether saints in heaven or on earth, is lost; on the other hand, where confidence in God diminishes, there a resort to, and confidence in the saints begin.

† A. Let it be admitted that some render service to the saints and to the mother of God, properly,—this is seldom, however,—even then, the example is dangerous, and should not be introduced into the congregation as a practice; but, according to the doctrine of Christ and all the Apostles, we should cheerfully approach God the Father alone, and through Christ alone. For it very readily happens that, in consequence of the abominable fall, persons endeavor to console themselves more with the saints than with God, and call upon their names and for their help rather than on God. This is, therefore, a very perverse, unchristian system; as I fear the world is now full, full, full of idolatry.

Now, although God permits *aid and signs to result* to these servers of saints, sometimes; yet they result through the devil. For God grants even to the servants of the devil bodies and lives as well as possessions and honors, through the devil, as it is clearly evident; precisely as a rich prince may grant a knave a treasure through another knave. Therefore we should base ourselves neither on the signs nor on the examples of the multitude, but alone on the doctrine of Christ, or of his Apostles, in this and in other cases.

ADMONITION TO BEAR THE IMPERFECTIONS OF OUR NEIGHBORS. 29

another. The *first* is because ye hear that the Scripture presents Christ to us as an example, upon whom the ignominies which were ignominious to to God, fell,—these are our sins,—and that he did not despise, reject, or revile us, but received us in order to redeem us from them. It is right, therefore, much more for us thus to act.

The *other reason* is, *because this example contributes to the praise and honor of God*; for through it God is praised and honored; and this is the case, because Christ everywhere testifies that all that he does, is his Father's will, and that he came merely for the purpose of doing his Father's will. Hence, it is certain that he also bore the ignominy of our sins simply because it was his Father's will.

Hence we perceive how superabundantly merciful the will of the Father is, which reigns over us, that he placed upon his beloved, his only Son our sins and his ignominy to bear; so that he would not have to condemn us on account of them. Now where this will of God is properly perceived, love and praise to God must result from the bottom of the heart, and his mercy be praised; for from it the individual secures a conscience so joyful and serene that he cannot restrain himself; he must honor and praise these rich blessings of God.

Behold, St. Paul says Christ has *established the honor of God through himself*, by receiving us, and by bearing and exterminating our sins. So, too, should we take upon ourselves the sins, burdens, and imperfections of our neighbors, and bear with them, and render them aid and relief. Now, when sinners or the infirm hear or perceive this, their hearts grow favorable towards God, and they must exclaim: "Why, this is indeed an excellent, gracious God and a righteous Father, who has such a people, and desires them not to judge, condemn, or reject us poor sinful and imperfect persons, but to receive, aid, and treat us as if our sins and imperfections were their own. Who would not love, extol, praise, and honor such a God, and, from the bottom of his heart, entrust all things to him? What must he be himself, if he desires his people thus to be?

Behold, such praise God desires to receive through us, by our receiving one another, and by regarding our neighbor's condition as our own. In this way persons would be incited to believe, and those who already believe, would be strengthened in their faith. But where now is this example in the world?*

"Now I say that Jesus Christ was a minister of the circumcision for the truth of God, to confirm the promises made unto the fathers; and that the Gentiles might glorify God for his mercy."

Having now submitted the sentiment, that they should receive one another, according to the example of Christ, to the honor of God, and allowing no difference among the people of Christ, whether saints or sinners, strong or weak, rich or poor,— for they are all entitled to the same privileges, having the same blessings, in Christ, who produces a unanimity of heart, spirit, mind, and mouth, making all things common, whether spiritual or temporal, however various they may be,—he proceeds to establish his position with strong declarations from the Scripture; and thus, too, by the Scripture he dissipates all the causes of discord, standing between the Jews and the Gentiles as an arbitrator and a mediator; as if he should say: "You Jews cannot reject the Gentiles, even if they do not eat and drink with you according to your custom, for they have even the same Christ whom you have as the Scripture has predicted:" again, "you Gentiles cannot contemn the Jews, if they do not conform to your manners in eating and drinking; for they, also have the same Christ promised to them in the Scripture.

Now, since, according to the Scripture, all have equal privileges in Christ, and since both Jews and Gentiles are gathered together under him, and since out of Christ no one has anything, and in him every one has all things; why then should you con-

---

* A. Nothing but tyrants, yes, devils, rule in ecclesiastic orders, who can do nothing but excommunicate, condemn, force, and repel.

tend, judge one another, and cause schisms, and not much rather receive each other in a friendly manner, as Christ received you? For no one has anything in preference to another, and no one has less than another; why then should you contend and create schisms on account of meats, drink, clothing, days, places, gestures, and the like, since nothing is depending on these, because they are temporal things out of Christ, which contribute nothing to the matter? Therefore, let every one who will, be at liberty in regard to these things. But if any one is yet weak in faith, and not free, have patience and bear with him till he becomes strong, seeing that this detracts nothing from you, as you still have Christ wholly and entirely.

Now, in order to understand these words of St. Paul, we must know that it is his custom to call the *Jewish people the circumcision*, because they were circumcised, and by this, as by a sign, they could be separated and distinguished from other people.

Thus, too, other things are designated by their signs; as, in regard to females, we say: "The veil or weft of hair produces many misfortunes in the world,"* and to priests: "How avaricious is the bald pate!" And horsemen are designated by their spurs and stirrups. Even in this way St. Paul calls the Jews according to their signs, the *circumcision*, and the Gentiles *præputium*, the *uncircumcision*, Gal. 2, 7, 8: "They saw that the Gospel of the uncircumcision was committed unto me," that is, of the Gentiles who are not circumcised, "as the *Gospel of the circumcision was unto Peter*," that is, of the Jews; and Eph. 2, 11: "Remember, that ye being in time past Gentiles in the flesh, who are called uncircumcision by that which is called the circumcision," &c. So here too: "I say that Jesus Christ was a minister of the circumcision;" that is, of the Jews, or Jewish people.

According to his custom he calls *Christ* also a *minister*, as he calls all preachers and apostles ministers; 1 Cor. 3, 5, : "Who then is Paul and who is Apollos? but ministers, by whom ye believed." Now this is the substance of the Apostle's words: "Jesus Christ was a minister of the circumcision;" that is, a preacher, teacher, apostle, messenger, sent from God to the Jewish people. For Christ never preached to the Gentiles, nor was he sent to them, but to the Jews alone.

This occurred, however, not for the sake of their merit, but, as he here says, *for the truth of God*. What truth is this? God promised Abraham, Isaac, and Jacob, that Christ should be born of their seed. Now, that God might be found faithful in his promises, Christ came according to this promise; and thus is the truth of God found, that he keeps what he promises. For the sake of this truth,—that God might stand as truthful,—and not for the sake of any one's merit, Christ became an apostle and a minister of the circumcision. This the following words, where he says, "to confirm the promises made unto the fathers," require. Observe what truth he means; namely, that by which the divine promise concerning Christ, made to the patriarchs, is established and fulfilled.

Now, although it is true that Christ, is common both to the Jews and the Gentiles, yet he was promised, not to the Gentiles, but to the Jews alone, as he says, Rom. 3, 2: "Unto them were committed the oracles of God;" Rom. 9, 4 : *The law was given to the Jews.* Thus, too, he came to them alone, as he also says himself, Matt. 15, 24: "I am not sent, but unto the house of the lost sheep of Israel." Thus the Jews have the prerogative that Christ was promised to them, and that they might await him. But to the Gentiles nothing was promised, and therefore, they could await nothing; although the Jews and the Gentiles are alike in this that, as Christ was promised out of pure grace, so he was given to the Gentiles. Yet, after he was promised, they had just reason also to expect him as the one who should be given to them.

Hence, the Jews have Christ, not only through the grace of the promise, but also through the truth of God

---

* A. And to the monks: "Behold, what may the cowl not do."

ADMONITION TO BEAR THE IMPERFECTIONS OF OUR NEIGHBORS. 31

who should fulfill his promise. But the Gentiles have neither the grace of the promise, nor the truth of the fulfillment, but the *mere naked, unadvised, unexpected mercy which Christ gives to them*, without any promise, without any obligation for the fulfillment of the truth of God. Yet, as the Scripture revealed that the Gentiles should obtain Christ, without any promise, without any hope and expectation however, this same Scripture too, must be fulfilled; and consequently, one party has nothing in preference to the other. But Christ was given to the Jews through divine promise and truth, to the Gentiles through pure, unexpected mercy.

Now, since the Scripture includes both, a promise to the Jews, and a prediction concerning the Gentiles, the unity is established, that *each one has Christ in common*, and henceforth one should receive another, as a participant in the common blessing. The Jews should not despise the Gentiles, because the Scripture says in regard to them, that they shall praise God for his mercy. How should they despise those who have and praise the mercy of God? On the other hand, the Gentiles should not despise the Jews; for Christ was promised to them, and according to the promise he became their minister and their preacher so that God stood faithful, and fulfilled his promise.

Observe this is the design of these words of Paul: "I say that Christ was a minister of the circumcision for the truth of God, to confirm the promises made unto the fathers." Wherefore sayest thou this? Doubtless, so that no one may despise the Jews, but receive them, because Christ received them, and did not despise them; yes, he was even manifested and given to them as their own promised preacher, minister, and apostle. But what sayest thou in regard to the Gentiles? I say not that anything is promised to them; but I say they praise and have the mercy of God, which is given to them without promise, as the Scripture intimates. Therefore no one should despise them, but receive them, because God has received them, and did not despise them. Now, as Christ is become common to all, the Jews and the Gentiles, although differently and through different reasons; so too we should become common among one another, receiving one another, bearing one another's burdens, and having patience with the imperfections of one another, regardless of distinction of external person, name, condition, and of anything else.

"For this cause I will confess to thee among the Gentiles, and sing unto thy name."

Here he begins to introduce some passages of Scripture, in which it is revealed *that the Gentiles will praise God* for his mercy; and this first one is in Ps. 18, 50, and in Ps. 108, 3, and it is spoken by the prophet in the person of Christ; as both the Psalms show. Now, if this declaration is to be verified, Christ must be among the Gentiles, not physically, but spiritually, for where Christ does not exist spiritually, there he is not yet praised; but wherever he is praised and sung, there is he spiritually. Thus this declaration forces the conclusion that *the Gentiles shall believe in Christ and have him*, which is, to have the mercy of God: yet in this nothing is promised to the Gentiles, but it is a mere revelation in reference to the Gentiles, as to what they will do.

We have already mentioned the proper service of God, which the prophet here styles *praise and singing of God's name*; as the whole Scripture styles it. Now, *praise* is nothing else but a confession of the blessings received. Hence, the Hebrew and Apostolic word reads: *confitebor*, I will confess thee; that is, thank and praise thee, and exclaim, all this have I received from thee.

"And again he saith, Rejoice ye Gentiles, with his people."

These words are a quotation from Deut. 32, 43, as it is said, where Moses says: "Rejoice, O ye nations, with his people." In Hebrew, however, it will admit of this reading: "Rejoice, ye Gentiles, with him;" (understand, his people); and thus, it seems to me, the Apostle introduces this passage. Yet whether the reading is otherwise, or thus, it is clear that no one either praises the people of God, or rejoices with him, unless he is a partaker of his blessings; and has that same God. For he that has not these, is an enemy to the people of God, and curses and persecutes them, as God says, Gen. 12, 3: "I will bless them that bless thee, and curse him that curseth thee." Here you perceive that those who bless the people of God, are partakers of his blessings. Hence this passage forces the conclusion that the *Gentiles shall become Christians.*

"And again, Praise the Lord, all ye Gentiles; and laud him, all ye people." This is the 117th Psalm, v. 1, 2, and it also speaks of the true service of God. Hence, too, it enforces the conclusion that the *Gentiles shall be the people of God.* Since no one serves, (that is, praises and honors,) God, but his people alone.

"And again, Esaias saith, There shall be a root of Jesse, and he that shall rise to reign over the Gentiles, in him shall the Gentiles trust."

This declaration stands in Isa. 11, 10; and it reads thus in Hebrew:— "And in that day there shall be a root of Jesse, which shall stand for an ensign of the people; to it shall the Gentiles seek: and his rest shall be glorious." The meaning of this passage evidently is that the Gentiles shall have Christ, and be subject to him. But St. Paul slightly changes the words, and follows the old translators, who formerly rendered the Bible in the Greek language. The import is the same however. *The root of Jesse* should not be understood here as the stem or tree of Jesse, as limners delineate it, a tree of Jesse, the father of David, with many branches; and as we sing in regard to the blessed Virgin, *germinavit radix Jesse*, the stem of Jesse has sprung forth; for this is wholly a forced construction. *Christ himself,* and no one else, *is this stem or root*; as this declaration of Isaiah clearly shows, which says: The Gentiles shall hope for the stem or root of Jesse, which shall rule the nations, &c. This cannot be attributed to the natural Jesse, or to our blessed Virgin.

But *Christ* is a *root of Jesse*, because he descended from the lineage of Jesse, through David, but in him the physical descent ceased. Through his sufferings he was buried in the grave, as an ill-favored root, he was concealed in the world, and out of him grew the beautiful tree, the Christian Church, spreading out in all the world. This were properly delineating the root Jesse, were the delineations so extended as to include the sufferings of Christ and their fruits.

But the declaration of Paul,—"And he shall rise to reign over the Gentiles,—is equivalent to the Hebrew: "Which shall stand as an ensign for the people." For by this *the government of Christ* is shown to be *spiritual*. By the Gospel he is set up in all the world as an ensign, to which we must look and hold, through faith. We see him not physically, but only in the sign, the Gospel; and thus, too, he rules the people through the Gospel, in the sign, and not in a physical presence.

Nor does his expression,—"In him shall the Gentiles trust,"—differ materially from the Hebrew text which says: "To it shall the Gentiles seek;" that is, they shall look unto him, and cleave unto him alone; they shall place all consolation, hope, and confidence in him, they shall enquire after nothing else, desire nothing else, but him.

But the phrase,—"And his grave (rest) shall be glorious,"—contained in our text, Isa. 11, 10, which the Apostle omitted, is not happily rendered by St. Hieronymus, where he thinks Isaiah wrote concerning the glorious grave of Christ. The design of Isaiah was that the rest of Christ should be glorious; that is, that his dying or death should not be like that of other persons who have their glory while they are alive; when they are dead, they have none. But in his death the glory of this root of Jesse first began. For after his death was he first raised to true life, power, glory, and honor, as a sign and regent of the Gentiles; yes, seated at the right hand of God, a Lord over all things.

"Now the God of hope fill you with all joy and peace in believing, that ye

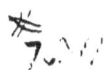

DR. LUTHER'S CHURCH-POSTIL.

SERMONS ON THE EPISTLES.

1 CORINTHIANS IV, 1-5.

may abound in hope, through the power of the Holy Ghost."

He concludes this Epistle with an excellent prayer, desiring them to be filled with joy and peace, saying:— "The God of hope," that is, which he gives them alone through and in Christ.

But the manner, in which this takes place, we have already mentioned;— namely, when *we perceive the will of God*, how he gave Christ to bear our sins, as we also should do. The more profoundly we perceive this will, the stronger will be our faith, hope, and love. We should, therefore, continually preach and hear it, and reflect on it; for this results through no other means, but the Gospel only.

Hence, the meaning of the Apostle is this: God, who works hope through the Gospel, grants you grace so that you may properly employ the Gospel and believe, through which you *first perceive Christ;* in consequence of which you will obtain *all peace* and a *good conscience,* as a common blessing, as well as *peace* among each other. For this *peace* and *joy* is received, not, like that which the world gives, through feeling and sensation, but *through faith.* For you neither feel nor see him who is your good, and from whom you derive your peace and joy. In this world, however, you will feel disquietude and grief. But if you learn that Christ is common and alike to all, you enjoy a blessed peace; for then there is nothing which one begrudges another, because you are all alike rich. Behold this is peace and joy through faith or in faith.

Hence, still further follow the words, *Abound in hope;* that is, that hope should ever increase. To this increase, suffering and persecution contribute. For hope does not increase so as to decrease adversity; no, adversity is increased so that our hope may not rely on our power, but exist through the power of the Holy Spirit, who assists us, and strengthens our hope, so that we may neither flee from nor fear the disasters of the world, but resist them until death, and overcome all evil, so that it must fly and dissipate before us. This is hope, not in human weakness, but in the *power of the Holy Spirit*, all of which, however, must result through the medium of the Gospel, as already stated:— "Through patience and consolation of the Scriptures we have hope." For where the Gospel does not exist, there is neither hope, consolation, peace, joy, faith, love, Christ, God, nor blessings; as we see before our eyes in the wretched, clergical, spiritless, carnal orders, who nevertheless pray much, and frequently hold masses; from which do thou God of hope, and of patience, and of consolation, graciously preserve us. Amen.

THIRD SUNDAY IN ADVENT.

EPISTLE, 1 COR. 4, 1-5.

Let a man so account of us, as of the ministers of Christ, and stewards of the mysteries of God.

Moreover, it is required in stewards that a man be found faithful.

But with me it is a very small thing that I should be judged of you, or of man's

judgment: yea, I judge not mine own self.
For I know nothing by myself; yet am I not hereby justified: but he that judgeth me is the Lord.
Therefore judge nothing before the time, until the Lord come, who both will bring to light the hidden things of darkness, and will make manifest the counsels of the hearts: and then shall every man have praise of God.

This Epistle presents an illustration of the Gospel for the first Sunday in Advent, in which we heard that the disciples did not ride on the colt themselves, but led it to Christ, and sat him thereon; this seems to be the design of the Apostle also here. For the Corinthians had begun to separate among themselves, and to cleave to the Apostles. One party boasted of Peter, another of Paul, another of Apollos; each one exalting the Apostle by whom he was baptized or taught, or whom he regarded as the most eminent. Here Paul comes and interposes, allowing none of them to boast of any Apostle, but of Christ alone, saying it matters not who he is, by whom they were baptized and taught; but it is of the utmost importance to hold to Christ unanimously, and be subject to him alone. Thus St. Paul beautifully illustrates how the Apostles are to be regarded, and this whole Epistle is a terrible thrust at Popery and* the clerical government; as we shall see.

"Let a man so account of us, as of the ministers of Christ, and stewards of the mysteries of God."

This is said in regard to all Apostles and all heirs to the Apostolic chair, whether it be St. Peter or St. Paul. Hence, we should be very cautious how we regard the Apostles and bishops, so that we may not attach too much, or too little importance to them. For St. Paul, yes, the Holy Spirit, did not fix this limit for nothing,—undoubtedly, that we should direct ourselves accordingly. Hereby, this same limit is laid down for bishops, designating the character of their office, and the extent of their power; so that, when we see a bishop, who assumes more than this text allows him, we may with certainty regard and avoid him as a wolf and an apostle of the devil; for undoubtedly he must be Antichrist, who exercises more authority in ecclesiastical government, than is here designated.

First, he says, we should not receive or regard them as anything else but *ministers of Christ;* nor should they desire to be regarded in any other light. But *minister of Christ* must not be understood here as service to God, which is now called service to Christ; as, praying, fasting, going to church, and all that the ecclesiastical rites, institutions, cloisters, and the whole clerical order, style divine service. For these are mere devised words and works, by which this declaration of Paul, and others, are entirely obscured, so that now no one can know any longer what Paul here calls ministry of Christ. He means the ministry which is an office. All Christians serve God, but they are not all in office. Thus too, Rom. 11, 13, does he call his office a ministry: "Inasmuch as I am the apostle of the Gentiles, I magnify mine office;" and in the preceding Epistle, Rom. 15, 8, [he says]: "I say that Jesus Christ was a minister of the circumcision;" and 2 Cor. 3, 6: "Who also hath made us able ministers of the new testament, not of the letter, but of the spirit."

Whence shall I get language strong enough to root out from the hearts of all Christians the error so deeply impressed through Popery, in which they interpret the ministry of Christ and the ministry of God, in no other light but as alluding to their own works which they perform towards Christ, without means? Only observe, beloved friend, *to serve Christ* and to serve God is styled, especially by St. Paul, bearing an office commanded by Christ, namely, preaching. It is a service or ministry which proceeds from Christ, not to Christ, and which comes not from us, but to us. This you should carefully mark; it is important; otherwise you cannot understand the design of the Pauline expression: *Ministerium, ministratio,*

---

* B. 118.

CONCERNING THE THREE-FOLD INSTRUCTION OF PAUL. 35

ministrare, etc. He always calls it *ministry, ministration, minister*, etc. But seldom does he mention the service, ministry, which ascends to God, but generally, that which descends to men. For also in the Gospel Christ bids the Apostles to be submissive and servants of others, Luke 22, 26.

And for the purpose of being understood in reference to such service, [ministry] he carefully asks, explaining himself, saying: *Minister* or *steward*, which can not be understood but of the office of the ministry.

But he, therefore, styles it service or ministry of Christ, and himself *minister of Christ*, because he received this office from him, and because he was commanded to preach. Thus all apostles and bishops are ministers of Christ; that is, preachers of Christ, messengers of Christ, stewards of Christ, dispatched to the people with his message; so that the meaning of this passage is this: Every one of you should be careful not to institute another head, to raise up another Lord, to constitute another Christ, but you should all unanimously adhere to the one only Christ; for we are not your lords, or your masters, or your heads; neither do we preach ourselves, nor do we teach our own word; we do not lead you into obedience to us, so that you must be subject to us, and observe our doctrine. Not thus, not t'us; but we are *messengers* and *ministers* of *him* who is your Master, Head, and Lord; we preach his word, enlist in his commandments, leading you into his obedience alone. Thus too should you regard us; you should expect nothing else from us, so that you, although we are different persons from Christ, may, however, not receive a different doctrine, different word, different government, different authority, from that of Christ, through us. Whoever thus receives and regards us, regards us properly, and receives, not us, but Christ himself, whom alone we preach. But whoever does not thus regard us, does us injustice, discards Christ, the common head, sets up another head, and makes gods of us.

Thus we read, in Judges 8, 22, 23, that the children of Israel said to Gideon: "Rule thou over us, both thou and thy son, and thy son's son also." But he answered: "I will not rule over you, neither shall my son rule over you: the Lord shall rule over you;" and 1 Samuel 8, 7, when the children of Israel desired a king of Samuel, God said: "They have not rejected thee, but they have rejected me, that I should not reign over them." Here we perceive that God cannot allow any authority but his own among his people and regiment.

If, however, you should inquire how they committed sin in this way, since God had given them Gideon as chief in the contest, and afterwards set apart many holy kings over them?—I reply that it was neither a sin, nor contrary to the will of God for them to have kings or princes; for authorities must exist on earth. But their crime consisted in the fact that they subjected themselves to human government and were not satisfied with the government of God. For Gideon and the holy kings extended their authority in reigning not a hair's breadth further than the command and injunction of God extended, and they regarded themselves not otherwise than as the servants [ministers] of God; that is, they ruled the people according to the word of God, and not according to their own word. Thus the government of God alone was perpetuated, and they were servants in it, as the Apostles were in the word of Christ. Hence, too, David sings concerning his own government, as if it were God's, saying, Ps. 7, 6, 8: "Arise, O Lord, in thine anger; lift up thyself, because of the rage of mine enemies; and awake for me to the judgment that thou has commanded So shall the congregation of the people compass thee about: for their sakes, therefore, return thou on high. The Lord shall judge the people."

But where more authority is assumed than the command of God grants, and where the magistrate undertakes, or the subjects seek, to rule with human doctrines, there arises idolatry and a new head; the magistrate is no longer a servant, [minister] but domineers himself without a command and injunction of God. Here God declares, as he said to Samuel:— "They have not rejected thee, but me, that I should not reign over them." This I say in regard to the government of the soul which is to stand before God; for civil government does not concern the soul; nor does it belong to this matter.

Now, where there is more than this one head, God or Christ, elevated, there too must there be a doctrine and word differing from the doctrine and words of Christ. There also must the service of Christ immediately cease, Christ be rejected, and a new domination be established. Any one may easily perceive that no one can be the servant of Christ, and a teacher of his own word at the same time, as the two cannot exist together. How can he be a servant of Christ, if he does not teach the word of Christ? Or, how can he teach his own word, when he should teach the word of Christ? If he teaches his own word, he is a lord himself, and does not serve Christ; if he teaches the word of Christ, he is not a lord himself.

Hence you may judge for yourself, from where Popery and its ecclesiastical rites with all the priests, monks, and teachers of their high schools, emanate. If they can prove that they teach nothing but the word of Christ, we must regard them as the ministers or servants of Christ. But if we can prove that they do not teach the word of Christ, we must regard them not as the servants of Christ. Now, it is clear, indeed, that their position is not the word of Christ, but their own.—Hence it is evident that they are the kingdom of Antichrist, and the servants of the devil. For here Paul stands firmly, and concludes: "Let a man account of us as of the ministers of Christ."

Their assertion, that besides the word of Christ, the commandments of the church may be taught, intimating that their teachings are the doctrines of the church, avails nothing. Paul continues to stand, however, and teaches that the *Church belongs* neither to Peter nor to Paul, but to *Christ only,* and acknowledges none but the servants [ministers] of Christ. Hence, you perceive how blasphemous it is for the Pope to cry out obedience to his doctrines as a road to salvation, and disobedience to them as a road to damnation. Paul attributes this obedience here to the devil, as he does, 1 Tim. 4, 1: "Now the Spirit speaketh expressly that in the latter times some shall depart from the faith, giving heed to seducing spirits, and doctrines of devils; speaking lies in hypocrisy; having their conscience seared with a hot iron; forbidding to marry, and commanding to abstain from meats, which God hath created to be received with thanksgiving of them which believe and know the truth;" and Christ, John 10, 5, says: My sheep know my voice. And a stranger will they not follow, but will flee from him: for they know not the voice of strangers. I know my sheep and am known of them.

Here you perceive how the fact that whatever is not the voice of Christ, is a strange voice, the doctrine of the devil, and to be avoided, accords with Paul. Here you learn the conclusion to which Christ himself comes in regard to doctrines, and to that which his Church hears and teaches, and which are the commandments of the Church. The Church has no other doctrine but that of Christ, and no other obedience but that of Christ. All, therefore, that the Papists say concerning the commandments and obedience of the Church, is of the same species as that, which Paul calls speaking lies in hypocrisy, from false spirits and doctrines of devils.

This is even the meaning of the following words, where he calls them *stewards of the mysteries of God.*— Steward indicates here a person who regulates the domestics of his lord, like the stewards in monasteries, the provosts in nunneries, and all similar governors, managers, and overseers, now do. For *oikonomous peritus rei familiaris,* is Greek, and signifies in English a steward, who knows how to provide for a house, and is able to rule the domestics, and whom Christ, Matt. 24, 45, simply calls a servant, where he says: "Who then is a faithful and wise servant, whom his lord hath made ruler over his household, to give them meat in due season?"— Such a servant was Eliezer, the Servant of Abraham.

Now, God has a house too, which we ourselves, the Christian Church, are. In this there are pastors and bishops, overseers and stewards, who are to preside over the house, to provide nourishment for it, and to superintend its members. But these blessings are not physical. St. Paul distinguishes the stewards of God, therefore, from all temporal stewards.— These furnish visible nourishment, and manage the bodies, but those, invisible food, and manage the souls. For this reason he calls them *mysteria*. This custom has so long discontinued, that we no longer know what a steward is, and who are the *mysteria*. They imagine that, when they baptize, celebrate mass, and administer other sacraments, they exercise the *mysteria*, and that now there is no proper *mysterium* but the mass; although they know not why it must be called *mysterium*.

I can find no word at this time in German, equivalent to *mysterion*, and it were well to retain the same Greek word, as we have many others. It is equivalent to *secretum, arcanum*, a thing hidden from our eyes, seen by no one, and generally pertaining to words; as, when something is said, which is not understood, we say this is hidden, in this there is a secret, this contains a *mysterion*, in this something is concealed. Even this same concealment properly signifies *mysterium*; I call it a secret.

What then are the *mysteria* of God? Nothing else but Christ himself; that is, faith and the Gospel concerning Christ. For all that is preached in the Gospel, is far removed from our senses and reason, and hidden to all the world; nor can it be attained except through faith alone, as he says himself, Matt. 11, 25: "I thank thee, O Father, Lord of heaven and earth, because thou hast hid these things from the wise and prudent, and hast revealed them unto babes;" and as Paul, 1 Cor. 1, 8, says: "We speak the wisdom of God in a mystery, which none of the princes of the world knew."

To express this matter in the clearest manner, *mysterium* is, your hearing the things which you hold in your faith, that Christ, the Son of God, was born of a virgin, died, and rose again, and all this for the forgiveness of our sins. For these things no eye sees, nor reason comprehends; yea, as St. Paul, 1 Cor. 1, 21, says; It is mere foolishness to the wise, and mere offence to the saints [self-righteous].

For how is it possible for nature to perceive, or reason to acknowledge that this man, Christ, is our life, salvation, peace, righteousness, redemption, strength, wisdom, Lord of all creatures, and God, and whatever else the Scripture says concerning him?— No one can know this except him who hears it from the Gospel and believes it; it is too far removed from our sense and reason. Thus, then, the *mysteria* of God are nothing else but the things or blessings, which are preached concerning Christ, through the Gospel, and which our faith alone apprehends and holds.

In reference to this matter Paul speaks, 1 Tim. 3, 16:* "Without controversy," says he, "great is the mystery of godliness: God was manifest in the flesh, justified in the Spirit, seen of angels, preached unto the Gentiles, believed on in the world, received up into glory." All this is said in regard to Christ, who was manifest in the flesh. For he dwelt among men, who had flesh and blood, as well as he himself had; yet, however, he continued to be a mystery. For, that he was Christ, the Son of God, the life, the way, the truth, and all good, was hidden.

Yet he was justified in the Spirit; that is, through the Spirit, believers thus received, acknowledged, and regarded him. For this justification is nothing else but to declare just, or to allow to be just; as it is said Luke 7, 29: "All the people that heard him, and the publicans, justified God." Again, Ps. 51, 4: "That thou mightest

---

* B. Where he also speaks and teaches concerning these matters, how he should walk in the house of God.

be justified when thou speakest." This is equivalent to saying: He that believes in Christ, justifies him, and acknowledges the truth that he alone is our life, righteousness, and wisdom, and that we are sinners, dead and condemned. For this is what he is and claims to be.† But he that does not do this, stands upon his works, and does not regard himself as condemned, contends with him, and condemns him.‡

The declaration, Rom. 1, 4, has reference to justification: "He is declared to be the Son of God with power, according to the Spirit of holiness." As it is said, among unbelievers he is disregarded, and not only weak, but entirely condemned. But among saints who live in the Spirit who sanctifies them, it is fully and effectually maintained that he is the Son of God; for to them it is shown, and firmly established.

Now, St. Paul might well have said here: "We are the stewards of the wisdom of God, or of the righteousness of God," &c. Since Christ is all this, as 1 Cor. 1, 30, he says: "Who of God is made unto us wisdom, and righteousness, and sanctification, and redemption." But this would have been specifying. He desired to embrace in one word all these blessings, which are to be preached concerning Christ, and styles them *mysteries.*— As if he should say, we are spiritual stewards whose duty it is to minister the grace of God, the truth of God, and who can enumerate all separately? I shall briefly, sum up, and say they are the mysteries of God. They are called mysteries, and things concealed, because they are attained by faith alone.

Thus too, Rom. 1, 4, he pursues a similar course, when he comprises all in a word, how Christ was manifested in the flesh, justified in the Spirit, preached to the Gentiles, &c. As 1 Tim. 3, he says briefly in Greek,

† A. And he that regards him as such, justifies him in his spirit.

‡ B. But this justification of Christ proceeds from no one but him who has the Holy Spirit, whose work alone it is. Flesh and blood cannot do it, even if it were clearly presented and preached before our eyes and ears.

oristhis definitus. In short, he was declared determined, received, and regarded as the Son of God, by angels, Gentiles, the world, heaven, and all; since, for this purpose, he was manifested, justified, revealed, preached, believed, received, &c. Therefore he also calls it mysteries here, and 1 Tim. 3, a mystery. These expressions are, however, equivalent; Christ is wholly and entirely one mystery and many mysteries; for many mysterious blessings do we derive from him.

This too is worthy of remark, that St. Paul adds the declaration: The mysteries of God; that is, those hidden things which God grants, and which exist in him. For the devil also has his mysteries, as Rev. 17, 5, it is said: "Upon her forehead was a name written, MYSTERY, BABYLON," &c. Again, Rev. 17, 7: "I will tell thee the mystery of the woman," &c. These are mysteries, over which the Pope and his priests now preside as stewards; for they intimate that their doctrine and work lead to heaven, whilst behind these are concealed nothing but death and hell, to all who trust in them. But the mysteries of God are those, in which there are life and salvation.

Thus, then, we arrive at the meaning of the Apostle in regard to these words, that a *minister of Christ is a steward in the mysteries of God;* that is, he should be, and admit of being regarded as one who preaches and administers to the household of God, nothing but that which is Christ, and is in Christ; that is, he should preach the pure Gospel, the pure Faith, that Christ alone is our life, way, wisdom, power, glory, salvation, &c., and that the things which we do of ourselves are nothing but death, error, foolishness, weakness, shame, and condemnation. Whoever preaches otherwise, should be regarded by no one either as a servant of Christ or as a steward in divine things, but should be avoided as a messenger of the devil. Hence the following:

"Moreover, it is required in stewards, that a man be found faithful."

Upon this all depends. After this God enquires; this, angels, men, and all creatures, seek and require; not whether any one is styled or regarded as steward, or not. Here no one enquires whether a person has a small of a large bishopric; no, not even so particularly, whether he is pious, or not, as to his person; but here we should enquire whether he faithfully executes his office, and sets as a steward in the blessings of God. Here Paul allows us great power to judge the doctrine and life of all our bishops, papists, cardinals. Such faithfulness Christ also requires, Matt. 24, 45:— "Who then is a faithful and wise servant, whom his lord hath made ruler over his household, to give them meat in due season."

What can this faithfulness be?— How does it hold itself? Tell me, who would be benefited, or who would be aided, if one bishop were so great as to possess every bishopric, according to the usurpation of the Pope?— Who would be benefited, if he were so holy as to be able to raise the dead with his shadow? Whom would it help, if he were as wise as all the Apostles and Prophets were? Here no enquiry is made in regard to any of these things; but the question is whether he is faithful, whether he administers to the household the word of God, preaches the Gospel, and dispenses the mysteries of God.— *Here, here, here,* is the enquiry; this helps every one, this benefits every one. Above all things, therefore, faithfulness is sought and required in these stewards.

Now, compare this text to the Pope and all the ecclesiastics, and tell me, after what the Pope is seeking. Are not all his raving and raging to enable him alone to become supreme and to rule with force? His whole concern is to become great, mighty, exalted, and wealthy, and to bring everybody else in subjection to himself. To this end, the devil most deceitfully endeavors, through his blasphemous lips, to make it appear that obedience to all his laws is very great, and that it is very dangerous to the salvation of the soul, not to be subject to this obedience. But he is not concerned about being faithful to this household.

For tell me, where, in all the deluge of his innumerable laws and commands, yes, in all his government, did you ever hear or read that he touched with a single word the mysteries of God, or preached the Gospel? Here all that is said, is in regard to quarrels, prebends, or, at best, concerning pates and apparel. Yes, he openly condemns the Gospel and the mysteries of God, besides. Him the bishops and ecclesiastics follow with their foundations, cloisters, and high schools.

This Apostolic faithfulness they have so perverted now, that among them, a faithful bishop, abbot, or ecclesiastical prelate, is one who faithfully manages, secures, improves, and increases the temporal possessions, the heritage of St. Peter, the castle of St. Moretz, the land of the holy cross, the interest of the Virgin, and other church interests, that is, their own emolument, under the name of God and of the saints, so that the world, even in its most worldly condition bears no comparison to them. Now, these* are the bishops and prelates who have well governed the Church, no matter whether they have ever during their whole life read or heard the Gospel, to say nothing about their duty to preach. Thus this blasphemous tongue now continues unconstrained in all the world, and calls good stewards in the blessings of God, those who are entirely useless, unless it is to perform under temporal lords the duties of treasurers, assessors, guardians, bailiffs, architects, mayors, ploughmen, butlers, and kitchen stewards. This, and no more, do they prove by their apostolic fidelity.

But, in the meantime, the souls are dying, all that is divine is going to ruin, the wolf reigns and devours. Here they see nothing; here they afford no security; here they sit still, and count over their registers, and attend to the interests of St. Lorentz, and in the most faithful manner provide for the property of the church,—a faithfulness, for which they are certain Christ has prepared for them not a low seat in heaven. O, wretched, lost, blinded

* A. princes.

multitude, how securely you are going on towards hell!

Here I cannot pass unnoticed, I must, as a warning against similar attempts, relate a trick of the devil, which I heard it said he exhibited in former times, at Merseburg, in our own country, with the golden cup of emperor Henry. Here the beloved people relate with great energy a falsehood for which they obtain indulgences, by asserting that the roasted Lorentz, by casting the golden cup in the balance, so overcome the devil that he had to release the soul of the emperor, in consequence of which the devil became so enraged that he broke off one of the ears of the cup. Such gross, doltish, idle falsehoods are intended to blind us Christians, so that we may not perceive the trickery of the devil. Why did the devil fabricate this? This whole affair is urged by him, in order to present a miracle for the purpose of establishing the wealth, luxury, and all the delicate faithfulness of the prelates, concerning which we have already spoken, so that the fools might be induced to believe that they can overcome the devil by presenting gifts to the Church; while, at the same time, Peter says, this can be done alone by the power of faith.[*]

But there exists a fidelity still more beautiful now even among these same spiritless lords and faithful stewards, actively engaged in the spiritual welfare of souls: these are indeed the right, true stewards. They are so very holy; St. Peter in heaven will have to be on his guard to maintain his seat for them. These are our spiritual fathers, priests, monks, and and nuns, who exercise themselves in obedience to the Pope, the holy Church, and every species of human institutions, orders, and statutes.[†]

Here indeed we perceive the right

[*] A. These are the signs, by which Christ and Paul predicted the elect might be misled from the faith. Now, let them go, they are now regarded as pious and faithful prelates.

[†] A. And among these exists the paragon, the quintessence, the kernel, the marrow, the fountain,—and how shall I enumerate all their honorable titles?—which are assumed and maintained from the *observance*, yes, far enough from the *observance*,—the beautiful little cat with a pretty smooth coat,

stewards and the unheard-of fidelity; how tenaciously, stringently, and earnestly they adhere to *that* obedience, and maintain their traditions. Ay, they are, indeed, the right saints. Few bishops, who strictly observe even the holy, spiritual law, can be ranked with them. But when we thoroughly examine all their cloisters, and view all their doctrines and conduct, we perceive that no people on earth are less acquainted with the mysteries of God, and farther from Christ; yea, they act as if they were mad, maliciously storming Christ with their own contrivances. They are the Gog and Magog in the Revelations, who are contending against the Lamb of God. For they set up their works, by which they exterminate faith; and yet they are called the faithful stewards of God; precisely as a wolf in the midst of sheep, is the shepherd.

Now, he that has ears, let him hear what St. Paul says: "It is required in stewards that a man be found faithful." But *he who* is occupied with the mysteries of God, *is faithful*. It is concluded, therefore, that the Pope, bishops, monks, nuns, universities, and *all* who with them build, or are occupied with anything else but Christ, the Gospel, and pure faith, have the name, indeed, of being the servants and stewards of Christ, but in reality they are the servants and stewards of the devil, and are engaged in the mysteries of the devil, their lord. Christ adds, therefore, saying, the servant of the house should be not only faithful, but also wise, so that he may distinguish between the mysteries of God and the mysteries of the devil, in order that he may guard and secure himself and those committed to him. For it happens as St. Paul, 2 Cor. 11, 13, says, the false apostles of Christ transform themselves into the true apostles of Christ, even as the devil transforms himself into an angel of light.

The greater the faithfulness the greater the danger, where there is no wisdom to distinguish the mysteries of God, as we perceive in the two aforesaid false, seductive faithfulness-es of those spiritless saints. St. Paul well knew that the mysteries of the devil would thus get the upper hand; silent, therefore, in regard to all else, he points out faithfulness. Had our bishops remained faithful stewards of God, Popery and its peculiar spiritual orders would undoubtedly not have been introduced, and the common order of faith would have been maintained; and if they were now faithful, or would become so, all these peculiar spiritual orders would soon pass away, and the common ones would be restored.

" But with me it is a very small thing that I should be judged of you, or of man's judgment."

But here, in the first place, we must comprehend the language, and explain the terms, with which we should be as familiar as with our mother-tongue. St. Paul uses the word to *judge* or *sentence*, here, in a favorable sense; that is, in a sense equivalent to esteem and regard for him. Although the word judgment in its common acceptation generally conveys the idea of condemnation, yet, however, in every judgment two things occur; one is condemned, the other liberated, one punished, the other rewarded, one dishonored, the other honored. This also occurs in all private judgment. For whilst the Pharisee in the Gospel praised himself, he censured the Publican and other persons;—whilst he honored himself, he dishonored others. Thus too does every one act towards his neighbor in praise or censure; a judgment must consist of these two parts. Hence St. Paul says here, that he is judged or sentenced by them; that is, one part of the sentence falls upon him, namely, the laudable and honorable part; by praising and extolling him above the other Apostles, they judged between him and them, to his advantage and to their prejudice. But some judged, that is praised, St. Peter, others Apollos. But that to judge here is equivalent to praise, is evident from the conclusion of this Epistle, where it is said: "Judge nothing before the time, until the Lord come, then shall every man have praise of God.' What else is this, but to say, praise not, let God praise? It belongs to God to judge, praise, and crown us; we should neither praise, judge, nor crown one another.

The expression, man's judgment, [*menschliche Tag*] here implies the decision, judgment, and praise, by which men elevate and render illustrious and renowned those whom they highly esteem. Even as the natural day with its own light illuminates and renders visible and perceptible the things which cannot be seen or known in the night and in darkness. Hence, in the Latin language, illustrious persons, of whom everybody speaks, are called *præclari, nobiles, illustres*, in German, *durchlauchtige*; that is, those who are highly renowned, and have a name and reputation far above others. On the other hand, those who are destitute of renown, are called *obscuri, ignobiles, humiles*, insignificant and unknown.

In like manner, the Holy Scripture styles kings and princes, *doxas, glorias, claritates*; that is, glory, splendor, &c. As St. Peter, 2 Peter 2, 10, says in allusion to the Pope and his adherents, they will defame and desecrate the *glorias*; that is, they will imprecate and curse majesties, kings, princes, and all that are high and glorious upon earth;—whilst at the same time, Christ has commanded us to love our enemies, to bless them that curse us, to do good to them that persecute us; —as we perceive that the Pope does on Maundy-Thursday, in the *Bulla Cœnae Domini*, and whenever it pleases him.

Man's judgment, [*menschliche Tag*,] therefore, is the clamor and ostentation which men make before the world. Thus, Jeremiah 17, 16, says; "I have not desired the woful day, thou knowest." As if he should say, they accuse me with preaching new things, for the purpose alone of gaining honor, a name, and praise before men, and of being esteemed by them; but thou knowest that it is not so; I have not sought such honor and praise. And Christ, John 5, 46' says: "I receive not honor from men;" that is, I do not desire men to boast of and extol me;

and John 8, 50: "I seek not mine own glory; again, John 5, 35, he says thus in regard to John the Baptist: "Ye were willing for a season to rejoice in his light;" that is, ye would have delighted in seeing John praise and extol you by his testimony, so that for this short season ye might have honor before the people. This is what ye sought, &c.

Thus, then, Paul regards it as a very small thing to gain such clamor, honor, praise, and reputation before men, and correctly calls it man's judgment, or a human day; for it proceeds from men, and not from God, and it shall also pass away with men: as if he should say, I have no desire to receive praise from you and all the world; let men seek after this; the servants of Christ and stewards of God expect judgment from Christ and from a divine day.

But the Apostle manifests his ingratitude indeed, by not sending them a bag full of bulls or letters, by not blessing them, and by not distributing indulgences among them, as those who hold the Apostolical see in high honor and esteem. The Pope would have conducted himself in a manner much more Apostolical; yes, he would have anathematized them, if they had not lighted up such a human day, judgment, and would have said: "I am papistical, the Pope is the highest, the holiest, the mightiest." Had St. Paul desired it he might have become Pope and the highest, by a single word, if he had fallen in with those who wished to connect themselves with him; the others would have had to submit. But since he sought faithfulness more than exaltation, in his stewardship, he must remain a common tent-maker, and travel on foot.

And from these words it is clear that the Corinthians judged according to the person, and hence preferred their baptism and Gospel to those of others, intimating that Paul, or Peter, or Apollos, is greater or better than others. This Paul could not grant, but holds that all are equal, let the person be as he may; the one baptized and taught by Paul is as much a Christian as the one baptized and taught by Peter or Apollos, or any one else. But in opposition to this, the Pope rages severely and terribly, admitting no one to be a Christian unless he be taught by him, and yet he teaches nothing but infidelity and the foolish works of men.

But whilst Paul rejects this undue respect of persons, and is concerned about faithfulness alone in the stewards of God, he removes in this way very clearly every reason for divisions among them, so that they cannot separate, but must remain united, and allow all things to be equal and common. For how could they separate, if one minister of Christ, is like another, and is as much a steward of God; so that in this respect there is no difference. For even if one is more faithful than another, it will not create sects, but it will only promulgate the common Gospel with greater energy.

Now, these words of Paul refer not to one, but to every apostle; for he does not say: "Let a man so account of *me*," but, "Let a man so account of *us*"—*us*, *us*, says he. What us? namely, me, Peter, Apollos, in regard to whom this matter arose.— Hence it must be concluded that St. Peter is to be regarded equal to St. Paul, one like the other; so that either St. Paul must teach incorrectly here, by viewing all the Apostles as equal servants of Christ and stewards of God, or the statement and government of the Pope must be false and fictitious, and this text a very powerful enemy to popedom.

" Yea, I judge not mine own self."

You may ask how he regards his own judgment greater than that of all other men; we perceive that the greater portion of mankind praise themselves, or highly esteem themselves; for naturally every one is well-pleasing to himself. But few are there who get this day, or judgment of man, or are judged favorably by others; so that he might have justly reversed it, and said; "With me it is a very small thing that I should judge myself; I desire neither this human [judgment] day, nor the praise of you and of all the world. But he speaks as a Christian according to his conscience before God. For the Corinthians exalted Paul in that which is acceptable before God. They desired him to be higher, greater, and better before God, than the others, but others extolled St. Peter.

Now, there is no greater evidence before God than that of the conscience. For *God judges not according to appearance*, like men, *but according to the heart*, as we perceive, 1 Kings 16, 7: Men judge according to external appearances, but God penetrates into the heart. Hence it is clear that the evidence of our consciences is of greater weight before God, than that of all the world; and this evidence alone will stand, as it is said, Rom. 2, 15: "Their conscience also bearing witness, and their thoughts the mean while accusing or else excusing one another; in the day when God shall judge the secrets of men."

Now, St. Paul desires to say here: "Why should parties arise among you in regard to us, even if one is regarded as greater or better than another by men, when it is of no consequence whatever. For even our own consciences dare not judge as to who is the best and highest before God. For Solomon, Prov. 28, 26, says: "He that trusteth in his own heart is a fool." Therefore, there are no grounds for parties. No one knows who is the highest in the sight of God. Even Christ does not claim the right to sit one on the right hand and the other on the left, Matt. 20, 23. Now, since they are all alike before God, and since one is a minister of Christ as well as the other, and since it is unknown who is the highest in the sight of God, no one should presume to judge or to decide, much less to exalt himself above another on account of his temporal power, wealth, and friends. Now, the exaltation of the Pope is also contrary to this principle, since they claim that his highness above others emanates from God. This Paul denies, since no one can know or judge before the last day.

But here the pointed tongues of the papists desire to effect a breach, assuming that Paul does not reject the highness of Peter or of the Pope, but prohibits the judging of the person himself, in regard to how good or bad he is before God; here I answer and confess that St. Paul does forbid the person's being judged, in regard to how he stands before God; but, notwithstanding, the Corinthians did this for the purpose of elevating also the office, baptism, and preaching, on account of the person; otherwise they had not said: "I am a good Pauline, I am a good Petrine," &c. For they well knew that the preaching, baptism, and office were one and the same; but they wished to elevate the office and its work in consequence of the highness of the individual. St. Paul, however, assumes the reverse; he makes the office alike, even because the persons are alike to us, since no one can know who is the highest and best in the sight of God. Had they wished to elevate the individual alone, and not the office, they would not have made sects; nor would they have said, "I am of Paul," &c. Precisely as it does not create sects, if we do hold St. Peter higher than St. Augustine, as to his person. But it does produce sects, if I say: "I am of Peter,' and you say: "I am of Augustine;" and if this is done as if the preaching which I hear were better and higher than that which you hear.

These hypocrites, the papists themselves, since they clearly perceive that their falsehoods, by which they make the pope the highest, cannot stand, unless the persons be pious and the best, proceed to amend their falsehood with a greater falsehood, endeavoring to make his person appear good also, by saying that the Pope cannot err, since the Holy Ghost never forsakes him, and Christ is always with and in him: Some of them open their blasphemous mouths so wide, and, since they cannot deny that the Pope does sin openly, exclaim: It is impossible for him to remain in fatal sins a quarter of an hour. So very accurately have they measured with hour-glasses and compasses the Holy Ghost in the Pope.

Why then do they tell such blasphemous falsehoods? Doubtless, because they perceive that this highness cannot be maintained, unless the person be rescued, and they would have to admit that this highness without piety, would be a thing of the devil. Thus too, it cannot be said that the Corinthians elevated the person and not the office, since the person was exalted on account of the office.

But if you further ask, why Paul did not judge himself, since he wishes to be regarded as a minister of Christ and a steward of God? I answer, as already stated, that the ministry and the office are not his, but God's, who enjoined them upon him. For as no man can make the word of God, so no man can send it out, or constitute an apostle. God has already accomplished this himself, and constituted them apostles. We should therefore, also glory in it, confess it, and spread it abroad as a treasure which God has given. Precisely as, although I cannot constitute myself a person, I should glory in it, and confess, that God has constituted me a human being. But as I cannot judge how I am and will remain in the sight of God; so I cannot* judge in reference to an apostle or a steward, who is the greatest before God.

You say moreover: You teach, however, that a Christian should not doubt that he is accepted of God, and he that doubts is no Christian; faith assures us that God is our father, and that as we believe, so it shall be to us.

Answer: To this adhere firmly indeed, that faith in the grace of God is sure; for faith is nothing else but a steadfast, indubitable, sure confidence in divine grace. But this is what I have said: the Corinthians desired to hold and judge the Apostles according to their persons and works, as to which was the holier, greater, and worthier in his person, so that in this way his office and those who adhere to him might secure some prerogative above others. Here Paul razes all works and worthiness,

Luther's Works, 7r. Bd.
* A. Nor can I judge any apostle or steward of God, &c,

places them before the judgment of God, and keeps all apostles in the same office and faith. The office which they bear is one and the same, the faith by which they are justified is one and the same; but as to who is better, higher, and worthier, and does most in this respect, must be left to God, and it is no cause for separation in the community; hence it follows:

"For I know nothing by myself; yet am I not thereby justified."

This declaration properly indicates that they judged the Apostles in respect to the worthiness of their persons and works; for Paul admits that he is irreproachable in regard to his conscience, and confesses that they judged correctly so far as his person and conscience were concerned. But such judgment is not sufficient before God; all decisions also, therefore, based on such principles are false.

In regard to this declaration much might be said. For here we perceive* that no one is rendered pious and happy by any work. For if Paul durst say: I know nothing by myself, he must have been full of good works indeed; notwithstanding he says, I am not thereby justified. Whereby then? By faith alone. For if any one could be justified by the fact that he knows nothing by himself, and that his conscience is clear, his confidence would rest on himself, and he might judge and praise himself, like the presumptuous saints do: thus too faith as well as the grace of God, would be useless and unnecessary; we would possess in ourselves whatever might be useful and necessary, and we might well do without God. But all depends on the fact that we rely on the grace of God, and are thereby justified. But as to how our works, persons, conditions, and worthiness are afterwards to be judged, must be left to God; we are certain that we are justified by none of these, but uncertain how God will praise and judge them.

It is easy also, I presume, for every one to understand that Paul here speaks concerning his life after his conversion, in which he knows noth-

* A, that all works, are rejected,

ing by himself; but in regard to his former life he himself, writes 1 Tim. 1, 13, that he was an unbeliever, a blasphemer, and a persecutor of the Christian community.

Here a question, however, arises: How he is not justified thereby, that he has no consciousness, when at the same time he says, 2 Cor. 1, 12: "For our rejoicing is this, the testimony of our conscience, that in simplicity and godly sincerity, not with fleshly wisdom, but by the grace of God, we have had our conversation in the world, and more abundantly to you-ward?" Here the answer is self evident, since he adds, by the grace of God. For we should indeed rejoice in, boast of, and glory in the grace of God, upon which the glory of our consciences rests; and even if he had not added these words, it would still have to be understood in reference to the glory in grace, or to the glory before the world.

For before men every one can and should acknowledge his innocence, and rejoice that he has injured no one; nor should he call that evil which he knows to be good. But before God this boasting is nothing; for God requires and judges the heart; men are satisfied with the deeds. Before God, therefore, there must be something higher than our good consciences; as Moses, Exod. 34, 7, says: "Forgiving iniquity and transgressions and sin, and that will by no means clear the guilty." Rom. 3, 27: "Where is boasting then?" 1 Cor. 1, 31: "He that glorieth, let him glory in the Lord;" that is in his grace.

"But he that judgeth me is the Lord." This is equivalent to saying I will wait till God judges and praises me; as he also says, 2 Cor. 10, 18: "For not he that commendeth himself is approved, but whom the Lord commendeth." This he says, however, in order not to deter them, but to incite them to a good life. For although no man can judge and commend another, yet he shall not pass unjudged and uncommended; for God himself will judge and commend whatever is well done. Therefore, we should be so much the more diligent in doing good, since God himself will judge, and not be remiss or negligent in this respect; although we may be uncertain as to what his judgment will be.

"Therefore judge nothing before the time until the Lord come, who both will bring to light the hidden things of darkness, and will make manifest the counsels of the hearts; and then shall every man have praise of God."

Here the question, whether we should not praise one another, may justly arise? Paul, however, Rom. 12, 10, says: "Be kindly affectioned one to another with brotherly love; in honor preferring one another;" and Christ, Matt. 5, 16: "Let your light so shine before men, that they may see your good works, and glorify your father which is in heaven;" and 2 Cor. 6, 8: We must walk, "by evil report and good report," here upon earth: answer, all this is to be done, not in view of our works, but of our faith alone. Good works we should do, and extol them in others, but on account of these, no one should be justified, judged, or preferred to another. For it may happen that before God, a farmer with his plow may be better than a nun with her chastity.

The five foolish virgins, Matt. 25. 2, were virgins, yet they are condemned. The widow, Mark 12, 42, who threw two mites into the treasury, did more than all the others, who nevertheless cast in much more. The work of the woman, Luke 7, 37, who was a sinner, is extolled above all the works of the Pharisees. Thus, moreover, it is simply impossible for us human beings to know or ascertain the distinction and difference between persons and their works, yet we should extol them all, and give them equal honors, not preferring one to another, and humbling ourselves among each other, and ever esteeming our neighbor higher than ourselves, and then we should let God alone judge who is the highest. Although the sentence has already gone forth from him, that whoever humbles himself shall be exalted, yet it is not clear who those are, who humble and exalt themselves. The reason is because their hearts according to which God judges, have not manifested themselves. One may indeed humble himself, who is secretly in his heart highminded; again, one who is humble in his heart, may exalt himself.

Therefore he says: "The Lord will come, who both will bring to light the hidden things of darkness, and will make manifest the counsels of the hearts;" here will appear the proper distinction, who is the worthier, higher, and better, and whose works are the best.

It is, therefore, most unchristian to base our judgment and opinion [in regard to individuals] upon their external character and works; as, if any one should say: A Carthusian's life is better in itself, than a farmer's, or a married man's, &c. The Carthusian, indeed, if disposed to act properly, should esteem his own life humbler and less important than the married man's life; since God judges, not according to the manner of being, but according to the secrets of darkness and the counsels of the heart. How can the Carthusian know whether his own or the farmer's heart is the humbler and better?

Here these two examples, which, in my opinion, are the best that stand in the whole *vitis patrum*, are applicable: The one, in regard to St. Antony, to whom it was revealed that a tanner at Alexandria, an humble, honest mechanic, who however did nothing of special note, was nevertheless far above St. Antony, on account of the humility of his heart; the other, relative to Paphnutio, who, with all his austere life was not superior to a fifer, and two married women. Through special grace, God permitted these two examples to be manifested at the time, when monachism was at its highest, and works prevailed prodigiously; in order to prevent our eyes from forming opinions and decisions according to works, and to teach us to regard all kinds of works alike, and to subject ourselves to one another.

You will then say: if all kinds of works and conditions are alike, and none is to have the preference, what do we make by forsaking the world and entering the best orders, by becoming monks, nuns, and priests, with a view to serve God? Answer: Why did Christ and Paul foretell that false Christs and prophets would arise, and deceive many? Had the doctrine, that service to God is alike in all conditions and works, continued, assuredly no monasteries or cloisters would have arisen, or, indeed, would not have so rapidly increased, and given rise to the illusion that their requirements alone are services to God. Who would have became a priest? Who would have became a monk,* had he known that his condition and work are no better, than [the condition and work of] the poorest nurse-maid, who rocks children, and washes swaddling cloths.

It would be a great, lamentable disturbance, yes, a shame, to the Pope, if he had to humble himself to a nurse-maid, and esteem his works beneath hers, when kings and all the saints of God are scarcely worthy to kiss his feet, on account of the great worthiness of his condition and works. These holy people, must, therefore, institute something better than St. Paul teaches here; they must judge themselves, and hold up their conditions and works as the best, in order to sell their merits, and procure heaven for poor laymen, married persons, and others in different conditions, as for those who live not in God's service.

Now, since you perceive that it is impossible for the present ecclesiastical order to stand, unless it exterminate this Epistle of Paul, make a distinction between it and other Christians, and adjudge itself the best, you see clear enough, indeed, that popery, monasteries, and cloisters are grounded on mere falsehoods and blasphemies. For they style themselves ecclesiastical, and the others secular, when in the eyes of God none are ecclesiastical, but believers, the most of which are found, not among the ecclesiastics, but among the laity. What, then, can be more false than to adjudge that order as ecclesiastical, and to separate it from those, among whom the real, true ecclesiastical order ex-

* A. Yes, who would have become pope and bishop?

ists? God alone is to judge who is ecclesiastical, and who is the best. They go on, and assume the title ecclesiastical, simply because they have shaved heads and long coats. Is this not madness and folly?

But you will say: If this is true, it were better for us to leave the cloisters and monasteries. Answer: Do one of these two: either adhere to this Epistle, judge not yourselves, and regard your order or condition no better, than if you were not an ecclesiastic, and your chastity not superior to that of an honest* wife who sleeps with her husband every night, and bears children,—if you are unwilling to do this, then drop your caps, bald pates, cloisters, and all,—or know that you are ecclesiastical, or spiritual, not from a good spirit, but from an evil spirit; you will never overthrow Paul here. It is better to bear children in the common faith of Christ, than to remain a virgin for the devil. Paul stands firm here: You must not judge yourselves.

But you will reply here: Why, St. Hieronymous and many others have highly applauded virginity; besides, St. Paul, 1 Cor. 7, 38, it is better to be a virgin than to be married. Answer: Hieronymous here, Hieronymous there, Ambrose there, Augustine here; you hear what God says here through St. Paul, that no one shall judge himself or another as the best: this is of more weight than Hieronymouses, were they as numerous as the sands upon the sea shore, or leaves in the woods. St Paul says it is better to be continent than to marry, but not before God; otherwise he would contradict himself at this place. For it is true, he that lives in a state of continence is freer, and can attend to the Gospel better than he who is married; and thus on account of the Gospel, Paul applauded virginity or continence; as he confesses himself, 1 Cor. 7, 32: "He that is unmarried careth for the things that belong to the Lord."

Thus Christ also, Matt, 17,12, applauds the eunuchs, not for the sake of their condition, but for the sake of the kingdom of heaven; that is, for the sake of the Gospel. But still they go on, although no one cares less for the Gospel, than these ecclesiastics, claim to be in a better state than others, and extol continence on account of its own worthiness and merit, not on account of its usefulness. Precisely as if I should say, it is better to learn a trade than to be a servant. Why? Not, because the condition is better before God, but because it has less hinderances. Thus too St. Paul applauds virginity and continence, in none, however, except in those alone who have a desire for it through the grace of God.*

The reason† for all this Paul gives in his declaration, that the hidden things of darkness and the heart-counsels are not yet brought to light. Since, therefore, God judges according to these, and we cannot perceive them, we should let these states or conditions and works remain unjudged and without distinction. The virgin should not elevate her state of virginity above that of the married woman; the Pope should subject his state or condition to that of the plow-boy, and no one should presume that his state or that of any one else, is better before God, than the state and occupation‡ of others.

* B. Married woman.

* A. But at present no one is concerned as to whether it is a hinderance or a furtherance. Every one plunges in, simply contemplating the exaltation, worthiness, and greatness of continence, with such pains, moreover, danger displeasure, unwillingness and impurity, as to render the wretchedness intolerable. Still they wish to be better than other people. In this way they have brought reproach upon the state of matrimony, so that it is looked upon as an impure, ignominious state. For this, then, God rewards them, by permitting their continence to pollute their garments and beds, with ceaseless flowings or burnings, so that in reality there is no greater or more polluted incontinence, than this inordinate, incarcerated, restrained, and intolerable continence.

† B. The hidden things of darkness and the counsels of the hearts.

‡ A. And each one should be free to choose whatever state suits him; all being alike, till the Lord come. But were this state of things introduced, where would the holy fathers and the ecclesiastical lords get their support, who are not accustomed to labor, and who secure their subsistence by making the impression that the common man is in error, by separating their states, and judging them as the best, with a view to enjoy some privilege, when at the same time their own self devised states are nothing? Hence arise so many foundations, and contributions for

By the hidden things of darkness and the counsels of the hearts, Paul implies the two principles, which are usually, but not very intelligibly, termed *will* and *reason*. For man possesses in his inmost parts these two principles: He loves, wills, desires, and delights: he understands, perceives, judges, decides. I shall now call them meaning and thoughts.

Now the thoughts and solicitations of man are so deep and deceitful that no one can see them, no saint can sufficiently comprehend them. Jeremiah, 17, 9, 10, says: "The heart is deceitful above all things, and desperately wicked; who can know it? I the Lord search the heart; I try the reins;" and David, Ps. 32, 2: "Blessed is the man, in whose spirit there is no guile."

Hence it is, that there are many pious, who do great works. But there is a design or solicitation in these. They seek their own interest, of which they never become certain. They serve God, not purely for God's sake, but for the sake of honor, profit, of gaining heaven or escaping the pains of hell. This false impression no one can experience, unless God permit him to endure many severe temptations. St. Paul therefore here calls such thoughts hidden things of darkness,—the most appropriate name that can be applied to them. They are not only concealed, but in darkness; that is, in the inmost parts, where neither the individual himself, but God alone can see them.

Behold, this sad, dark intent and ground of the heart, should induce us to subject ourselves to one another, and not to hold or weigh one work or state against another. For the intention is the whole weight and doom of every work, condition, life, and conduct.* Now, since in her darkness, a married woman may have something good concealed, and a virgin something evil, it is entirely preposterous and unchristian, to exalt above a married woman, a virgin on account of her continence, which is simply external. Precisely as if I should weigh eggs in a balance, according to their shells alone, leaving out the yelks and whites.

Now, our thoughts correspond with our views, whether they be good or false. For we direct our aims, counsels, and thoughts according to our intentions and solicitations. These Paul here calls counsels of the hearts; that is, the thoughts, with which we are occupied, in order to accomplish our intentions and solicitations.

These Mary touches in her song of praise, Luke 1, 51: "He hath scattered the proud in the imagination of their hearts." Here she calls the intentions the hidden things of darkness, that is the solicitations; and the heart, the counsels and imaginations. Again, Moses, Gen. 6, 5, says in regard to these: "Every imagination of the thoughts of his heart was only evil continually;" and Christ, Matt. 6, 22, 23, diligently warns us against the same false views, saying: "The light of the body is the eye: if therefore thine eye be single, thy whole body shall be full of light. But if thine eye be evil, thy whole body shall be full of darkness. If therefore the light that is in thee be darkness, how great is that darkness!" All this is said in reference to the hidden operations of darkness, which can by no means be overcome, except by despair in regard to our works, and by strong faith in the pure grace of God; and for this purpose nothing is more profitable than many severe sufferings, together with all kinds of misfortune. Under such influences we may learn to perceive to some extent, otherwise all must be lost.

FOURTH SUNDAY IN ADVENT.

EPISTLE, PHILIPPIANS 4, 4-7.

Rejoice in the Lord always: and again I say, Rejoice.

Let your moderation be known unto all men. The Lord is at hand.

Be careful for nothing; but in every thing by prayer and supplication with thanksgiving let your requests be made known unto God.

---

cloisters, chapels, and churches, and especially for those idle, beloved bellies and gluttons. All these would fall and pass away, if this doctrine of St. Paul were introduced.

* A. As Solomon, Prov. 16, 2, says: "The Lord weigheth the spirit." God is the weigh-master of the spirits.

And the peace of God, which passeth all understanding, shall keep your hearts and minds through Christ Jesus.

WHILST THIS EPISTLE is short, it is a rich and important lesson of Christian faith. It teaches us how we should conduct ourselves towards God and towards our neighbor, saying:

"Rejoice in the Lord alway."

This rejoicing is a fruit and result of faith, as he says, Gal. 6, 22: "The fruit of the Spirit is love, joy, peace, long-suffering, gentleness, goodness, faith, meekness, temperance." For it is impossible for a heart to rejoice in God, which does not first believe in him. Where faith does not exist, the individual is filled with fear, timidity, sadness, and a disposition to flee, at the mere thought or mention of God. Yes, such a heart is full of enmity and hatred against God; because it feels itself guilty in its conscience, and has no confidence that God is gracious and merciful to it; while it knows that God is an enemy to sin, and will dreadfully punish it.

Since, then, these two exist in the heart, a consciousness of sin, and a perception of God's chastisement, it must always be depressed, faint, and terrified, continually apprehensive that God is standing behind it with a club, as Solomon, Prov. 28, 1, says: "The wicked flee when no man pursueth;" and, Deut. 28, 65: "The Lord shall give thee there a trembling heart, and thy life shall hang in doubt," &c. To speak much to such a heart in regard to joy in God, is like persuading water to burn; it has no effect on it; for it feels the hand of God pressing it in its conscience.—Hence the prophet also says, Ps. 32, 11: "Be glad in the Lord, and rejoice, ye righteous: and shout for joy, all ye that are upright in heart." It must be the just and the righteous, who are to rejoice in the Lord. This Epistle is, therefore, written, not for the sinner, but for the saint. We must first tell sinners how they can be liberated from their sins, and secure a merciful God; this rejoicing will then, when they have been liberated from their evil consciences, follow of itself.

But how shall we be liberated from our evil consciences, and feel satisfied that God is merciful to us. Answer: This has been sufficiently stated already in the foregoing postils, and it will still be frequently indicated hereafter. Whoever desires to have a peaceful conscience, and to feel that God is merciful, must not depend on works, like the perverters do, murdering the heart still more, and increasing its hatred to God; but he must despair in regard to all works, and apprehend God in Christ, comprehend the Gospel, and believe what it promises.

But what does the Gospel promise, but that Christ is given for us, that he bears our sins, is our bishop, mediator, advocate before God, and thus only through Christ and his work, God is reconciled, our sins are forgiven, and our consciences liberated and cheered? When this faith of the Gospel really exists in the heart, God is fair and lovely; for it feels in all confidence nothing but his favor and grace; it fears not his chastisement; its mood is secure and peaceful, because God has conferred upon it such superabundant goodness and grace, through Christ. Hence from such a heart must follow love, peace, joy, singing, thanksgiving, praise; it will enjoy a full, a cordial pleasure in God, as in its most beloved and gracious father, who has conducted himself so paternally towards it, and without any of its merit, has so richly poured out upon it his goodness.

Behold, concerning such rejoicing St. Paul here speaks; here there is no sin, no fear of death or hell, but a joyful, all-powerful confidence in God and his kindness. Hence it is called a *rejoicing in the Lord*, not in silver or gold, not in eating or drinking, not in pleasure or chanting, not in strength or health, not in skill or wisdom, not in power or honor, not in friendship or favor, yea, not even in good works or holiness. For these are mere deceptive, false joys, which never touch or affect the bottom of the heart, and concerning which we may well say the individual rejoices, but his heart experiences not.

But to rejoice in the Lord, that is, to trust, confide, glory, and pride in the Lord, as in a gracious father, is a rejoicing which rejects every thing that is not the Lord, as well as that self-righteousness, of which Jeremiah, 9, 24, speaks: "Let not the wise man glory in his wisdom, neither let the mighty man glory in his might, let not the rich man glory in his riches: but let him that glorieth glory in this, that he understandeth and knoweth me." Again, Paul, 1 Cor. 10, 31: He who glories let him glory in the Lord.

He also says: *The rejoicing should be always.* Here he hits those who rejoice in God, praise and thank him half of their time; that is, when it is well with them, when not, their rejoicing ceases.* But not so with David, Ps. 34, 1: "I will bless the Lord at all times: his praise shall continually be in my mouth." For this he had good reason; for who shall injure or harm him, who has the favor of God? Sin harms him not, neither death, nor hell, as David, Ps. 23, 4, sings: "Yea, though I walk through the valley of the shadow of death, I will fear no evil;" and Paul, Rom. 8, 35, 38, 39: "Who shall separate us from the love of Christ? Shall tribulation, or distress, or persecution, or famine, or nakedness, or peril, or sword? For I am persuaded, that neither death, nor life, nor angels, nor principalities, nor powers, nor things present, nor things to come, nor light, nor depth, nor any other creature, shall be able to separate us from the love of God, which is in Christ Jesus."

"And again I say, rejoice."

This repetition of the Apostle adds strength to his admonition. This is highly necessary. For since we live in the midst of sin and evil, both of which drive us into sorrowfulness, the Apostle desires to cheer us up against this, so that, if even we should sometimes fall into sin, our joy in God may be stronger than our sorrowfulness in sin. It is true, indeed, that sin naturally brings with it fear and sorrowfulness of conscience, and we cannot always escape sin; hence we should let our rejoicing rule, and Christ be greater than our sins, as John, 1 John 2, 1, says: "If any man sin, we have an advocate with the Father, Jesus Christ the righteous: and he is the propitiation for our sins;" also, 1 John, 3, 20: "For if our heart condemn us, God is greater than our heart, and knoweth all things."

"Let your moderation be known unto all men."

Now, whilst he instructs them how to conduct themselves before God, to serve him with joyful hearts, he proceeds briefly to teach them how to conduct themselves before men, saying: "Let your moderation be known unto all men." This is equivalent to saying: Rejoice always before God, but before men be moderate: regulate your conduct so as to do, bear, and suffer whatever may be admissible, and not contrary to the commandments of God, that you may render yourselves agreeable to all; not only, not to give offence to any one, but also to put the best constructions on what others may do, that you may be clearly recognized as those, to whom all things are alike, and who are satisfied with whatever hits or misses you, cleaving to nothing that might bring you into conflict or discord with any one. With the rich, be rich, with the poor, poor, with the joyful, rejoice, with the weeping, weep: and finally, be all things to all men; so that every one must confess that you are not disagreeable to any one, but pleasant to all, uniform, alike, and common.

Such is the meaning of the little word *epeikia, æquitas, clementia, commoditas,* which the Apostle employs here, and which we cannot render better than by the word moderation,* in which one suits and accommodates, confirms, and equalizes himself to another, and is to one like he is to another, and alike to all, not setting himself up as a model and patron, and not desiring every one to bow, conform, and moderate himself to him. Hence, too, justice is divided into strict and mild justice, and that which is too strict is

---

* A. Concerning which, Ps. 48: He will praise thee, when thou favorest him.

* A. That is, a virtue

mitigated; that is, *æquitas, moderatio, clementia juris*. The Latin translator has rendered it *modestiam, moderation;* and this would convey the proper sense, were moderation not generally understood in reference to eating, drinking, and apparel. But the word here is designed to indicate a moderation of life, which mitigates, adjusts, and adapts itself to the abilities and circumstances of others, yielding, accepting, following, mitigating, doing, allowing, tolerating, in such a way as it conceives necessary to the capacity and condition of its neighbor, even to the detriment and disparagement of its possessions, honors, and life.

This we must illustrate by examples, in order that it may be more clearly understood. Paul, 1 Cor. 9, 19, 22, [says]: "For though I be free from all men, yet have I made myself servant unto all, that I might gain the more. And unto the Jews I became a Jew, that I might gain the Jews; to them that are under the law, as under the law, that I might gain them that are under the law; To them that are without law, as without law, (being not without law to God, but under the law to Christ,) that I might gain them that are without law. * * I am made all things to all men, that I might by all means save some;"— that is, he ate, drank, and acted with the Jews according to the law; although it was not necessary for him so to do; and with the Gentiles he ate, drank, and acted, without law, like the Gentiles, since only faith and love are required; all else is free to be omitted or observed. Hence, for the sake of one, all this may be observed; for the sake of another, omitted, and thus adapted to each one.

Now, if a blind, capricious individual were to intrude here, demanding this to be omitted or that to be observed, like some of the Jews did, as necessary, and requiring every one to follow after him, and he after no one, equality would be destroyed; yes, even Christian liberty and faith exterminated. To this, like St. Paul, no one should yield, in order that liberty and truth may be maintained.

Again, Matt. 12, 1, and Mark 2, Christ suffered his disciples to break the Sabbath, and broke it himself frequently, where it was necessary:— where it was not necessary, he observed it, assigning this reason, saying: "The Son of Man is Lord even of the Sabbath day;" that is, the Sabbath is free; for the sake of love and service to one it may be broken; on the other hand, for the sake of love to another it may be observed.

Thus for the sake of the Jews, St. Paul circumcised Timothy, says Luke; but he would not permit Titus to be circumcised, because they insisted on it, and were unwilling to leave it free. He claimed authority both to do it, or not do it, so as to benefit others, but deemed neither the one nor the other as necessary, simply for the sake of the work itself, as if it must be performed.

But, to make the application to ourselves: When the Pope commands us to confess, to receive the Sacrament, to fast, to eat fish, and to perform any of his other commands, and insists that these things must be done in obedience to the Church, we should calmly put our foot on such injunctions, and do the contrary, simply because he commands them; so that liberty may be maintained. But, when he does not enjoin these things, we should according to his desire, observe them with those who observe them, and, on the other hand, omit them with those who omit them, saying like Christ said: "The Son of Man is Lord even of the Sabbath day," much more of such human laws. For to observe these things with such liberty, injures nothing, either in regard to faith or the Gospel; but to observe them through compulsion as an act of obedience, exterminates faith and the Gospel.

*Thus, in regard to all other external institutions or ordinances, which are free in themselves, and not contrary to faith or love, we should maintain the privilege of observing them in love and liberty, for the sake of those with whom we are, so that we

---

* A. Thus, through love, &c., we should observe monastic vows, rules, and statutes.

may agree and unite with them. But if they insist that these things shall and must be observed as an act of obedience, as necessary to salvation, we should* desist from them, and do the contrary, to show that nothing, but faith and love, is necessary for a Christian; all else, we are at liberty, through love, to observe or omit, according to our associations. For to observe these things through love and liberty, injures nothing; but to observe them through necessity and obedience, is reprehensible. This should also be understood in regard† to ceremonies, hymns, prayers, and all other‡ church ordinances, whilst they are observed through love and liberty. Only for the service and the pleasure of the company present, should they be observed, when it is a work otherwise not evil in itself.—But when these things are urged as necessary, we should desist from them, and act against them, in order to maintain the liberty of faith.§

Again, moreover, when civil government enjoins its laws, and demands its tribute, we should freely render our services to them, even if they do constrain us. For here there is no danger in reference to our liberty or faith; since it does not claim that the observance of its laws is essential to salvation, but to civil dominion, protection and government. Hence our conscience maintains its liberty, and our faith is not impaired, by submitting to these things. But to that which does not injure us in regard to our faith, and which benefits others, we may adequately adapt ourselves. But were it to insist that the observance of its laws is essential to salvation, we should pursue the same course as that already suggested relative to the laws of the Pope and the cloisters.

Now every one should act according to these examples, in all other instances, and, as St. Paul says here, put himself on an equality with all men, acting complacently, so as not to take into consideration simply his own claims or rights, but the wishes and advantages of others. For here St. Paul with a single word has razed all rights. If you have a right or a demand, and the condition of your neighbor really requires you to yield it, you act contrary to the principle of love and this equality, and are reprehensible indeed, if you seek and demand it; since by it, you sustain no injury relative to your faith, and your neighbor secures an advantage. For you would desire any one to act thus towards you, as the natural law says.

Yes, we also remark here, that, if any one should harm or injure you, you should put the best construction on it, and excuse it, thinking like that holy martyr, who, when all his possessions were taken, said: They cannot, indeed, take Christ away from me. Thus, too, should you say: It does not injure me as to my faith, why should I not excuse him, submit and accommodate myself to him?

I cannot better illustrate this subject than by the introduction of an example of two good friends; and as they conducted themselves towards each other, so should we act towards all men. But how did they? Each one did what was agreeable to the other; each one yielded, submitted, suffered, did, and allowed whatever he conceived to be useful or agreeable to the other, freely and without constraint. Thus each one adapted and accommodated himself to the other,

---

* **A.** Cloisters, plates, caps, vows, rules, and statutes.
Luther's Works, 7r Bd.

† **A.** Instituted Masses, singing, &c.

‡ **A.** Ordinances of the collegiate churches, &c.

§ **A.** And here you perceive how diabolical these institutions, cloisters, and all popedom, are, since they do nothing else but make out of liberty and love, necessity and obedience, by which the Gospel together with faith is exterminated, to say nothing of the wretchedness of the common populace who submit to these things, for the sake of their bellies. For how many now attend choir and pray *Horas*, hours, for God's sake? A general destruction of these institutions and cloisters would be the best reformation, in this respect. For they are of no benefit to Christianity, and could easily be dispensed with. And before such liberty could be established in one such institution or cloister, a hundred thousand souls might be lost in the others. Therefore whatever is not beneficial and useful, and does such unspeakable injury, and cannot be remedied, would much better be wholly and entirely exterminated.

not restraining each other by any selfish motives; and if one infringed on the property of the other, he was excused; and, in a word, here there was neither law, demand, restraint, nor fear, but pure freedom and good-will, and yet everything passed along so harmoniously, that the one hundredth part of the harmony would not be secured by any laws or restraints.

The headstrong, however, and the inflexible, who excuse no one, and determine to control and govern everything according to their own minds, lead the whole world into error, and are the cause of all wars and calamities on earth; and yet they claim to do it all for the sake of justice; so that a heathen has well said: *Summum jus, summa injustitia*; that is, the most extreme justice is the greatest injustice. Again, Prov. 7, 17, it is said: "Be not righteous over much; neither make thyself over wise." For as the most extreme justice is the greatest injustice, so the most extreme wisdom is the greatest folly. Hence the old adage: "When the wise act the fool, they act the fool too grossly." If God were always to execute the most extreme justice, we could not live a moment. St. Paul, 2 Cor. 10, 1, commends such gentleness in Christ, saying: I beseech you by the meekness and apppproving of Christ; so we may moderate our minds, demands, wisdom, and wit, and adapt ourselves according to the circumstances of others, in all respects.

But observe the beautiful arrangement of these words: "Let your moderation be known to all men." You may say: How can any one become known to all men? Again, must we boast of our moderation and proclaim it to all men? God forbid. He does not say: Boast of it and proclaim it; but let it be known, or experienced by all men; that is, exercise it in deed before men, not by thinking or speaking about it, but by showing it in your actions and conduct, so that every one must see, comprehend, and experience it: so that no one can say anything else in regard to you, but that you are moderate, being overcome by real experience, even if he wished to speak otherwise in reference to you; so that his mouth may be stopped by the knowledge of everybody relative to your moderation; as Christ, Matt. 5, 16, says: "Let your light so shine before men, that they may see your good works, and glorify your father which is in heaven;" and 1 Pet. 2, 12: "Having your conversation honest among the Gentiles: that, whereas they speak against you as evil doers, they may by your good works, which they shall behold, glorify God in the day of visitation." For it does not lie in our power to make our moderation acceptable to all men. But it is enough for us to enable every one to perceive and experience it in our lives.

By the phrase, *all men*, we are not to understand all persons on earth, but *all kinds of persons*, both friends and foes, great and small, lords and servants, rich and poor, natives and foreigners, relatives and strangers.—For there are some who conduct themselves in the most friendly and complacent manner towards strangers, but towards their own families or domestics, to whom they are accustomed, they manifest nothing but rigor and austerity. How many are there, who excuse, twist, and construe in the most favorable manner all that the great and the rich do and say, but to servants, or to the poor and inferior they are severe and hard, or put the most unfavorable construction on all they say or do? Again, to his children, parents, friends and relatives, everybody is affectionate, and everything is construed and borne in the most favorable manner. How often does one friend flatter another, till it becomes a public vice, imitating and apppproving, as excellent, everything he does? But towards his foes and adversaries he pursues the contrary course. In these he can find no good, no reason for toleration or favorable construction, but censures according to appearances.

In opposition to such unequal and partial moderation St. Paul speaks here. He desires the *moderation* of a *Christian* to be full and complete, to one like to another, whether friend or foe, bearing with and excusing every one, without respect to person or merit. For it is essentially good, and naturally mild, precisely as gold remains gold, whether secured by a pious or an impious individual. For the silver did not become ashes when Judas the traitor, received it. Thus, all creatures that are of God, are real and remain alike to every one. Thus, too, the *moderation* received in *the Spirit*, continues mild, whether directed to a friend or an enemy, to the rich or the poor. But pale, insidious nature acts as if gold in the hand of St. Peter remains gold, but in the hand of Judas becomes ashes.

Thus, the moderation arising from our reason and nature is mild, not to all men, but to the rich and the great, to strangers and friends. Hence, it is false, empty, deceptive—mere dissimulation, treachery, and deception before God. Observe, therefore, how impossible it is for nature to exercise this full, spiritual moderation, and how few people become conscious of the imperfections of that beautiful, transcendent moderation which they manifest towards some people, presuming they do right and proper by being immoderate towards others.— For, thus, our mean, filthy nature, with her beautiful reason, which always acts and decides contrary to the Spirit and that which is of the Spirit, teaches. As St. Paul, Rom. 8, 5, says: "They that are after the flesh do mind the things of the flesh."

Now, St. Paul has comprehended in these few words the *whole* of a *Christian's conduct towards his neighbor*. For he that is moderate, treats every one right, both in regard to body and soul, in words and actions, bearing with his evils and imperfections. This then, is nothing else but love, peace, long-suffering, gentleness, goodness, meekness, and everything that belongs to the fruits of the Spirit, Gal. 5, 22.

But, you will say: Yes, who would, then, be able to keep a bit of bread, in consequence of wicked people, who would abuse such equality, take everything we have, and not allow us even to live on the earth? Listen how beautifully St. Paul replies in the conclusion of this Epistle. First, he says:

"The Lord is at hand."

Were there no God, you might well thus fear the wicked. But there is not only a God, but he is at hand.— He will neither forget nor forsake you; only be moderate to all men, and let him care for you, how he will support and protect you. Has he given you Christ, how shall he not give you the necessaries for a support? He still has much more than any one can take from you: you, too, have more already, than all the goods of this world, since you have Christ. Concerning this the Psalmist, Ps. 55, 22, speaks: "Cast thy burden upon the Lord, and he shall sustain thee;" and 1 Pet. 5, 7: "Casting all your care upon him; for he careth for you;" and Christ, Matt. 6, 25: Behold the lilies of the field, and the fowls of the air, &c. This is equivalent to saying:— "The Lord is at hand." Then follows

"Be careful for nothing."

Take no thought for yourselves; let him care for you; he whom you now acknowledge, is able to care for you. The heathen, who knows not that he has a God, takes thought for himself. Christ, Matt. 6, 31, 32, says: "Take no thought, saying, What shall we eat? or, What shall we drink? or, Wherewithal shall we be clothed? (For after all these things do the Gentiles seek:) for your heavenly Father knoweth that ye have need of all these things." Let the whole world, then, grasp, and deal unrighteously, you shall have enough; you shall not die of hunger or cold, unless some one shall have taken away your God, who cares for you. But who shall take him from you, if you do not let him go yourself? We have no reason, therefore, to take thought for ourselves, since we have, as a father and a protector, him who has all things in his hand, even those who, with all their possessions, would rob or injure us. But we should always rejoice in him, and be moderate to all men, as those who are certain that they shall have enough for body and soul, especially as we have a gracious God;—those who have not, may well be concerned about themselves. Our care or concern should be, not to be concerned indeed, and to rejoice in God alone, and to be mild to man. In regard to this the Psalmist, Ps. 37, 25, speaks: "I have been young, and now am old; yet have I not seen the righteous forsaken, nor his seed begging bread." And Ps. 40, 17: "The Lord thinketh upon me."

"But in everything by prayer and supplication with thanksgiving let your request be made known unto God."

Here he teaches us to cast our care upon God; and this is his meaning: Take no thought for yourselves. If, however, anything occurs to produce care or anxiety in you, as must be the case, since many trials will befall you on earth, act thus: Make no effort to evade it, let it be what it may, but cease your care or anxiety, turn to God with prayer and supplication, and entreat him to accomplish all for you, that you wished to effect by your care. This do with thanksgiving, because you have a God who cares for you, and to whom you may freely bring home all your cares. He, however, who does not act in this way, when anything befalls him, but wishes first to measure it by his reason, overrule it by his counsels, and falls into anxiety, plunges himself into deep wretchedness, and loses the joy and peace in God, and yet accomplishes nothing; but digs only in the sand, sinks himself still deeper, and effects nothing; as we daily learn from our own experience and that of others.

It may be necessary to say that no one should, therefore, come to the conclusion that he will let everything go, and rest upon God, without doing anything, or using any exertion, not even prayer; for any one who would thus act, would soon fail, and fall into care or anxiety. We must strive; and even for this reason much falls on us, which gives us care, that we may be driven by it from our cares to prayer; and not without reason does the Apostle place in opposition the two clauses: *Be careful for nothing*, and *in all things flee to God*. Nothing and *all* are opposed to each other. By this he shows sufficiently that many things occur which drive us to care. About all these, however, we should not be over-anxious, but commit ourselves to God, and entreat him for what we need.

Now, let us examine here how prayer should be formed, and what manner is proper in praying. He seems to make prayer consist of four parts, namely, *praying, supplication, thanksgiving*, and *petitioning*. *Prayer* is nothing else but the words or expressions,—as, for instance, the Lord's Prayer, the Psalms, and the like,—in which sometimes something else, besides that for which we petition, is stated. *Supplication* is enforcing and strengthening prayer by something; as, when I entreat any one for the sake of his father, or for the sake of anything that he loves, or highly esteems. Thus we entreat God through his Son, through his saints, through his promises, through his name, as Solomon does, Ps. 132, 1: "Lord, remember David, and all his afflictions;" and Paul also, Rom. 12, 1: "I beseech you, therefore, brethren, by the mercies of God;" and 2 Cor. 10, 1: "I beseech you by the meekness and gentleness of Christ," &c. *Petitioning*, is to state what we have at heart, and what we desire in prayer and supplication; as in the Lord's Prayer, in which there are prayer and seven petitions. Christ, Matt. 7, 7, 8, says:— "Ask, and it shall be given you: seek and ye shall find; knock, and it shall be opened unto you: for every one that asketh receiveth; and he that seeketh findeth; and to him that knocketh it shall be opened." *Thanksgiving* is to relate the blessings received, and thus to strengthen our confidence to await that for which we pray.

In this way the prayer becomes vigorous, and through supplication urgent, but through thanksgiving, sweet and acceptable: and thus, with its strength and its sweetness, it overcomes and receives whatever it petitions. This manner of praying we see in the practice of the Church, and of all the holy fathers in the Old Tesment, who always offered supplication and thanks in prayer. Thus, too, the Lord's Prayer begins with praise, thanking, and acknowledging God as a father, and presses forward to him, through fatherly and filial love. Its supplication has no equal. Hence it is the highest and noblest prayer under the sun.

With these words St. Paul has most beautifully spiritualized the golden censer, and disclosed its mystery, concerning which Moses has written much in the Old Testament, how the priest should burn incense in the temple. For we are all priests, and our prayer is the censer. The priest is the golden vessel which signifies the words in prayer, which are dear and precious; as, the words in the Lord's Prayer, the psalms, and other prayers. For in the entire Scripture, the vessel is taken for the words, because in and with the words, the sense is comprehended, presented, and received; precisely as in the vessel, the wine, the water, the coals, and whatever else, are contained. Thus too, by the golden cup in Babylon, Rev. 17, 4, human doctrine is understood, and by the cup, in which the blood of Christ is, the Gospel.

But the fire coals are the thanksgiving and enumerating of the benefits in prayer; for, that the coals signify benefits, Paul, Rom. 12, 20, indicates, where he quotes the declaration of Solomon, Prov. 25, 22: "If thine enemy hunger, feed him: if he thirst, give him drink: for in so doing, thou shalt heap coals of fire on his head." They are, however, fiery and burning coals; for the benefits overcome and enkindle the heart most powerfully. But in the law it was forbidden to take fire coals from any other place, but the altar; that is, in prayer we must not refer to our works and merits, like the Pharisee did in the Gospel, Luke 18, 11, but receive the benefits in Christ. He is our altar, upon whom we are offered; on this benefit we must render thanks, and in it pray; as St. Paul, Col. 3: 17, says: "Do all in the name of the Lord Jesus, giving thanks to God and the Father by him." For he can allow nothing else, as he shows, Lev. 10: 1, where [it is said] the sons of Aaron, Nadab and Abihu, were burnt before the altar, because they took coals for the censer from another place, than the altar.

The petition is the volume of smoke, as the incense or the thyme, which is laid thereon, and which completes the prayer. The declaration of St. Paul, "Let your request be made known unto God," is made in view and explanation of the smoke of the censer; as if he should say: If you wish to offer incense as a sweet savor before God, let your petition be made known through supplication and thanksgiving; this is the right, the sweet smoke or fume, which is recognized and rises up before God, like a small taper and a straight rod; precisely as the natural smoke rises up from the incensory. Such a prayer penetrates through heaven. For the gratitude and benefit induce us to pray freely and forcibly, as well as with ease, pleasure, and delight; like the coals of fire make the smoke strong; otherwise the prayer is cold, sluggish, and heavy, especially if the heat be not first enkindled with the coals of benefits.

But how shall our prayer be made known to God when it is not only known to him before we begin; but he himself also comes to us first, and induces us to pray? Answer: St. Paul makes this statement for the purpose of teaching how *a real, true prayer should be;* namely, that it should not be made in vain or on a venture, like those do, who care not whether God hears them or not, ever uncertain, yea, rather thinking they will not be heard. This, however, is neither praying nor petitioning, but tempting and mocking God. For if any one should entreat me for a penny, and did not believe or think that I would give it to him, I would not be disposed to hear him, but would come to the conclusion that he was either mocking me, or else was not in earnest; how much less will God hear such blare? For a prayer should be made known to God; that is, we should not doubt that God hears us, and that our prayer reaches him, and that our request shall assuredly be granted. For if we do not believe that God hears our prayer, or that it reaches him, it will undoubtedly not reach him. As we believe, so it will be.

The rising smoke is, therefore, nothing else but the faith in prayer, when we believe that it reaches him and is heard. With these words St. Paul touches that which is often alleged in the Psalms: "My cry comes before him, even into his ears, Ps. 18, 6: again, Ps. 141, 2: " Let my prayer be set forth before thee," &c. Relative to this, Christ, Matt. 31, 29, and Mark 11, 24, says: "All things, whatsoever ye shall ask in prayer, believing, ye shall receive;" and James 1, 6: " But let him ask in faith, nothing wavering, for he that wavereth, let him not think that he shall receive anything from the Lord."

It is easy, therefore, to perceive that the bawling in the institutions and cloisters in all the world, is mere mockery and temptation of God. For such prayer indeed is well known to men, for those who offer it, continually exclaim, cry out, and blare; but to God it is unknown; it reaches him not, because they themselves do not believe, or are not certain, that it reaches him. As they believe, so it is; so that it is time indeed for this mocking and tempting of God to be rejected at once, and to exterminate such mock-houses, as Amos calls them, ch. 7. O, if we would observe the true manner of praying, what could we not accomplish? But now we pray much, and have nothing; for our prayers never reach God. Wo to unbelief and distrust.

"And the peace of God, which passeth all understanding, shall keep your hearts and minds through Christ Jesus."

Behold, how orderly and beautifully St. Paul teaches a Christian. He should first rejoice in God through faith, and then manifest moderation and kindness to men. But should he say: How can I? He answers: The Lord is at hand; but how, if I am persecuted and robbed? He says: Be careful for nothing, pray God, and let him care; yes, meanwhile, I shall become weary and desolate? Not so: The peace of God shall keep you. Let us now take this into consideration.

By the phrase, *the peace of God*, we must understand, not that peace, in which God himself dwells calmly and contentedly, but that *peace which he produces in our hearts*, and *which makes us contented*, precisely as that which we speak, hear, and believe from God, is styled the Word. It is the gift of God, and hence it is styled the *peace of God*, because it effects peace with him, even if we have displeasure with men.

This *peace transcends all mind, reason, and understanding*. By this we must not understand that it cannot be felt or experienced by any one. For, if we are to have peace with God, we must feel it in our hearts and consciences. How else could our hearts and minds be preserved through him? The difference between this peace and that which reason comprehends, will be understood by the following illustration: Those who do not know how to flee to God in prayer, proceed, when tribulation and adversity overtake them, and when they are filled with care or anxiety, to seek peace, but it is only that which reason apprehends and obtains. But reason knows of no peace except that which exists after the evil shall have been removed. This peace does not transcend reason, but it is compatible with it. Hence they rage and strive according to their reason, until they obtain this peace by the removal of the evil, by force or fraud. But those who rejoice in God, are satisfied when they have peace with God. They calmly endure tribulation; they do not desire that peace which reason dictates; namely, the removal of the evil; but they stand firm, and await internal strength through faith; they enquire not whether the evil will be of short, long, temporal, or eternal duration; they give themselves no anxiety or concern about its termination; they always leave this matter to the regulation of God; they are not anxious to know when, how, where, or by whom it will be terminated. God, therefore, in return affords them grace, and removes their evils with advantages so great as to exceed all their expectations and desires.

Behold, this is the peace of the cross, the peace of God, the peace of the conscience, the Christian peace, which makes us, even externally, calm, and satisfied with every one, and unwilling to disturb any one. For reason cannot comprehend how we can have pleasure in crosses, and peace in disquietude, nor can it accomplish this. It is the work of God, which no one can know, but him who has experienced it. In regard to this it is said above, in the Epistle for the second Sunday: "The God of hope fill you with all joy and peace in believing." What he there calls *peace in faith*, he calls here *peace of God*.

In this way, St. Paul indicates that for him who *rejoices in God*, and leads a moderate life, the devil will raise up a cross, to drive and turn his heart away from this course of conduct. He should, therefore, be well fortified, so as to rest his peace where the devil cannot reach it, namely, in God; he must not be anxious about getting rid of what the devil has forced upon him, but he must suffer him to exercise his wantonness, till God himself comes and exterminates it. Thus his heart, mind, and affection will be kept and preserved in peace. For even his patience could not long endure, if his heart did not exist above itself in a higher peace, satisfied that it has peace with God.

By the words heart and mind here, we must not understand the natural will and understanding, but, as Paul himself explains it, the heart and mind in Christ Jesus; that is the will and understanding which we have and bear in Christ, of Christ, and under Christ. This is the faith and love with all their operations, according to their dispositions and inclinations towards God and man. This is nothing else but a disposition to trust and love God from the heart, and to feel disposed from the heart and mind to serve God and man, in every respect and as far as possible. Such a heart and mind the devil seeks to avert with fear, terror, death, and every species of misfortunes, and to set up for it human devices, to induce it to seek consolation and help in itself and in man, and thus it falls from God upon its own care.

Now, in a word, this Epistle is a *lesson of Christian life towards God and man*, teaching us, really, to let God be everything to us, and ourselves everything to all men; to be to men, as God is to us, to receive from God, and to give to men: this is the sum and substance, *faith* and *love*.

CHRISTMAS-DAY.*

EPISTLE, TIT. 2, 11-15.

For the grace of God that bringeth salvation hath appeared to all men.

Teaching us, that denying ungodliness, and wordly lusts, we should live soberly, righteously, and godly, in this present world;

Looking for that blessed hope, and the glorious appearing of the great God, and our Savior Jesus Christ;

Who gave himself for us, that he might redeem us from all iniquity, and purify unto himself a peculiar people, zealous of good works.

These things speak, and exhort, and rebuke with all authority. Let no man despise thee.

---

†In the first place, St. Paul teaches in this Epistle what Titus and every

---

* At the mass on Christmas night.

† It is written in the book of Nehemiah, ch. 4, that when they were rebuilding Jerusalem, they wrought with one hand, and with the other they held the sword, on account of the enemy who wished to hinder the building. This St. Paul, Tit. 1, 9, explains thus, that a bishop, pastor, or a preacher, should be mighty in the Holy Scripture to teach and admonish, as well as to resist the gainsayers. Thus we should use the Word of God in a two-fold manner, as bread and as a weapon, in feeding and in resisting, in times of peace and of war; and thus with one hand we should build, improve, teach, feed all Christendom, and with the other, make opposition to the devil, the heretics, the world. For where there is no defence, the devil will soon destroy the pasture, to which he is so bitterly opposed. We shall, therefore, (if God grant grace.) handle the Gospel in this manner, not only for the purpose of feeding our souls on it, but also to learn to put it on as armor, and with it to fight against all enemies, so that we may be provided with pasture and weapons.

preacher should preach to the people, namely, Christ, and nothing else, so that the people may know what Christ is, why he came, and what blessings he accomplished for us, saying: "The grace of God hath appeared," &c., that is, it is manifest and clear. How was this accomplished? Through the Apostles and their preaching, it was proclaimed in all the world. For previous to the resurrection of Christ, it was still concealed, and Christ dwelling in the Jewish country only, was not yet glorified. But after his ascension, he gave the Holy Spirit, concerning whom he has said before, John 16, 13: The spirit of truth, whom I will send, shall glorify me.

Now this is the meaning of the Apostle: Christ came not for the purpose of dwelling here on earth simply for his own advantage, but for our good. He therefore permitted his goodness and grace, not to remain and continue with and in himself, but, after his ascension, to be proclaimed, preached, and spoken publicly in all the world, before everybody; nor did he permit such revelation and proclamation to be made, simply as such, and only as a rumor or report, but to bring fruit in us. For it is a revelation and proclamation, teaching us to deny, refuse, and reject all that is ungodly, and all earthly, worldly lusts or desires, and thus henceforth to lead a sober, righteous, and godly life.

By the declaration, "The saving grace of God hath appeared," &c., he condemns the favors of the world and of men, as pernicious, condemnable, and ineffectual, and wishes to incite in us a desire for divine favor and grace, teaching us to contemn human favor and grace. For he that desires to have the grace and favor of God, must consider all other graces and favors, as he says, Matt. 10, 22 : "Ye shall be hated of all men for my name's sake;"* and Paul, Gal. 1, 10 : "If I yet pleased men, I should not be the servant of Christ." Therefore, where the saving grace of God appears and is proclaimed, there the pernicious grace of men must be passed in silence and obscurity; and he that wishes to perceive and taste the former, must reject and forget the latter.

He says it has appeared or is proclaimed to all men; for Christ, Mark 16, 15, commanded the Gospel to be preached to all creatures in all the world; and in many places, and especially in Col. 1, 23, Paul also says: "The gospel, which ye have heard * * was preached to every creature which is under heaven:" that is, it is preached publicly, so that all creatures, much more all men, might have heard it. For in the first place Christ preached only in the Jewish country, and the Holy Scripture was confined to the Jews, as the 2d ver. of the 76th Ps. and 19th ver. of the 147th Ps. say. But afterwards it was left free, not being confined to any particular place, as the 4th ver. of the 19th Ps. says: "Their line is gone out through all the earth, and their words to the end of the world." This is said in regard to the Apostles.

You may say, however: Surely this did not occur in the time of the Apostles. For Germany was converted nearly eight hundred years after the Apostolic age: and now, recently many islands and countries are discovered, in which nothing of this grace had appeared until in the fifteenth century. Answer: the Apostle speaks concerning the character of the Gospel; for it is a sermon so commenced and ordained as to go into all the world, and at the time of the Apostles it had already gone into the greatest and best part of the world. Before this, however, no sermon of such character was commenced or ordained. For the law of Moses was confined to the Jewish nation alone. Therefore, since this was accomplished for the most part, and must be completed, as is still the case, the Scripture speaks of it, as if it had already been accomplished.

For there is a manner of speaking employed in the Scriptures, called synecdoche, which is very common, that is, when the whole of a thing is spoken of, and only a part is meant;

---

* A. And Ps. 5, 2· God has destroyed the bones of those who desire to please men.
Luther's Works, 7r Bd.

as Christ is said to have laid in the grave three days and three nights, when at the same time he was there only one day, two nights, and two parts of two days. Thus, Matt. 23, 23, 37, it is said, Jerusalem stoned the prophets, yet a great portion of its inhabitants were pious. Thus too, it is said, the ecclesiastics are avaricious, still there are many pious persons among them. This manner of speaking is very common in all languages, and especially in the Holy Scripture.

Thus the Gospel was preached at that time to all creatures; for it is a sermon, designed, introduced, and ordained to reach all creatures. In this way a prince might say, having dispatched a message at his residence, and it having entered upon the way, the message is gone to the place or individual, for which it was designed, even if it had not already reached the point. Thus too God lets his Gospel go forth to all creatures, even if it has not already entirely reached all.— Hence the prophet, Ps. 18, 5, said: "Their voice is gone forth into all the world;" he does not say that it has already reached all the world; but it is on the way, going out into all the world. Thus too Paul means, it is preached, and made manifest without intermission to all men; it is already on the way, and is already accomplished, although not completed.

This appearing of grace teaches us two points, as St. Paul says here; "Denying ungodliness and worldly lusts." These we must explain. The little word *Impietas*, which the Apostle styles in the Greek, *Asebia*, and in the Hebrew it is *Resa*, I cannot render by a single word in the German. I have, therefore rendered it, *ungœttlich Wesen*, *ungodliness*. The Latin and Greek terms do not fully express the Hebrew. For *Resa* is properly the sin of not honoring God; that is, of not believing, trusting, fearing him, of not surrendering to him, of not submitting to his providence, and of not recognizing him as God. In this sin, gross, outward sinners are deeply implicated indeed; but much more deeply are the wise, sainted, learned, ecclesiastics, who, relying upon their works, seem to themselves and in the eyes of the world, to be pious. In a word, all who do not give themselves over to the pure goodness and grace of God, and live accordingly, are all *Impii*, ungodly, even if on account of their great holiness they could raise the dead, or were full of continence and all virtues. It would seem proper to call them graceless or faithless persons. However, I shall call them *ungodly*. Therefore Paul says the saving grace has appeared to graceless persons, so that they may become rich in grace and rich in God; that is, that they may believe, trust, fear, honor, love, and praise him, and thus change ungodliness into godliness.

For what would it profit for the saving grace of God to appear, if we should attempt, through something else to become pious, or to lead godly lives, when St. Paul says here, it was revealed and proclaimed in order that we might deny ungodliness, and henceforth live piously, not through or of ourselves, but through it? No one, therefore, more disparages this grace, and more gainsays its appearing, than do hypocrites and ungodly saints, who are unwilling to regard their own works as nugatory, sinful, and reprehensible, still discovering much good in themselves, and, according to their own good meaning, as they imagine, deserve, without grace, great merit. God, however, regards no work as good,—nor is it really good,—unless he produces it in us himself, through his grace. In order, therefore, that he may work many of these in us all, and that our efforts or works may cease, he manifested his saving grace to all men.

Now, the first great evil of all men, is their godlessness, impiety, and gracelessness. In this is comprehended first the faithless heart, and then all the thoughts, words, works, and the whole course of conduct, accomplished in and through this faithless heart. The individual left to himself, lives and acts only according to his natural abilities and reason, and in these he is sometimes so beautiful and brilliant as to out-shine the real saints.

But in this he seeks simply his own interest, unable to live and act to the honor of God, even if he does secure more praise and glory in this direction, than the real saints, about whom the Scripture frequently speaks.— For this godless, graceless conduct is an evil so great, so extensive, and so deeply subtile as to prevent those who walk in it from ever being able to perceive or believe it, even when it is presented to them. The Prophet, Ps. 32, 2, calls it, not a reasonable, worldly, fleshly, but a spiritual deception, which deceives not only the reason, but also the spirit of man.

In short, it must be believed rather than felt. For if God permitted his grace to be made manifest to all men, so that they might deny ungodliness, we must believe him to be that being who knows our hearts better than we do, and we must confess that, were our deeds not impious and reprehensible, he would not have permitted his grace to be proclaimed to ameliorate us. A person who would administer medicine to an individual who is not sick, would be regarded as a fool; God must, therefore, be regarded as a fool, by those who, according to their good meaning and feeling, are unwilling to believe that all their deeds are godless and condemnable, and that his saving grace is necessary. This is terrible. He therefore says, Matt. 21, 32, that the chief priests, doctors, and ecclesiastics, (elders) did not believe John, the Baptist, who called on them to repent; they would know of no sin.— All the Prophets were killed because they accused the people of this sin; no one however believed them; not one thought that such sins were in himself. They judged according to their feelings and thoughts and works, not according to God's word and counsel, which he delivered through the Prophets.

St. Paul, therefore, employs a very forcible term here, in Greek, *paedeuusa*, which means to instruct, like we instruct children in the beginning, in regard to what they never heard or knew before. They regulate themselves, not according to their reason, but according to the word and instruction of the father. Whatever he represents to them as useful or injurious, they so regard, and believe and follow him. But for the intelligent and great we assign some cause, which they may comprehend with their reason, why a thing is useful or useless. Such children the saving grace of God desires as scholars, so that, if they cannot imagine, they may still believe, that their deeds are godless and reprehensible, and thus receive this grace, and follow it.— Christ, therefore, well says, Matt. 18, 3: "Except ye be converted, and become as little children, ye shall not enter into the kingdom of heaven."— And Isaiah, 7, 9: "If ye will not believe, surely ye shall not be established." Thus the divine, saving grace has appeared not only to help us, but also to teach us to know that we need it, since by its appearance it indicates that all our works are ungodly, graceless, and condemned. Hence the Psalmist, Ps. 119, 7, so fervently entreats God to teach him his judgments, laws, and commands, so that he might not follow after his own opinions and feelings, as God forbade, Deut. 12, 8: "Ye shall not do * * every man whatsoever is right in his own eyes."

The other evil in man he calls *worldly lusts*. In these are comprehended all disorderly conduct, which an individual performs towards himself and his neighbor; like the first, ungodliness, comprehends all disorders towards God. Observe, however, how judiciously the words *lusts, worldly*, are arranged. He calls them worldly, for the purpose of including all evil lusts, whether of goods, luxuries, honor, favors, and all that belongs to the world, in which a person may commit sin with his lusts. He does not say, however, that we must deny worldly goods, or their use. These are good, and the creatures of God.— We must avail ourselves of their use in eating, drinking, clothing, and other necessaries of life. None of these are forbidden. Only the lusts after these, the undue attachment and craving, are forbidden. These we must deny. For these lead us into all sins against ourselves and our neighbors.

By this, the conduct of godless hypocrites,—who, although they may be clad in sheep's clothing, and sometimes resist an evil deed, through fear or shame, or the punishment of hell, are still filled with evil desires for wealth, honor, and power,—is also condemned. No person loves life more dearly, fears death more terribly, and desires more ardently to remain here in this world, than they do; and yet they do not recognize these worldly lusts, in which they are drowned, performing many works in vain. It is not enough to put away only worldly works or words, worldly desires or lusts must be removed, so that we may use this life and all that belongs to it, without placing our affections on it, with a view to the future life; as follows in this Epistle: "Looking for * * the glorious appearing of," &c.

But here we perceive that the grace of God reveals the fact, that all men are full of worldly lusts, although some may conceal it by their hypocrisy. Were any one not subject to such desires, there could be no necessity for a revelation of this grace, or for its being salutary, or for its manifestation to all men, or for its showing that such lusts must be put off.— For whoever is not subject to such lusts, has no need to put them off; nor has this declaration of Paul any reference to him; neither can he be a human being, and hence he has no necessity for this grace, or its manifestation. What must he be? Without doubt, a devil, eternally condemned with all his holiness and purity. If, however, they could hide all their worldly lusts, they cannot conceal the fact that they ardently desire to continue in this life, and that they are unwilling to die. By this they show how graceless they are, and that all their works are ungodly and worldly; and yet they do not perceive their graceless, perilous infirmity.

He also says: We must deny or renounce. By this he rejects many foolish means, devised by men, in order to become pious. For some run into the wilderness, some into cloisters, and others separate themselves from society, presuming by bodily flight to run away from ungodliness and worldly lusts; and others again resort to tortures and injuries of their bodies, by imposing, beyond their natural abilities to endure, upon themselves hunger, thirst, wakefulness, labor, and uncomfortable apparel. Yes, if ungodliness and worldly lusts were painted upon the wall of the house, you might run out of it; or if they were knit in a red coat, you might pull it off, and put on a grey one; or if they grew in your hair, you might have it shaved off, and go with a bald pate; or if they were baked in the bread, you might eat roots instead of bread. But since they inhere in your heart, and occupy you through and through, where will you run, so as not to carry them with you? What will you put on, so as not to be under it? What will you eat and drink, without being present with it? In a word: What will you do without being there yourself, as you are in yourself? Beloved man, the great enticement is in you, and you must first run and fly away from yourself, as James 1, 14, says: "But every man is tempted, when he is drawn away of his own lusts, and enticed."

The design of the Apostle, therefore, is not for us simply to flee from the external causes which lead to sin, but as St. Paul says here, *to deny them*, so that the lusts or desires which are in us may be mortified.— Then no external enticement can injure us. This is fleeing properly. If these are not mortified, fleeing from external enticement will avail nothing. Yes, we must remain in the midst of enticement, and there learn through grace to deny lusts and ungodliness, as it is said Ps. 110, 2: "Rule thou," or apply thyself "in the midst of thine enemies." Conflict, not fleeing, energy, not rest, must prevail here, if we are to win the crown.

We read of an old father who, being unable to continue in a cloister, because he could not endure the enticement, concluded to go into the wilderness to serve God in peace.—

Now whilst he was there, his little jug of water turned over; he set it up again, but it turned over a second time. He then became enraged, and dashed it to pieces. He then concluded in himself, saying, behold, I cannot have peace by myself alone; I perceive that the defect is in me.— He then returned to the cloister, submitting to the sufferings of enticement, and teaching from that time on, that we must triumph, not by fleeing from, but by denying worldly lusts.

He indicates, moreover, how we should live after we have denied ungodliness and worldly lusts, saying, that "we should live soberly, righteously, and godly, in this present world." What an excellent, general rule and life, suited and adapted to all conditions, he here designates.— He gives no occasion for sects, introducing no difference among men, like human doctrines do. He first introduces *soberness*, in which he includes all that relates to man, in regard to how he should act towards himself.— This consists in subduing his own body, and in keeping it under good discipline. Our text, in all respects, calls that *soberness* which St. Paul calls *sophron* in Greek, which implies not only soberness, but temperance in the entire conduct of the body or flesh; as for instance, in eating, drinking, sleeping, apparel, talking, mien, and gestures,—which is called an honorable life, and good breeding. A person thus acting, knows how to conduct himself in all these particulars temperately, soberly, and vigorously, so as not to lead a wild, shameless, loose, disorderly life, in eating, drinking, sleeping, talking, mien, and gestures. Thus, too, he says in the 4th verse; that the aged women should "teach the young women to be sober" and blameless.

It is true, excessive eating and drinking very greatly impede and obstruct our efforts to lead an honorable life. Temperance, on the other hand, contributes much to enable us to accomplish it. For as soon as a person indulges his appetite to excess, he cannot fully control himself; his five senses become wild and intractable.—

Experience teaches us that, when the stomach is full of meat and drink, the mouth is full of words, the ears of lust to hear, the eyes of lust to see, the whole system becomes indolent, drowsy and dull, or too wild and dissolute, and all the members soon over-leap the bounds of reason and propriety, until there is neither discipline nor moderation left. The word in our text, therefore, is not so improperly Latenized *sobrius*, soberness. For also in the Greek language, the words *Asotos* and *sophron* are opposed to each other, like *Vœllerei* and *Mœszigkeit*, drunkenness and soberness, in the German. When we examine the word in Latin, we find that *sobrius*, soberness, does not mean, that an individual has neither ate nor drank anything for breakfast; but *sobrius* and *ebrius* stand in opposition to each other, like *Trunkenheit oder Vœllerei* and *Nuchterkeit*, drunkenness or ebriety and soberness, in the German. We Germans also call the individual *nuchtern*, sober, who is not drunken or intoxicated, but has full control over himself, although he has eaten and drank.

Now you perceive what kind of good works the Apostle teaches. He does not require us to make pilgrimages; neither does he forbid particular kinds of diet, nor does he teach us to wear a particular kind of clothing, or to fast on certain days, like those do, who by human laws separate or exclude themselves, basing their spiritual, good life on the dissimulation of their clothing, diet, hair, and seasons, and desiring to become pious by not going in the ordinary style, in regard to their clothing, situations, diet, seasons, and gestures. They have an appropriate name in the Gospel, *Pharisaei*, which means, excluded or separated, and whom the prophet, Ps. 80, 14, calls *Monios*, which implies a singular person, and that is called a wild hog, which goes alone and singularly. We shall also hereafter call them singular, so that they may be known. But they destroy in a dreadful manner the vineyard of God, of which the Psalmist complains. For such pharisees and singular persons make a great show with their traditions, singularly chosen garments, meats, days, and gestures, and easily draw the multitude away from the common walks to their ways, so that, as Christ says, even the elect can scarcely resist.

Let us learn, then, from St. Paul here, that no meats, no drinks, no colors, no clothing, no days, no gestures, are forbidden or appointed, but all these things are free for every one, to be used in soberness and moderation. These things are not forbidden, as already stated; it is only the disorder, the excess, the abuse, that is prohibited. But where there is a separation or exclusion of meats, clothing, places, days, there you will certainly find human laws, not evangelical Christian doctrine and liberty; but dissimulation and hypocrisy must be the ultimate result, without soberness and moderation. Use all things, therefore, that are upon the earth, when and where you please, thanking God, as Paul teaches; only guard against excess, disorder, misuse, or licentiousness, relative to them, and you will be in the right way. Do not permit yourself to be misled by the fact that the holy fathers established orders and sects, used certain meats and clothing, and acted thus and so. They did not do this in order to single out themselves above others—otherwise they were unholy—but they preferred to pursue this course, and exercise their moderation in so doing. Exercise your moderation also in whatever you think proper, and maintain your freedom. Do not confine yourself to manners and modes as if they were right ways and pious life. For if you do, you will be singular, and deprived of the community of saints. Diligently guard against this. We must fast, we must watch, we must labor, we must wear inferior clothing, &c. But do this when you think your body needs subduing and moderation. Do not set apart specified days or places for this purpose, but do it on whatever day necessity and moderation require it.— This then, is fasting properly, and you will fast every day, denying worldly lusts. Thus teaches the Gospel, and those who thus act, are the people of the New Testament.

In the second place, we should be *righteous* in our lives. No work, however, or time is appointed and singled out here. The ways of God are left free and universal. Everything is left free to the supervision of each one to do right, when, where, and to whom it may be necessary. For by this St. Paul teaches how we should conduct ourselves towards our neighbor.— To him righteousness is due from us, which consists in doing to him, as we would wish him to do to us, and in granting to him what we wish him to grant to us; that is, we should do him no harm or injury, in regard to his body, wife, children, friends, possessions, honor, and all that belongs to him. We should, moreover, aid him and stand by him, wherever we see that he needs our assistance, with our bodies, property, honor, and all that belongs to us. For righteousness consists in rendering to each one whatever is due to him. O, what a little word this is, to comprehend so much. O, how few, who otherwise live properly, walk in this way of righteousness. We do everything else, but that which saving grace reveals, and directs us to do.

The word neighbor must be so construed as to include even our enemy. But this way is entirely grown over, much more so than the way of moderation. This too is almost entirely devastated and untrodden, in consequence of the introduction of certain meats, clothing, gestures, ostentations, which have been so superabundantly and more than profusely insinuated; and yet we ape after and make fools of ourselves with rosaries, with ecclesiastical and feudal institutions, with hearing of masses, with festivals, and our own self-devised works, concerning which there is no divine command. O, Lord God, how wide hell has opened her mouth, as Isaiah, 5, 14, says: and how narrow has the gate of heaven become, in consequence of the accursed doctrines and devices of these singular and pharisaical persons. The prophets are painters, unconsciously indicating the present state

DR. LUTHER'S CHURCH-POSTIL.

SERMONS ON THE EPISTLES.

VOL. I.] TITUS II, 11-15. [NO. 3.

of things. They represent hell by a dragon's mouth, wide open, and the door to heaven as closed. O, the wretchedness of the picture!

It is not necessary, therefore, for you to make inquiry relative to what you should do externally. Look to your neighbor; there you will find enough to do, even if you have a thousand kind offices to render. Only do not suffer yourself to be misled; think not that you will go to heaven by praying and attending church, or by the influence of institutions and monuments, whilst you are passing your neighbor. If you pass him in this life, he will lie in your way in that which is to come, so that you must pass by the door of heaven, like the rich man who left Lazarus lying at his gate. O, woe to us, priests, monks, bishops, and pope! What do we preach? What do we teach?— How we lead the poor multitude from the way. The blind leading the blind, both shall fall in the ditch. Such doctrines, as St. Paul declares in the conclusion of this Epistle, we should teach.

In the third place, we are taught to *live godly*. This shows us how we should conduct ourselves towards God. Thus we are fully prepared for our duties towards ourselves, towards our neighbors, and towards God.— Now, as we have already stated, *impietas* implies wickedness, gracelessness, ungodliness. So, on the other hand, *pietas* means gracefulness, godliness, faithfulness. This consists in trusting God, in relying on his grace alone, in esteeming no work, unless it is wrought in us by him, through grace; so that he is thus recognized, honored, adored, praised, and beloved by us. In short, it consists in fearing and trusting him, as it is said, Ps. 33, 18, and 147, 11: "The Lord taketh pleasure in them that fear him, in those that hope in his mercy." To fear is, to believe that all our contrivances are ungodliness, as the appearing of his grace shows; we should, therefore, fear him, and freely forsake these, and henceforth guard against them. To hope is, not to doubt that he will be gracious to us and make us graceful and godly.

Behold, thus the individual yields to God, giving himself away to him, doing nothing of himself, but permitting him to work and rule in him; so that his whole care, fear, prayer, and desire are, continually, for God not to let him follow his own works and ways, which he regards as godless and deserving of wrath, but to rule over him, and work in him through grace. From this will result a good conscience, and love, and praise to God. Behold, those are *pii*, pious, graceful persons, who do not walk and trust in reason or nature, but in the grace of God alone, ever fearing, lest they should fall from it into their reason, self-conceit, good meaning, and self-devised works. Upon this David based the whole of the 119th Psalm,— every verse, although there are a hundred and seventy-six, breathing the same prayer. This is a subject of such vital importance, and so many dangers and difficulties connect themselves with nature, reason, and human doctrine, that we cannot be too much on our guard.

Behold, in this way God does not require us to build churches or cathedrals, to make pilgrimages, to hear mass, &c.; but he requires a heart and a life, which move in his grace, and fear all ways and conduct that do not result from grace. Nothing more can you render him. For all else he gives you, as he says, Ps. 50, 14, 15: O, Israel, think not that I inquire after thy gifts and offerings; for every thing in heaven and on earth, is mine already. This is my service, that thou offerest unto me thanksgiving, and payest thy vows unto me. Call upon me in the day of trouble: I will deliver thee, and thou shalt glorify me; as if he should say: Thou hast vowed unto me, I shall be thy God; this keep. Let me work; perform not thine own works; let me help thee in thy need; look to me for every thing, that I alone, may direct and control the life which thou livest. Then thou wilt be able to know me and my grace,—to love and praise me. This is the right road to salvation. Otherwise, if thou, thyself, workest, thou wilt, also, praise thyself, disregard me, and not let me be thy God; thou wilt prove treacherous, and break thy vow.

This, you perceive, is real divine service. For this we need neither bells nor churches, neither vessels nor ornaments, neither lights nor candles, neither organs nor singing, neither images nor pictures, neither tables nor altars, neither pates nor caps, neither fumifications nor sprinklings, neither processions nor movements with the cross, neither indulgences nor briefs. For these are all human inventions and ornaments, which God does not regard, and which too often obscure, with their glitter, the real service of God. One thing only, is necessary for this service, the Gospel. This should be properly urged, and through it, this divine service made known to the people. This is the true bell and organ for this divine service.

He also says, we *should thus live in this present world.* First, because this cannot be accomplished by works.— Our whole life, must be thus, whilst we remain here. For, as Christ, Matt. 10, 22, says: "He that endureth to the end shall be saved." It is true, some persons occasionally accomplish something. This, however, does not include their whole life, nor does it endure to the end. Secondly, no one should spare his good course of conduct till after this life, or till in death. For that which we await in the life to come, must be secured in this life.— Now, many depend on purgatory, and live, as they list, till their end, and expect to profit afterwards by vigils and soul-masses. They shall fail indeed. It were well, had purgatory never been conceived of; by it much good is suppressed, and many cloisters, monasteries, priests, and monks, are established and employed. In this way these three parts of Christian life are very much suppressed; when, at the same time, God has neither commanded nor spoken anything about purgatory, and it may not,* God pardon, be void of false, foul deception. For it is dangerous, at least, to accept or build upon any thing that God has not designated, when we are scarcely able to stand when we build upon the institutions of God, which can never waver. This declaration of Paul, indeed, is a severe thrust at purgatory, since he desires us to live properly in this life: so that we may not sustain a blow to our faith. Not that I deny the existence of purgatory at this time;† but it is dangerous to preach about it, even if there were some truth connected with it, because the Word of God, or the Scripture, says nothing about it.

But he has the greater reason for saying, *in this present world,* for the purpose of showing the power of the saving grace of God, because the world is so wicked, that a pious person must live in it alone, without example, as it were, like a rose among thorns, and endure in consequence of it, all manner of misfortune, censure, shame, and sins. As if he should say: Whoever desires to live soberly, righteously, and godly, must expect all manner of enmity, and take up the cross. He must not allow himself to

* A. It may be wholly, or for the most part, deception, &c.

† C. Namely, when we count 1522 years.

be misled, even if he has to live alone, like Lot in Sodom and Abraham in Canaan, among nothing but gluttonous, drunken, incontinent, unrighteous, false, ungodly persons. It is world, and it will remain world. This he must resist and overcome, censuring its worldly desires. Behold, this is living soberly in an ale-house, chastely in a brothel, godly in a house of mirth, justly in a den of murderers. Such a world renders this life strait and distressing, so that we wish and cry out, and ask for death and the day of judgment, awaiting the same with ardent desire,—as follows.— A life subject to so many evils, must be led by grace. Nature and reason are lost here.

"Looking for that blessed hope."

Here he makes a very clear distinction between a godly life and every other life. By this, every one is enabled to perceive how near to, or how far from a gracious life, he is. Let all, who presume they live so piously, step forward, and let us ask them whether they delight in this declaration; whether they are so prepared as to await with pleasure the day of judgment; whether they regard it not only as tolerable, but also as a blessed event, to be looked for with ardent desire and cheerful confidence. Is it not true that all human nature shrinks from that day? Is it not true that, if this day were dependent on them for its approach, they would prefer it never to appear; and especially would not this be the case with hypocritical saints? Where then is nature?— Where is reason? Where is free-will, which is so highly extolled as inclined to, and potent for good? Why does it flee and shrink not only from that good, but also from the honor and salvation of God, which the Apostle here calls a blessed hope, in which we shall be blessed? What then prevents the conclusion here, that such persons lead impious, graceless, reprehensible lives,—the evils and ungodliness of which, but for the appearing of this day, they might conceal? What is more ungodly than to strive against the will of God? But does not the individual, who flees from the day, in which the honor of God shall be revealed, and who does not await it with love and joy, strive against the will of God?

Observe then, he that does not desire this day and await it with love and delight, is not living a godly life, even if he were able to raise the dead. But you may say: Yes, then few persons are leading pious lives, especially of the singular and spiritual, who, above all others, flee death and that day. This is what I have said already. These singular persons simply lead themselves and others from the right path, destroying the ways of God. For here we clearly perceive how little, except to strive against God, reason and nature are able to accomplish, and how necessary this saving grace is, so that, our own works ceasing, God alone may work in us, so that we may rise from ourselves and our godless conduct to a supernatural, graceful, godly life; so that we may not only not fear that day, but ardently and cheerfully await it with joy and pleasure, as has already been further illustrated in the Gospel for the second Sunday.

This, you perceive, is taught, not by nature or reason, but by the grace of God, which has appeared. This, observe, enables us not only to deny worldly lusts, but also to feel an aversion to them, desiring to be liberated from them, and feeling our whole course of conduct to be rather unsatisfactory. It, moreover, produces in us an essential disposition to entreat God in all confidence, and to await his coming with pleasure.

Now, let us carefully weigh these words. He calls it a *blessed hope*. This he brings in contrast with that miserable, unhappy life, in which nothing but misfortune, danger, and sin, worry and harrass us when we wish to act uprightly; so that we have reason to feel vexed by everything that exists here, and to be encouraged by that hope. This is the case with those who earnestly endeavor to live soberly, righteously, and godly. For the world cannot long endure such persons, and they must soon be regarded by it as repulsive; as Paul, Rom. 5,

3, says: "We glory in tribulations also: knowing that tribulation worketh patience: and patience, experience; and experience, hope; and hope maketh not ashamed." Thus our eyes stand closed against things, worldly and visible, and open to things, eternal and invisible. All this is produced by grace, through the cross, which we must endure in consequence of our efforts to lead a godly life, which the world cannot tolerate.

"And the glorious appearing."

St. Paul calls this advent *Epiphaniam*; that is, appearing or manifestation; as he said above in regard to grace, that it has appeared or has been manifested. The word advent, therefore, is not sufficient in the Latin.— For the Apostle wishes to distinguish the last advent from the first. The first took place in humility and disparagement, so as to attract little attention, and secure no other manifestation but that which was made in faith through the Gospel. He is still concealed; but on the day of judgment, he will appear in clear, effulgent splendor and honor, so that his splendor and honor will be manifest to all creatures, and this manifestation shall thus continue forever. For the last day will be an eternal day; as it appears in its first instant, all, every heart, all things will stand open. This he calls his glorious appearing, or the appearing of his honor. Then no one will preach or believe. Then every one will see and feel every thing, as in a bright day. Therefore, he also says: "Of the great God;" not that there is another God somewhere, who is little, but because God has not as yet, and will not till the last day, display his greatness, his majesty, his glory, his effulgence. Now we see him in the Gospel and in faith. This is a little, narrow view; here God is little, and slightly comprehended; but then he will permit us to see him according to his greatness and majesty.

These words afford consolation to all who live soberly, righteously, and godly. For he declares that the glory shall belong, not to our enemy or judge, but to our Savior, Jesus Christ,

———

Luther's Works 7r. B.d.

who will then render us perfectly happy. For he will employ that day and glorious appearing for the purpose of liberating us from this world, in which we must endure so much in consequence of our efforts to lead a pious life in submission to his will. Hence, in view of that advent, and of that great and glorious redemption, we should the more firmly and cheerfully bear up under the persecution, murder, shame, and misfortunes of the world, and in the midst of death, and persevere the more steadfastly in a godly life, relying with boldness upon the Savior, Jesus Christ.

These words, on the other hand, are terrible to worldly-minded and wicked persons who are unwilling to endure, for the sake of godliness, the persecution of the world. They prefer to live here in peace, and thus to be pious, in order that they may meet with no enmity and difficulty. But the dissolute, the impudent, the obdurate, disregard these words, without a thought that they will have to appear on that day. Like furious animals, they run blindly and heedlessly along into this day, and into the abyss of hell. You may, perhaps, ask: How, then, shall I attain such godliness, as will enable me thus to await that day, since my nature and reason flee from it, and are unable to attain it? If so, observe what follows:

"Who gave himself for us."

These things are, therefore, so fully presented to you, for the purpose of enabling you to perceive and acknowledge your inabilities, to despair wholly and entirely of yourself; thus to humble yourself in truth and reality, and to learn how vain you are, and how ungodly, gracelessly, and impiously you live. Observe, the grace which has appeared through the Gospel teaches humility, and this humility fills you with a desire for grace, and a disposition to seek salvation. Where such humble desire for grace exists, there the door of grace is open to you, there it cannot be void; as St. Peter says, 1 Pet. 5, 5: "God resisteth the proud, and giveth grace to the humble;" and, as Christ has frequently said in the Gospel: "Every one that exalteth himself shall be abased, and he that humbleth himself shall be exalted," &c.

For this reason the blessed Gospel is now presented to you. It lets this saving grace shine forth and appear in you, showing what more is required to prevent you from falling into despair. This is the Gospel, this is the light and appearing of grace, this the Apostle here declares, namely, that Christ gave himself for us, &c. Therefore, hearken to the Gospel; open the eyes of your heart, and let this saving grace shine forth, to enlighten and teach you what you should do. This is the sermon which is proclaimed to all men, as already said; and here we have the explanation of this appearing of grace.

Banish, then, far from your mind, the error into which you may have fallen, that, when you hear the Epistles of St. Paul or of St. Peter, you are not hearing the Gospel. Do not allow yourself to be misled by the name *Epistle*. For all that St. Paul writes in his Epistles, is the pure Gospel, as he says himself, Rom. 1, 1, and 1 Cor. 4, 15. Yes, I dare say, that the Gospel is clearer and more brilliant in the Epistles of St. Paul, than it is in the four Evangelists. The Evangelists describe the life and words of Christ, which, however, were not understood till after the advent of the Holy Ghost, who glorified him; as he says himself. But St. Paul, whilst he writes nothing concerning the life of Christ, clearly expresses why he came, and what advantages result to us from him. *What else is the Gospel but the sermon, that Christ gave himself for us, so that he might redeem us from sin, that all who believe this shall certainly be saved?*— Thus, we should despair of our own efforts, and cleave to Christ alone, relying upon him. This is a very lovely, consolatory declaration; and it is readily perceived by such hearts as despair of their own efforts. Hence, *Evangelium* implies a sweet, a kind, gracious message, which gladdens and cheers a sorrowful and terrified heart.

You should be careful, therefore, to believe that to be true, which the Apostle declares through the Gospel, namely, that Christ gave himself for you, in order that he might redeem you from all unrighteousness, and to purify you for a peculiar inheritance. Here, in the first place, it follows, that you must believe and confess that all your efforts are impure and unrighteous, and that your nature, reason, skill, and free-will, apart from Christ, are ineffectual. Otherwise you would make void this gospel. For, according to the Gospel, Christ did not give himself for the righteous and the pure. Had righteousness and purity existed; why should he have given himself, in vain? It would have been a foolish giving.

In the second place, you must believe the truth of the fact that he gave himself for you, in order that through this giving of himself, your impurity and unrighteousness may be put away, and through him you may become pure and righteous. If you believe this, such faith will accomplish all this. For his giving himself for you can render you pure and righteous in no other way, but through such faith, as St. Peter, Acts 15, 9, says: *Through faith he purifies the heart.* Hence you perceive that Christ is not presented to you in your hand; nor is he placed in a coffer, or in your bosom, or in your mouth, but he is presented to you through the Word and the Gospel, held up before you, in your heart, through your ears, and is offered to you as the being who gave himself for you, for your unrighteousness, for your impurity. Hence, you can receive him in no other way, but with your heart. This you do when you open your mind, and exclaim in your heart: Yes, I believe, it is so. Behold, thus by means of the Gospel, he penetrates your heart through your ears, and dwells there through your faith. Then you are pure and righteous, not through your effort, but, in consequence of the guest, whom you have received in your heart, through faith. Behold what rich, precious blessings these are.

Now, when such faith dwells in you, and you have Christ in your heart, you dare not think that he is poor and destitute. He brings with him his life, his spirit, and all that he is, has, and controls. Hence, St. Paul says, that the spirit is given, not for the sake of any work, but for the sake of the Gospel. When this comes, it brings Christ, and Christ brings with himself his spirit. Then the individual is new and godly. All that he does then, is well done. He is not idle. For faith is neither idle nor inactive. It acts, and speaks in regard to Christ, without intermission. Then the world is aroused against him, and will not hear or tolerate him. Crosses will then be incurred, and these render this life loathsome, and the day of judgment desirable. Behold, this is the Gospel and the appearing of the saving grace of God.

Now, how can death and the day of judgment be terrible to an individual who has such a heart? Who shall injure him, when the great God and Savior, Jesus Christ, to whom the day of judgment belongs, stands by his side and before him, with all his glory, greatness, majesty, and might? None other, than him, who gave himself for us, will control the day of judgment. He will assuredly not gainsay himself, but will declare that he gave himself for your sins, as you believe. What, then, will sin do, when the judge himself confesses that he has taken it away, through himself? Who shall judge the Judge?— Who will overpower him? He will avail more than all the world with its innumerable sins. Had he given, not himself, but something else, for you, we might fall into great error. What can terrify you, since he has given himself for you? He would have to condemn himself, rather than sin should condemn those, for whom he gave himself.

O, here is great, indubitable security. It depends upon the fact that our faith is strong and unwavering.— Christ will undoubtedly not waver.— He is sufficiently steadfast. We should, therefore, urge and enforce faith by preaching, by our efforts, and sufferings, so that it may be secure and steadfast. For works will avail nothing here. The evil spirit will assail our faith alone, knowing well, that all depends on it.

O, how unfortunate is it, that we do not perceive our advantages, permitting the Gospel with the saving grace to lie in darkness. Wo unto you, the Pope, bishops, priests, and monks! What do you do, in the churches and on the pulpits? Now, let us take into special consideration, the words,

"That he might redeem us."

He gave himself for the purpose of redeeming, not himself, but us. It is evident then, that we were held as captives. How then can we be so presumptuous and ungrateful as to attribute so much to our own free-will and natural reason? If we claim something in us that is not held captive in sin, we disparage his grace, by which we are redeemed, according to the Gospel. Who can accomplish anything good, whilst he lies captivated in sin and unrighteousness?— Our own efforts may seem good indeed, but they are not good in truth, or the Gospel in regard to Christ must be false.

"From all iniquity."

Iniquity he calls *Anomias*, which is, specially, everything that does not conform to the law, including the transgressions both of the soul and of the body; the former designated by ungodliness, which is impiety, and the latter by worldly lusts. Hence, he adds the word "all," so as to include the sins and unrighteousness both of the body and the soul, from which Christ has wholly and entirely redeemed us. This is said in opposition to the self-righteous and singular, who redeem themselves and others from certain species of unrighteousness, through the law, or their own reason or free-will; that is, they resist and avoid, indeed, the outward actions, through prohibitions, or the fear of pain or punishment, or the expectation of rewards or profits. But this is only the scum of unrighteousness—the heart still remains full of ungodly, graceless inclinations and worldly lusts, and they are righteous in regard neither to their bodies nor their souls. But through faith, Christ redeems us from all unrighteousness, liberating us again, so that we may live heavenly and godly,—a power which we did not possess before, whilst we were in the prison of unrighteousness.

"And purify unto himself."

Sin is attended with two evils.—First, it takes us captive, so that we are unable to do, perceive, or desire anything good, thus robbing us of freedom, light, and power. From this the second evil readily follows, our forsaking good, and engaging in nothing but sin and impurity, cultivating the land of wicked Pharaoh in Egypt, with hard and heavy labor. But when Christ comes through faith, he liberates us from the bondage of Egypt, giving us power to do good. This is the first gain.

Afterwards all our efforts during our whole life should be to purge out from our bodies and souls the unrighteousness of our graceless, worldly conduct, so that until death, our whole life should be nothing but a purification. For, although faith truly redeems us at once from all legal guilt, and sets us free, yet evil desires still remain in the body and soul, like the stench and sickness of a prison. With this, faith is occupied, in order that everything may be purified. Even as in the gospel, John 11, 44, Lazarus was raised from the dead by a single word, but afterwards the shroud and the napkin had to be removed; and as the half-dead man, whose wounds were bound up, and who was carried home, by the Samaritan, had to remain in the inn, till he was perfectly restored.

"A peculiar people."

By these words is implied something that is owned, like a peculiar inheritance or possession is held.—The people of God are called in the Scripture the inheritance of God; and as a house-keeper cultivates, nourishes, and improves his inheritance; so, through faith, Christ, who inherited us, impels and cultivates us, so that we may daily grow better and more fruitful. Thus you perceive that faith not only liberates us from sin, but constitutes us the inheritance of Christ, which he accepts and protects as his own. Who, then, can injure us, when a God so great possesses us as his inheritance?

"Zealous of good works."

The fact that we are his inheritance stands in opposition to ungodliness; whilst the circumstance that we should be zealous or diligent in our efforts for good, is opposed to worldly lusts. Thus through a godly walk and conduct we are his heritage, and through a sober and righteous life, we do good works. By this heritage we serve him, and by good works, our neighbors and ourselves. But first the heritage, and then the good works. For good works are not performed without godliness, and it is said we must be zealous, *zelotæ*, that is, we should emulate each other in doing good, as if we should vie with each other in our efforts to accomplish good for all. This is the proper meaning of the word *Zelotæ*. But where now are these?

"These things speak and exhort."

O, Lord God, it is a useful charge, not only to preach the principles inculcated in this Epistle, but also to urge, admonish, and arouse continually, leading the people to faith and real good works. Although we may be already informed, we must continually persevere and admonish, so that the Word of God may have its sway.

O, Pope, bishops, priests, and monks, who are now flooding the Church with fables and human doctrines, let these things be deeply impressed upon your minds. You will have more than enough to preach, if you preach nothing more than this Epistle and its import, continually admonishing, and enforcing it. The life of a Christian is beautifully portrayed in it. This, and nothing else,* you should preach and enforce. May God grant this! Amen.

Mark, two principles must be observed in the office of a minister, *teaching* and *admonition*. We must teach those who are uninformed; we must admonish those who are already informed, so that they may not decrease, grow indolent, or fall away en-

---

* A. Let no one despise you.

tirely, but persevere against all temptations.

The armor of this Epistle.*

In the first place, from this Epistle we may maintain the position that without grace no good can be accomplished, and all human efforts are sinful. This is established by his declaration: Grace hath appeared. Hence it is evident that previous to this no grace existed here. If no grace existed here, it is evident that there was nothing but wrath. Hence it follows that, without grace, instead of good, there is nothing in us but gracelessness and wrath.

Again, his declaration, the saving grace, clearly indicates that all that is destitute of grace, is already condemned, and beyond the limits of help and salvation. Where, then, is free-will? Where are human virtues, reason, and opinions? All are without the salvation of grace, all are condemned, all are sinful and shameful before God, even if they appear precious to us.

His language, *to all men*, is still more impressive. Here none are excepted. Hence it is manifest that before the Gospel was recognized, nothing but wrath must have ruled in all men; as he says, Eph. 3, 2: We were formerly by nature the children of wrath, even as others. Here, then, the Apostle stops the mouths of, and repels with secure armor, all who boast of their reason, works, opinions, free-will, light of nature, &c., without grace, regarding all as corrupt, *impii*, impious, graceless, and godless.

He says, moreover, that the grace of God appeared to all men, that they might deny ungodliness and worldly lusts. Who can stand before such armor? What else follows from this, but that without the grace of God all our works are ungodliness and worldly lusts? For, if there were any godliness and spiritual desires in any, it would not be necessary for all to deny ungodliness and worldly lusts;—neither would grace, nor its saving appearance be necessary for them.

---

* Here is inserted, in the edition B, that which appears below in the note at the beginning of this sermon.

Observe, thus we should use the Scripture as armor against false teachers, not only to exercise our faith in our lives, but also to defend and protect it openly against error.

Here all hypocrites, all ecclesiastics must, therefore, lie prostrate, no matter how much they may have fasted, prayed, watched, and toiled. All this will avail nothing; ungodliness and worldly lusts will still continue in them. Although, for the sake of shame, they may conceal and cover themselves, yet the heart is still impure. For, if our works, clothing, cloisters, fasting, and prayers, could render us pious, the Apostle should more properly have said: A prayer, or a fast, or a pilgrimage, or an order, &c., has appeared, teaching us to become godly. No, no, neither of these, but the saving grace has appeared. This, this, this alone, and nothing else, renders us pious.

Hence, it is easy to perceive how dangerous and reprehensible are these human laws, orders, sects, vows, and the like. For all these are, not grace, but works, leading, by their appearance, all the world into error, distress, and misery, so that it forgets grace and faith, and expects through such errors to become pious and happy.

His declaration likewise, that we should look for the blessed and the glorious appearing of the great God, establishes the fact that there is another life beyond this life. Hence, it is clearly evident that the soul is immortal; yes, even that the body must come forth again; as we pray in the creed: "I believe in the resurrection of the body, and life everlasting."

It may be clearly inferred, moreover, from this language which he employs, The great God and our Savior Jesus Christ, that Christ is true God. This clearly implies that the being who shall come in glory on the day of judgment, is the great God and our Savior, Jesus Christ.

Should any one endeavor to raise a cavil here, by attributing to the Father, what is said here in regard to the great God, it would still not hold, since the appearing and the glory are common to the great God and our

Savior, Jesus Christ. Were he not true God, this glory and splendor of the great God, would not be attributed to him. Since, then, it is the splendor, the glory, the work of the great God and our Savior, he must also be God with the great God. For, through Isaiah, he has said more than once: "My glory will I not give to another," and yet he here gives it to Christ; hence, Christ must be none other but God, whose own is the glory of God, and yet he is a distinct person from the Father.

Again, we might also draw a strong argument against human doctrines, from these words of St. Paul: "These things speak and exhort;" for had he designed anything else to be taught, he surely would have indicated it. But our bishops and popes now think if they permit these things to be written in books and on little slips of paper, they have done enough, their own commands notwithstanding;— when, at the same time, they ought with their own voice to preach and enforce the Gospel, without intermission. O, wo unto them!

SECOND CHRISTMAS.*

EPISTLE, TIT. 3, 4-8.

But after that the kindness and love of God our Savior toward man appeared, Not by works of righteousness which we have done, but according to his mercy he saved us, by the washing of regeneration, and renewing of the Holy Ghost; Which he shed on us abundantly, through Jesus Christ our Savior; That being justified by his grace, we should be made heirs according to the hope of eternal life. This is a faithful saying, and these things I will that thou affirm constantly, that they which have believed in God might be careful to maintain good works. These things are good and profitable unto men."

THIS EPISTLE teaches and impresses the same principle already expressed in the conclusion of the

* A. In the earlier Christmas-matins.

Gospel, in regard to contentment or good-will, as well as relative to love for our neighbors; and the substance is this: Why should we be unwilling to do that which God has already done for us, in whose sight we are much less worthy of such blessings, than any one can be in our sight?— Now, since God has conducted himself friendly and kindly towards us, in conferring mercy upon us; so let us conduct ourselves towards our neighbors, even if they are unworthy; since we, ourselves, are also unworthy.

Now, in order that this Epistle may be the more readily understood, it may be necessary for us to know what introduced, and gave rise to such language. A little before he spake these words, he said to Titus, his disciple, Tit. 3, 1, 4: "Put them in mind to be subject to principalities and powers, to obey magistrates, to be ready to every good work, to speak evil of no man, to be no brawler, but gentle, showing all meekness unto all men. For we ourselves also were sometimes foolish, disobedient, deceived, serving diverse lusts and pleasures, living in malice and envy, hateful and hating one another. But after that the kindness and love, appeared," &c.

Here you perceive that St. Paul indicates the relation we sustain to God and man, desiring us to render obedience to magistrates, and to conduct ourselves in a manner friendly towards our neighbors; and notwithstanding they may be wicked, blind, erring individuals, yet we should view them in the most favorable light, cheerfully endeavoring to make ourselves agreeable to them; remembering that God acted in a similar manner towards us, when we were like they now are.

The little word *appeared*, which implies the revelation of the Gospel, through which Christ appeared in all the world, is sufficiently defined in the foregoing Epistle; and although this Epistle is applied to the birth of Christ, yet little depends on this circumstance. He does not employ the little word *grace*, here, which he did above; but he ascribes to the God of grace, two other lovely words, "kindness and love." The first is *Christotes*, in Greek, and implies that friendly, lovely course of conduct which renders an individual attractive to all, and makes his society so sweet as to provoke every one to love and affection. Such an individual is capable of bearing with all, having no disposition to neglect or repel any one in a harsh, uncouth manner. In him all can repose confidence; all can approach him, and deal with him. Even as the Gospel represents Christ to the people, as kind to all, rejecting and repelling no one, but pleasant and amiable to all.

Thus too, through the Gospel, God presents himself to us in a manner altogether lovely and friendly; adapting himself to all, rejecting no one, passing over all our defects, and repelling none by severity. For there nothing but grace is revealed, by which he sustains us; and through which he approaches us most kindly, regardless of merit or worthiness.—This is the day of grace; here every one may approach with all confidence the throne of his grace; as it is written, Heb. 4, 16, and Ps. 34, 5: "They looked unto him, and were lightened; and their faces were not ashamed;" that is, he will not let us come and ask in vain, or go away empty, with shame.

The second is *Philanthropia*, the love of mankind; as for illustration, avarice may be termed the love of money; and, as David, 2 Kings 1, calls a fondness for women, the love of women. Thus naturalists call some animals philanthropical, or humane; as, for instance, the dog, the horse, the dolphin. For these animals have a natural fondness and love for man, adapt themselves to him, and serve him, as if they were endowed with reason and understanding, relative to him.

Such a disposition and love the Apostle attributes here to our God, as Moses also has done, Deut. 33, 2, 3, where he says, concerning God:—"From his right hand went a fiery law for them. Yea, he loved the people." This indicates, that God not only presents himself in the Gospel, in a friendly manner, desiring to draw all to himself, and bearing with them, but also offers himself to them, seeking to be with them, and holding out to them his grace and friendship.

These two words, the kindness and love of our God, are sweet and consolatory indeed, in which he offers his grace, and draws near to us, receiving all in the most lovely manner, who come to him, and desire him. What more should he do? Now, observe why the Gospel is styled a consolatory, lovely sermon of God in Christ. What can be conceived that is more lovely than these words, to a poor, sinful conscience? O, how wretchedly the devil has perverted for us, through the laws of the Pope, these pure words of God.

These words should be viewed in their free and full import. No distinction of persons among men should be made, since such heavenly love and kindness are secured not on account of our merit or worthiness, but in consequence of his grace alone, and extend to all that is called man, no matter how insignificant. For God loves, not the person, but the nature. The idea involved is not love for the person, but for the nature; so that his honor is entirely maintained, and no one can boast of his worthiness, or despair on account of his unworthiness; but all, one like another, may console themselves in consequence of the unmerited grace, which he so kindly and humanely offers and gives.

For had there existed, anywhere, a consideration or person worthy of anything, it surely would have been found in those who had performed works of righteousness. But Paul rather rejects these, saying: "Not by works of righteousness, which we have done," &c. How much less, should this appearing be in consequence of your wisdom, power, nobility, wealth, and hair turned yellow. The grace, which blots out all our honor and boasting, and ascribes all honor to God alone, who bestows it upon the unworthy without merit, is pure as well as great.

Now, this Epistle, moreover, inculcates two principles, *believing* and *loving*, or the receiving of favors from God, and the granting of favors to our neighbors. Now the entire Scripture enforces these two principles, and the one cannot exist without the other. For he that does not firmly believe in this grace of God, will most assuredly not extend it towards his neighbor, and is slow and indolent in assisting. But the more firmly any one believes, the more diligent and willing will he be in assisting. Thus *faith incites love, and love increases faith.*

Here we perceive how very imperfectly we,[*] who presume to become pious and happy through any other means, walk in faith. So many new works and doctrines are daily devised, that everything like a correct conception of a really good life, is entirely destroyed; when, at the same time, all Christian doctrines, works, and life are briefly, clearly, and superabundantly comprehended in these two principles—faith and love—through which man is placed between God and his neighbor, as a medium, which receives from above, and distributes below, and becomes a vessel or channel, through which the fountain of divine blessings flow incessantly to other individuals.

Behold, these are the really godlike persons, who receive from God all that he has in Christ, and, in return, approve themselves by their beneficence, as if they were gods to other persons. To this the 82d Ps. v. 6, is applicable: "I have said, Ye are gods; and all of you are children of the Most High." Children of God are we through faith, which constitutes us heirs of all divine blessings. But children are we through love, which makes us beneficent towards our neighbor. For divine nature is nothing else but pure beneficence, and, as St. Paul says here, kindness and love, which daily pour out all their blessings, in abundance, upon all creatures.

Now, you should be careful to accept the declaration of these words,

[*] A. Presume to become pious, &c., through other works, than beneficence towards our neighbor.

through which the kindness and love of God are revealed and offered to all, reposing your faith on them, thus daily exercising and strengthening it, and entertaining no doubt in regard to the fact that God is and will be lovely and kind to you, and you shall realize these blessings. Then you may ask and seek with perfect confidence whatever you may wish, whatever lies near to you, and whatever may be necessary for you and your fellow-man. But if you do not maintain such a belief, it were much better you had never heard them. For by your unbelief you falsify these precious, consolatory, grace-abounding words, and act, as if you do not regard them as truth; which would be a great, a high dishonor and disrespect to God,—a sin so enormous, that you could perpetrate no greater one.

But if you are in possession of faith, it will be impossible for your heart not to laugh for joy in God, and to grow bold, secure, and courageous. For, how can a heart continue sorrowful and cast-down, when it entertains no doubt that God is kind to it, and conducts himself towards it as a good friend, with whom, as with itself, it may freely enjoy all things? Such joy and pleasure must follow; if they do not, most assuredly there is something wrong about our faith. This the Apostle calls, in the Galatians, receiving the Holy Spirit in and through the Gospel. For, the Gospel is a declaration or sermon concerning the sweetness and grace of God, so lovely as to bear along with it the Holy Ghost, in preaching and hearing; as the rays of the sun naturally transmit heat with themselves.

But how could St. Paul have presented words sweeter and more lovely? I venture to assert, that I never read, in all the Scripture, words expressed relative to the grace of God, more lovely, than these two, *Christotes* and *Philanthropia*. In these, grace is so represented as not only to secure the remission of sins, but as also to dwell with us, to surround us with friendship, ever willing to assist, and offering to do for us all that we may desire; as a good, willing friend, to whom we may look for every favor and accommodation. Imagine to yourself a good friend, and you will have a picture of the manner in which God offers himself to you, in Christ, yet a very imperfect picture, however, of such super-abundant grace.

Now, if you thus believe, rejoice in God, your Lord, are alive, are satisfied in his grace, have all that you may need, what will you, then, do on earth, in this life? You cannot be inactive! Yes, such a disposition and love towards God cannot rest. You will grow warm and zealous in doing all that you know will contribute to the praise, honor, and glory of God, who is so kind and gracious. Here is no longer a distinction of works. Here all commands terminate. Here is neither restraint nor compulsion, but a joyful will and disposition to do that which is good, whether the object to be accomplished is insignificant or costly, small or great, short or long.

It will be your desire for all persons to obtain this knowledge of divine grace. Hence your love will break forth, and do all that it can for every one, preaching and proclaiming this truth wherever it can, and rejecting all that is not preached or practiced according to this doctrine. Behold, the devil and the world cannot endure to hear or see this, unwilling for their devices to be rejected by you. They will bring, in opposition to you, all that is great and learned and rich and powerful, representing you as a heretic and insane.

Observe, you will be brought to the cross for the sake of the truth, like Christ, your Lord. You will have to endure extreme reproach, and endanger your body, life, property, honor, and friends, until you are driven from this life into eternity. In the midst of all these difficulties, however, you should rejoice, freely enduring all these, viewing them in the most favorable light, acting kindly, and always bearing in mind, that you, too, were once, like they are, in the sight of God. For this faith and love can most assuredly do this. Behold, this is really a Christian life, which does to others as God has done to it.

This is the import of the Apostle, when he says: The kindness of God did not appear unto us, or save us, on account of our righteousness. As if he had said, if we were unworthy, and yet through mercy were received, and enjoyed the favors of God, notwithstanding the enormity of our demerits and sins, why should we be sparing in our favors to all, whose merits or worthiness have claims upon us? No, not thus, but let us be children of God, and do good even to our enemies and evil-doers, as God has done, and still does to us, his enemies and evil-doers. This accords with the declaration of Christ, Matt. 5, 44, 45, 46: "Love your enemies, * * * that ye may be children of your Father which is in heaven: for he maketh his sun to rise on the evil and on the good, and sendeth rain on the just and on the unjust. For if ye love them which love you, what reward have ye? do not even the publicans the same?"

St. Paul not only rejects us in a remarkable manner, on account of our evil deeds, but says: "Not by works of righteousness, which we have done." By this he indicates the works, which we regarded as good,* which may be regarded as a righteousness in our eyes and those of others, and which still render us more unfit for the reception of God's grace, since they are false in themselves, and since, on account of them, we commit a two-fold sin, by regarding them as good, and by depending upon them,—a position which rather incites the bitterness of God.

In a similar manner do our enemies, who are in the wrong, and still maintain in opposition to us that they are in the right, for the most part, incite in us feelings of bitterness; yet we should not refuse to favor them; precisely as God, through pure mercy, did not refuse to confer his favors upon us, in similar errors, when we were foolish and imagined that whatever we did was right and proper. Now as he

---

Luther's Works, 7r Bd.
* B. God.

did not deal with us according to our imagined righteousness; so, in return, we, too, should not deal with them according to their merits or demerits, but assist them from the principles of pure love, awaiting thanks and reward, not from them, but from God. Let this suffice in regard to the sum of this Epistle.

Now, let us take into consideration the words which he employs in expressing and commending this grace. In the first place, he extols it so high as to reject all our righteousness and good works. For we must not come to the conclusion that the thing which he rejects by these words, is a matter of no importance, but that it is the very best that man can accomplish on earth, namely, righteousness. If all men were to concentrate all their diligence in the accomplishment of wisdom and virtue according to their reason, knowledge, and free-will,—as the illustrious virtues and wisdom of certain pagan teachers and princes, as Socrates, Trajanus, &c., of which we read, and which all the world applaud in writing and conversation,—yet such wisdom and virtue are nothing in the sight of God, but sin, and altogether reprehensible; because they are not accomplished in the grace of God; that is, those who accomplish these, neither know God, nor honor him in this way, presuming they have achieved them through their own abilities. This is taught by nothing else, but grace in the Gospel.

Thus, too, St. Paul boasts that he rather than any of his equals led a life altogether irreproachable, presuming too that he did right in persecuting the Christians who rejected this pious life. But afterwards, when he learned to know Christ, he said, that he regarded his righteousness as filth and dirt, in order that he might be found, not in his own righteousness, but in Christ and in faith; as he further indicates all this in Phil. 3, 9, and Gal. 1, 14.

Here he sets aside, therefore, all boasting of free-will, all human virtue, righteousness and good works, concluding that all these are nothing but perversion, no matter how dazzling, how great, they may be, and that we must be saved by the grace of God alone, and that it saves all who possess this faith, and desire it in a correct conception of their own corruption and justness.

Now it is necessary for us to accustom ourselves to that portion of Scripture, which inculcates two kinds of righteousness: A human righteousness, as St. Paul here and in many other places styles it; and a divine righteousness, that is, divine grace which justifies us through faith, as St. Paul here expresses it, saying in the conclusion of this Epistle: "That being justified by his grace, we should be made heirs according to the hope of eternal life. Here you perceive that the grace of God and righteousness—which is also called the righteousness of God, because he gives it to us, and ours, because we receive it—become ours.

Thus, he says, Rom. 1, 17: It is declared in the Gospel, relative to the righteousness of God, that it is secured through faith: "as it is written, The just shall live by faith." Again, it is thus stated, Gen. 15, 6: "Abraham believed in the Lord; and he counted it to him for righteousness." Thus the Scripture concludes, that no one is justified before God, except him that believes, as just stated, and as quoted by St. Paul from Habak. 2, 4: "The just shall live by his faith."—Thus faith, grace, mercy, truth, is a thing which God works in us through Christ and his Gospel; as it stands written, Ps. 25, 10: "All the paths of the Lord are mercy and truth."

But we walk in the ways of God, and he in us, when we observe his commandments. These ways must all proceed in divine mercy and truth, and not in our abilities or powers which are ways of wrath and falsehood in the eyes of God, as he says, Isa. 55, 9: "For as the heavens are higher than the earth, so are my ways higher than your ways;" as if he should say, your ways are earthly and nugatory; you must walk in my heavenly ways, if you are to be saved.

"But according to his mercy he saved us."

How may these words, which read as if we were already saved, pass criticism? Are we not still on earth, in the midst of afflictions? Reply: They are thus declared, in order that the power of divine grace and the character of faith may be expressed in opposition to the erring self-righteous, who desire to secure and obtain salvation for themselves, through their works, as if it were still far from them. Not thus, Christ has saved us at once in two diverse ways: In the first place, he has done everything that is necessary for our salvation; namely, he has subdued and destroyed sin, death, and hell, so that in this respect there is nothing more for any one to do. In the second place, he has given all this to all of us in Baptism, so that whoever believes in Christ, that he has accomplished this, assuredly, immediately, in the twinkling of an eye has it, and all his sins with death and hell are removed, so that he needs nothing more in order to salvation, than such faith.

Behold, blessings so superabundant God pours out upon us in Baptism, so as to exclude the works, by which foolish persons presume to merit heaven and to become happy. No, dear friend, you must have heaven, and be in a state of salvation before you can do good works. Works merit not heaven, but heaven is conferred out of pure grace. Good works should be performed, without any expectation of merit, simply for the benefit of our neighbors, and to the honor of God, until the body is also liberated from sin, death, and hell. All the life, therefore, that a truly believing Christian leads after his baptism, is but a waiting for the manifestation of the salvation he already has.

Most assuredly he is in full possession of it, but it is still concealed in faith. Were this faith taken away, it would be manifest in him; this occurs in physical death, as it stands written, 1 John 3, 2: "Beloved, now are we the sons of God, and it doth not yet appear what we shall be: but we know that when he shall appear we shall be like him; for we shall see him as he is. And every man that hath this hope in him purifieth himself, even as he is pure."

Therefore, let not the self-righteous who disregard faith, mislead you, removing your salvation from you, and compelling you to secure it by works. No, beloved friend, it is within you; it is already secured, as Christ, Luke 17, 21, says; "The kingdom of God is within you." The life, therefore, which we live after our baptism, is nothing else but a tarrying, a waiting, and a longing for a manifestation of that which is in us, and an apprehension of that, for which we are also apprehended, as St. Paul, Phil. 3, 12, says: "I follow after, if that I may apprehend that for which also I am apprehended of Christ Jesus;" that is, that we may see the blessings which are given us in the shrine of faith. He is eager and desires to see his treasure, which Baptism has given and sealed to him in faith.

Thus, too, he says in this same chapter: "Our conversation is" already "in heaven; from whence also we look for the Saviour, the Lord Jesus Christ: who shall change our vile body, that it may be fashioned like unto his glorious body." Again, Gal. 4, 9, where he says, "After that ye have known God," he repeats the words, saying, "or rather known of God." Whilst both these are true, there is still a difference: we are known of God, and are already apprehended; but we do not yet know and apprehend him. For our knowledge is yet covered and locked up in faith.

Thus too he says, Rom. 8, 24: "We are saved," already in hope; that is, we do not yet see it. "But hope that is seen is not hope," says he; "for what a man seeth, why doth he yet hope for? But if we hope for that we see not, then do we with patience wait for it." Again, also Christ, Luke 12, 35, 36, says: "Let your loins be girded about, and your lights burning; and ye yourselves like unto men that wait for their lord, when he will return from the wedding; that when he cometh and knocketh, they may open unto him immediately." Again, St. Paul also said in the foregoing Epistle,

Tit. 2, 12, 13.—"We should live soberly, righteously, and godly, in this present world; looking for that blessed hope, and the glorious appearing of the great God and our Saviour Jesus Christ."

Behold, these and similar texts all show that we are already saved, and that a Christian should not seek after works, for the purpose of being saved by them. For such illusion and doctrine blind his Christian eyes, pervert the proper understanding of faith; and force him from the way of truth and salvation. This is implied in the words: "According to his mercy he saved us;" and at the end of this Epistle: "We should be made heirs according to the hope of eternal life." We are heirs,—yet this is concealed in faith,—and wait in hope for its manifestation.

This waiting, however, and the life we live after we are baptized, are designed to subdue the body, and to display the power of grace in the conflict against the flesh, the world, and the devil; and yet all this finally, to enable us to work for the benefit of our neighbors, and to bring them also to the faith by our preaching and examples. For, although he might accomplish this through angels, he desires to do it through us, human beings, so that faith may be perpetuated and completed in a more congenial manner; for faith would not continue here, if angels were continually to dwell with us. Neither would it be so agreeable, as if effected through creatures, like us, to which we are accustomed, and which we understand.

The fact, therefore, that we spend so much for the sake of purgatory, and forgetful of such faith, presume to secure ourselves against it, or to liberate ourselves from it, by good works, is, without doubt, an indication that we are under the influence of the devil and of Antichrist; as if our salvation were not already secured, and as if we must get it in some other way, than through faith; even when we see that it is contrary to all Scripture and the principles of Christianity. For whoever does not receive salvation through pure grace, independent of all good works, will most assuredly never secure it; and whoever turns his good works to his own advantage, and endeavors to profit himself and not his neighbors by them, performs no good work. For all this is faithless, and pernicious error and deceit.*

Now the devil has exerted such an influence that very nearly all institutions, cloisters, masses and prayers, have reference to purgatory alone, with a view so pernicious, moreover, that through works we must improve our condition and secure salvation. The blessings, therefore, of Baptism and faith must be obscured, and Christians ultimately become heathens.

O, Lord God, what abomination! Whilst, like Christ and St. Paul, we should teach Christians to consider themselves, after baptism or Absolution, ready for all hours of death, waiting for a manifestation of the salvation which they have already received, we, by a dependence on purgatory, afford them very sluggish security, in which they take into consideration simply this life, and defer and procrastinate till they come to their death-beds, and there effect sorrow and repentance, and presume by institutions, soul-masses, and testaments or wills, to liberate themselves from purgatory. But such hopes are vain and futile. Now follows:—

"By the washing of regeneration, and renewing of the Holy Ghost."

How beautifully does the Apostle, in explicit terms, extol the grace of God, given us in Baptism. He calls Baptism a washing, by which not only our feet or hands, but our whole bodies are cleansed. Thus too, Baptism wholly and at once cleanses and saves an individual, so that for the chief part and inheritance of salvation, nothing more is necessary, but such faith in such grace of God; so that we are saved, indeed, through pure grace, without works and merit; and thus love, praise, thanks, and honor for divine mercy, shall continue

* A. That I wish purgatory had never been devised, or introduced into the pulpit, as it is so abominably destructive of such Christian truth and correct faith.

in us eternally pure, without any boasting of, or pleasure in our own powers or performances; as has been already sufficiently and frequently stated.

The righteousness of man is not such a washing, but simply a washing of garments and vessels, as it is written in regard to hypocrites, Matt. 23, 25, in which they appear externally clean to themselves and others, but internally they continue full, full of filth. Thus he calls this washing, not a bodily washing, but a "washing of regeneration," which is a washing that does not wash the skin superficially and cleanse men bodily, but converts and changes the whole nature into another nature, so that the first birth, the birth of the flesh, is destroyed with all the inheritance of sin and condemnation.

In this way, moreover, it is clearly indicated that our salvation is not to be secured by works, but is given to us at once. By our birth we get not only one member, as our hands or feet, but the whole life, the whole person, which acts not in order to be born, but because it is born. Thus works do not render us clean and pious or save us; but we are first made clean and pious and saved, and then we freely perform works to the honor of God, and for the benefit of our neighbor.

Behold, this is the pure knowledge of the pure grace of God. Here then we learn to know God and ourselves, to praise God, to reject ourselves, to seek consolation from God, and to despair of ourselves. At this doctrine, those who presume to compel persons to endeavor to obtain salvation by laws, commands and works, stumble very much.

In order, moreover, that this washing and this regeneration may be the more clearly understood, he adds, saying: *Renewing*, because here there is a new man, a new nature, a new creature, which has altogether a different disposition, loves differently, and lives and speaks and acts differently from the manner in which it did before. As he says, Gal. 6, 15: "In Christ Jesus neither circumcision availeth anything, nor uncircumcision,' (that is, no work of the law,) 'but a new creature;" as if he should say: It will not thus admit of being patched and mended here and there with works. There must be an entirely new disposition; the nature must be changed; then works will follow of themselves.

Concerning this birth Christ, also, says, John 3, 3: "Except a man be born again, he cannot see the kingdom of God." Here we see that works will not do; the individual himself must die, and secure a different nature, which occurs in Baptism, when he believes; for faith is this renewing. For the damned also will be born differently in the last day. But this will be a birth without a renewing. They will be unclean, as they were here in their old Adamic life. Wherefore, this is a washing, a regeneration, which makes new creatures.

Relative to this birth there is much said in various places in the Scripture. For God calls his Word and Gospel *matricem* and *vulvam*, Isa. 46, 3:— "Hearken unto me, O house of Jacob, and all the remnant of the house of Israel, which are borne by me from the belly, which are carried from the womb:" as women speak in regard to the bearing of children. Whoever believes the Gospel, is conceived and born of God. But more in reference to this at some other time.

All these are such words, we perceive, as overthrow works and human presumption in regard to commands, and clearly point out the nature of faith, that an individual at once fully receives grace and is saved, so that works do not come to his assistance, but must follow. Precisely as if God would produce out of a dry log, a fresh, green tree, which would then bring forth its natural fruit. The grace of God is great, strong, powerful and effective. It does not lie, as visionary preachers presume, in the soul, asleep; nor does it permit itself to be borne, as a painted board bears its paint. No, not thus, it bears, it leads, it drives, it draws, it changes, it works all in man, and lets itself be felt and experienced. It is concealed, but its works are manifest; words and works show where it dwells; as the fruit and leaves of a tree indicate its kind and nature.

Therefore, to attribute nothing more to it, but that it aids in adorning and accomplishing works, like the sophists, Thomas and Scotus, and the masses, erroneously and perversely do, is a doctrine which falls far short of its import and significance. It not only aids in the accomplishment of works, but it alone accomplishes them; yes, not only the works, it changes and renews the whole person, and its object is to change the person, rather than to accomplish the works of the person. Its design is to effect a washing, a regeneration, a renewing, not only of the works, but, of the whole man.

Behold this is preaching freely and fully concerning the grace of God. For Paul does not say here, that God has saved us by works; but he exclaims in a full voice, that God saved us by regeneration and renewing. To patch up this matter with works avails nothing; an entire conversion of our nature is necessary. Therefore, it happens, too, that those who believe right, must suffer much, and die, in order that grace may manifest its nature and presence.*.

Finally, he calls this washing, "regeneration, renewing," in order that the greatness and efficacy of grace may be, in deed, fully expressed.— Thus this washing is a matter of such great importance, that it must be effected, not by a creature, but by the Holy Ghost. Ay, how completely dost thou, thou holy St. Paul, reject the free-will, the good works, and great merits of presumptuous saints! How high thou exaltest our salvation, and yet bringest it so near to us, yes, in us! How clearly and purely thou

---

* A. Observe, in regard to this, David says, Ps. 111, 2: "The works of the Lord are great, sought out of all them that have pleasure therein." Who are these, his works? We are, sought through his grace in Baptism. We are great works, new works, new-born. For it is a great matter to be saved so quickly, to be liberated from sin, death, and hell, eternally. For this reason he says: They are "sought out of all them that have pleasure therein," or desire; God has devised this, and he does all that man desires. But what more can he desire than to be saved, and redeemed from sin, death, and hell?

preachest grace! Therefore, work here or work there; to renew the man, and to change the person, are impossible, except by the washing of regeneration of the Holy Ghost.

This we clearly perceive in the self-righteous; there are none more intolerant, presumptuous, proud, and faithless than they are. For they are intractable, unrenewed, obdurate, hardened, and immovable, in their old Adamic nature, which they clothe and adorn with their good works; their evil nature is unchanged; they have nothing but outward works. O, they are a pernicious people, and in the eyes of God wholly destitute of grace, although they imagine they sit in his lap.

Now, St. Paul accords here with Christ, John 3, 5, where he says, in reference to this washing: "Except a man be born of water and of the Spirit, he cannot enter into the kingdom of God." Here you perceive that the water is the washing; moreover, that to be born again is the regeneration and renewing, and that the Spirit whom St. Paul mentions here, is the Holy Ghost.

It should also be observed here, that the Apostle seems to know nothing of the sacrament of confirmation. For he teaches, as Christ also teaches, that the Holy Spirit is given in Baptism; yes, in Baptism we are born of the Holy Spirit. We read, it is true, in the Acts of the Apostles, 8, 17, that the Apostles laid their hands on the heads of those who had been baptized, that they might receive the Holy Ghost. This is so construed as to make it apply to confirmation, when at the same time, it was done that they might receive the Holy Ghost as external evidence, and speak with divers tongues in preaching the Gospel. But this in the course of time ceased, and no longer exists, except in the ordination or consecration to the priestly or ministerial office; and even this is dreadfully abused. But, more of this at some other time.

"Which he shed on us abundantly through Jesus Christ our Savior."

Observe, the Holy Spirit is not only

given, but *shed;* not only shed, but *abundantly shed.* The Apostle cannot sufficiently magnify grace and its works, and yet we, alas, place such a low estimate on it, in comparison with our works. It were absurd for God and his Holy Spirit to pour out the Spirit upon us, so abundantly, and still to seek something from us and in us, by which we might be justified and saved,—as if such divine, superabundant works were insufficient.

Thus, too, St. Paul had spoken too inconsiderately, and might justly have been accused of falsehood. But he speaks in terms so full and excellent, that it is clear that no one can rely too much upon such washing and regeneration,—they are inexhaustible;—and that no one can place too much confidence in them,—there is still room for more. And even for this reason, God has embraced, in the word and faith, blessings so great, that the nature of this life could neither bear nor comprehend them, if they would begin to manifest themselves. And, at the same time too, when they begin to be manifested, the individual must die, and leave this life, so as entirely to sink and disappear in the blessings which he now apprehends in faith, as in the limits of a little point. Behold, so superabundantly are we justified and saved without any works, if we only believe it.

Wherefore, St. Peter also, 2 Peter 1, 4, says: "Whereby are given unto us exceeding great and precious promises: that by these ye might be partakers of the divine nature." He does not say they *will be* given to us, but they *are* given to us. And Christ, John 3, 16, says: "For God so loved the world, that he gave his only begotten Son, that all who believe in him, perish not, but have everlasting life."* Observe here, that they, all who believe, have eternal life. If so, they are certainly just and holy without any of their works; and works contribute nothing thereto; but it is effected by pure grace and mercy, so richly shed upon us.

But you may say: "How does it happen, then, that it is so frequently said in the Scripture, that those who do good shall be saved?" as, Christ, John 5, 29, says: "And shall come forth: they that have done good, unto the resurrection of life; and they that have done evil, unto the resurrection of damnation;" and Paul, Rom. 2, 7: Honor and glory to all who do good; indignation and wrath to all who do evil; and many other similar declarations. Answer: How is this to be viewed? Not otherwise than the words indicate, without any gloss. He that does good shall be saved; he that does evil shall be damned. The error, however, arises from the fact that we judge good works according to external appearances. This is not the case in the Scriptures, which teach that no one can do good, unless he himself is good first. Now, he does not become good through good works, but the works become good through him. But he becomes good through this washing of regeneration, and in no other way. This is what Christ means, Matt. 7, 17: "Every good tree bringeth forth good fruit; but a corrupt tree bringeth forth evil fruit;— Matt. 12, 33: "Either make the tree good, and his fruit good; or else make the tree corrupt, and his fruit corrupt."

It is true indeed, the self-righteous perform works similar to the regenerated; yes, their works are frequently more brilliant than those of the regenerated. They pray, fast, contribute, aid in the erection of institutions, make pilgrimages, and conduct themselves very splendidly. But Christ, Matt. 7, 15, calls this *sheep's clothing*, in which ravening wolves move. None of them are really humble, mild, moderate, and good in their hearts. This they show when any one crosses them and rejects their works; then they bring forth their natural fruits, by which they may be known; as temerity, impatience, arbitrariness, obstinacy, and slander, with many other evil propensities.

It is true therefore, he that does

---

* As there seems to be some discrepancy between the English version and the German, of this passage, we have adhered to the German. —(Translator.)

good shall be saved; that is, his salvation shall be made manifest; but he would do nothing good, were he not already saved in the new birth. The Scriptures, therefore, sometimes designate such persons according to their external conduct in regard to good works, and at other times, according to their internal nature, which produces such external conduct, in regard to good works, saying: They are already saved in view of their internal nature, and they shall be saved, if they do good; that is, if they remain steadfast, their salvation shall be made manifest.

The works, therefore, which we performed in our old, unregenerate state and Adamic nature, are the works which the Apostle rejects in this Epistle, saying: "Not by works of righteousness, which we have done," &c. They may be good works, but not before God, who regards personal goodness, and afterwards the works; as, Gen. 4, 4, 5, he had respect first for Abel, and then for his offering; and he turned away from Cain first, and then from his offering, which according to its external appearance, however, was an offering and a good thing, as well as the offering of Abel.

He adds too in a remarkable manner: "Jesus Christ our Savior," in order to keep us under Christ, as young chickens are gathered under the wings of the hen. For he himself thus says, Matt. 23, 37: "O Jerusalem, * * * how often would I have gathered thy children together, even as a hen gathereth her chickens under her wings, and ye would not!" In this is taught the nature of true and living faith. It is of such a character, that it is not enough in order to salvation for you to believe in God like the Jews and many others did, upon whom he also conferred many blessings and temporal advantages; but you must believe in God through Jesus Christ. In the first place, you must not doubt that he is your gracious God and Father, that he has forgiven you all your sins, and saved you in Baptism. In the second place, you must know besides, that all this has not been effected without reason, or without satisfaction having been rendered to his righteousness. For there is no occasion for mercy or grace to operate on and in us, or to aid us in eternal blessings and salvation: justice must first be satisfied to the fullest extent; as Christ, Matt. 5, 18, says: "One jot or one tittle shall in no wise pass from the law till all be fulfilled."

For whatever is said in regard to the grace and goodness of God, must be understood in reference to those alone, who most purely fulfill his commands; as he says, Mich. 2, 7, when the Jews presumed they were great in the sight of God, and continually exclaimed: "Peace, peace;" again, "Should God be so angry? should his benign Spirit have thus broken from us," &c.; he answers: Yes, "do not my words do good to him that walketh uprightly?" No one, therefore, can attain the rich grace of God, unless he shall have rendered the fullest satisfaction to the commands of God.

Now, enough has been said to show, that our works are nothing before God, and that we cannot fulfill the least of his commands in a single work; how much less then can we render full satisfaction to his justice, so as to become worthy of his grace? If, moreover, we were even able to keep all his commandments, and to make full satisfaction to his justice, still we would not thereby be worthy of his grace and salvation; nor would he be under any obligation to confer them upon us. But he might require all that from us as obligatory service of his creatures, who are under obligation to serve him. But whatever he grants besides, is pure grace and mercy.

This Christ clearly taught, Luke 17, 7, 10, where he thus says in a parable: "But which of you, having a servant plowing or feeding cattle, will say unto him by and by, when he is come from the field, Go and sit down to meat? And will not rather say unto him, Make ready wherewith I may sup, and gird thyself, and serve me, till I have eaten and drunken; and afterwards thou shalt eat and drink?

Doth he thank that servant because he did the things that were commanded him? I trow not. So likewise ye, when ye shall have done all those things which are commanded you, say, We are unprofitable servants: we have done that which was our duty to do."

Now, if through grace, and not in consequence of any obligation, heaven is given to those, who do all that they are under obligation to do, and if also to such persons, (if there be any such,) heaven is given, not in consequence of merit, but through divine, gracious promises; as it is said, Matt. 19, 17, "If thou wilt enter into life, keep the commandments; what then shall we presume upon our wretched works? Why extol them as if, in consequence of their nature, and not in consequence of the pure promise and gracious word of God, they are worthy of the kingdom of heaven?

In the first place, therefore, God has given us a being, who has fully satisfied divine justice for us all. And in the second place, he has, also, through this same being, shed abroad his grace and rich blessings, so that, notwithstanding this grace is received without price or merit, yea, with great demerit and unworthiness, it is still not given to us without cause and deserved merit. But as St. Paul, Rom. 5, 18, teaches, that, as we fell into sin, which is born in us in our natural birth, through Adam, without our own deserts and actions; so, on the other hand, in the new birth, we enter into grace and salvation, through Christ, without our merit and works.

For this reason, the holy Apostle is so careful, in every place where he speaks of grace and faith, to add, Through Jesus Christ, so that no one come, and say, Yes, I believe in God, and am thus satisfied. No, beloved friend, you must believe so as to know how, and through whom you must believe, that God requires of you the fulfillment of all his commandments and satisfaction of his justice, before he accepts your faith unto salvation; and if you could render full satisfaction, you should still await salvation, through grace alone, and not on account of any duties you may perform; so that your pride and presumption must fall to the ground before the eyes of God.

Observe, such are the advantages you have in Christ, through whom grace and salvation are conferred upon you, as through him, who has rendered full satisfaction to all the commandments and justice of God, in your stead and for you. Besides, he is worthy of grace and salvation being conferred upon you, through him. This is true and Christian faith.

For no faith is sufficient, but the Christian faith, which believes in Christ, and accepts, through him, and in no other way, these two principles; namely, the satisfaction of divine justice, and grace, or the gracious bestowment of eternal salvation. Thus says Paul, Rom. 4, 25: "Who was delivered for our offences, and was raised again for our justification;" not only for the purpose of putting away sin and of fulfilling the commandments of God, but also for the purpose of rendering us worthy, through him, of being righteous, and the children of grace.

Again, Rom. 3, 25: "Whom God hath set forth to be a propitiation through faith in his blood;" not only simple faith, but faith in his blood, with which, in our nature, he has rendered full satisfaction, and become a throne of grace for us, so that we receive both absolution and grace, without any cost and labor to us, but not without cost and labor to Christ.

We must, therefore, shelter ourselves under his wings, Matt. 23, 37, and not in the security of our own faith, flee away, as the hawk would soon devour us. Our salvation must exist, not in our righteousness, but, as I have often said, in the righteousness of Christ himself, as a tabernacle and wing spread out for us.

For our faith, and all that we may have from God, is insufficient; yes, it is inadequate, unless it rests itself beneath the wings of Christ, and firmly trusts, that, not we, but he can render and has rendered full satisfaction to the justice of God for us, and that grace and salvation are conferred upon us, not on account of our faith, but through the will of Christ; so that God's pure grace, promised, procured, and given for us, may be fully and clearly recognized.

This is implied in his declaration, John 14, 6: "No man cometh unto the Father, but by me;" and he does nothing more in the whole Gospel, than draw us out to himself, spreading out his wings, and calling us together under him. This is the design of St. Paul also, in the conclusion of this Epistle, where he says:

"That being justified by his grace, we should be made heirs according to the hope of eternal life. This is a faithful saying."

He does not say, by our faith, but, by the grace of Christ; that is, Christ alone is in favor with God; he alone has done the will of God, and merited eternal life. Now, since he has done this, not for himself, but for us, all who believe in him, should be so deeply absorbed in him, that through him and his grace, all that he has done for them, should be regarded as if they, themselves had accomplished it. Behold what a rich, inexpressible thing Christian faith is; what great and incomprehensible blessings it brings to all believers!

Let us learn from this how precious the Gospel is, which proclaims these blessings, and what injuries and destruction to souls, those who silently pass over the Gospel, and preach the works of the law, yea their own human doctrines, effect. Therefore, guard against false preachers, yes, against false faith also; rely not upon yourself, or upon your faith; flee to Christ, keep under his wings, stay under his shelter, let not yours, but his righteousness and grace be your shelter; so that you may be made an heir of eternal life, not by the grace which you have received, but, as Paul says here, by his grace.

Thus, too, it is said, Ps. 91, 4: "He shall cover thee with his feathers, and under his wings shalt thou trust;"—and, in the Song of Solomon, 2, 14: "O my dove, that art in the clefts of the rock, in the secret places of the stairs." That is, in the wounds of Christ the soul is preserved. Behold, this is the true Christian faith, which does not flee to, and rely upon itself, as the sophists dream, but it flees to, and relies upon Christ, and is preserved under and through him.

It has been sufficiently stated already, that we are heirs of eternal life, in hope, and that grace, without any works, confers at once, all, salvation, inheritance, &c., yet in hope. For these are concealed until death, and then we shall see what we have received and what we possess in faith.

The Armor of this Epistle.

This Epistle militates forcibly and in express terms against all righteousness devised by human reason, as well as against all human powers and free-will. The words are clear, in which he says: "Not by works of righteousness, which we have done, but according to his mercy he saved us," &c. And, in fact, all the words militate against such righteousness. For he attributes all to the washing of regeneration, to renewing, to the Holy Spirit, to Jesus Christ, and his grace. How then can the least particle of presumption continue in us, before such claps of thunder?

Wherefore, it matters not how brilliant secular and ecclesiastical laws may be, how splendid the position of priests, monks, and nuns, how dazzling gentlemen of honor and ladies of uprightness,—even if they could raise the dead,—without faith in Christ, all is nothing. Such hypocrisy blinds and misleads the whole world, and obscures for us the holy gospel and Christian faith.

As little, then, as the works of beasts, or the occupations of men help us in procuring salvation, so little do such brilliant works and conditions of men, as we have just mentioned, assist us in our salvation; yea, they obstruct it in a most pernicious manner. For this reason, you should guard against wolves in sheep's clothing, and learn to cleave to Christ in true and firm faith.

THIRD CHRISTMAS.*

EPISTLE, HEB. 1, 1-12.

God, who at sundry times and in divers manners spake in time past unto the fathers by the prophets,
Hath in these last days spoken unto us by his Son, whom he hath appointed heir of all things, by whom also he made the worlds;
Who being the brightness of his glory, and the express image of his person, and upholding all things by the word of his power, when he had by himself purged our sins, sat down on the right hand of the Majesty on high;
Being made so much better than the angels, as he hath by inheritance obtained a more excellent name than they.
For unto which of the angels said he at any time, Thou art my Son, this day have I begotten thee? And again, I will be to him a Father, and he shall be to me a Son?
And again, when he bringeth in the first-begotten into the world, he saith, And let all the angels of God worship him.
And of the angels he saith, Who maketh his angels spirits, and his ministers a flame of fire.
But unto the Son he saith, Thy throne, O God, is for ever and ever: a sceptre of righteousness is the sceptre of thy kingdom:
Thou hast loved righteousness, and hated iniquity; therefore God, even thy God, hath anointed thee with the oil of gladness above thy fellows.
And, Thou, Lord, in the beginning hast laid the foundation of the earth; and the heavens are the works of thine hands:
They shall perish; but thou remainest; and they all shall wax old as doth a garment;
And as a vesture shalt thou fold them up, and they shall be changed; but thou art the same, and thy years shall not fail.

THIS is a strong, a forcible, a lofty Epistle, pre-eminently presenting and enforcing the high article of faith concerning the Godhead, (the divinity) of Christ: and the presumption, that it was not written by St. Paul, is rather plausible, because it presents a style altogether more ornamented, than he is accustomed to use in other places. Some are of the opinion that it was written by St. Luke, and others, by St. Apollos, whom St. Luke represents as having been mighty in the

* A. Of High Mass.

Scriptures, in opposition to the Jews, Acts 18, 24. It is true indeed, that no Epistle enforces the Scriptures with greater power, than that employed in this Epistle; so that it is evident that its author was an eminent, Apostolical individual, no matter who he may have been. Now the object of this Epistle is to establish and advance the faith concerning the divinity of Christ, and as I have already said, there is scarcely any portion of the Bible that more strenuously enforces it. We must, therefore, adhere to it, and treat it in its regular order.

In the first place, it was the design of the Apostle to bring the Jews to the Christian faith; and he presses them so closely indeed, as we shall hear, that they cannot deny that Christ is true God. Now, if he is God and the son of God, and he himself has preached to us, and suffered for us, necessity and justice demand that we should much rather believe in him: the fathers in times past believed, when God spake simply through the prophets.

Thus he contrasts the preachers and the disciples; the fathers and us, who are the disciples; the Prophets and Christ, who are the preachers. The Son, the Lord himself, preaches to us; his servants preached to the fathers. Now, if the fathers believed the servants, how much more would they have believed the Lord himself? And if we believe not the Lord, how much less would we have believed the servants? Thus he urges the one by the other; so that our unbelief in comparison with the faith of the fathers, is an enormous disgrace; and on the other hand, the faith of the fathers, in comparison with our unbelief, is a very great honor.

Our shame appears still greater, when we bear in mind the fact, that God spake to the fathers, not only once, but at sundry times, and not only in one manner, but in divers manners, and still they always believed, whilst we are not once induced by such examples to believe the Lord himself. Observe, thus he proceeds with a powerful discourse to convert the Jews, and yet it availed nothing.

"At sundry times and in divers manners."

In my view, there seems to be this difference between these two phrases. The phrase, *at sundry times*, implies that there were many prophets succeeding each other, and that all the prophecies were not made through one prophet, at the same time. The phrase, *in divers manners*, implies, that through one prophet, to say nothing of the many, God spake at one time, in one manner, and at other times, in different manners. As for instance, some times, he expressed himself in clear terms, and at other times, through figures and visions :— Ezekiel described the four Evangelists by the four beasts; again, Isaiah sometimes clearly says that Christ shall be a king, and, at other times, he calls him a rod and a branch of the stem, Jesse; again, excellent fruit of the earth, and thus they speak of Christ in divers manners.

The words, *in divers manners*, moreover, may also be understood as referring to the fact that, for the purpose of aiding the people of Israel in their temporal matters also, God spoke in various ways. For his leading them out of Egypt, by Moses, was one thing, and his leading them through the Red Sea was another thing; and his commanding Moses to fight, &c., was still a different thing. There was not simply one declaration, but divers declarations were employed. The objects accomplished differed; but the faith was, nevertheless, always the same, at all times and in all manners.

How beautifully and kindly the Apostle persuades and invites the Jews, by calling to their minds the fathers, the prophets, and God himself. They had unbounded confidence in the fathers, the prophets, and God who spake to them in times past. But now they will not believe him;— nor will they take to heart the fact, that he spake to the fathers, not only once, but frequently, not in one manner, but in divers manners, as they well know, and must confess; nor will they believe now, since he speaks in another time and in another manner. In this manner he never spake before, nor will he ever speak in it again. The manner of speaking, therefore, which they so ardently desire, will never be employed. For he has never yet spoken, in former times, in the manner designated by them. For that would obstruct the faith and the object of God. We must leave to him the time, the person, and the manner, to speak, and be concerned about the faith only.

Wherefore, he may well say, "*In these last days.*" For, previous to the last day, no other mode of preaching will be employed. For this is the last time and the last manner, in which he designs to speak. He has commanded this word alone, and left it on record, to be preached until the end, as St. Paul, 1 Cor. 11, 26, says: "For as often as ye eat this bread, and drink this cup, ye do show the Lord's death till he come." He also arrests their gazing, by saying, *In these days*; so that they need not gaze after other days to come. The days, in which the last time and the last manner of speaking have commenced, are already at hand.

"*By his Son.*"

Here he begins to praise Christ, the last teacher, speaker, and apostle, and so praises him, as to show from forcible, well-grounded Scripture, that he is the real Son of God, and Lord over all. Here we should first learn to know Christ rightly, and how he exists in two natures, the divine and the human. In regard to this many persons fall into error. In some respects, they manufacture fables out of his words. They apply to the divine nature such declarations as really belong to the human nature, and thus delude themselves by such passages of Scripture. For, in regard to the declarations concerning Christ, it is of the utmost importance to determine which ones belong to the divine nature, and which to the human.— Then all will be clear and easy.

But, before we do this, we must attend to the inquiry, which some one may institute: If this is the last sermon, [or proclamation,] why is it said concerning Elias and Enoch, that they shall come in opposition to Antichrist? *Answer:* Concerning the advent of Elias,[*] I maintain that he will not come bodily[†] or physically. I know very well that St. Augustine has somewhere said; The advent of Elias and Antichrist is firmly fixed in the minds of all Christians. But I also know that there is no declaration of Scripture extant to prove this assertion. For what Malachi, ch. 4, v. 5, says concerning the coming of Elias, the angel Gabriel refers to John the Baptist, Luke 1, 17, and Christ does the same thing still more clearly, where he says, Mark 9, 13: " But I say unto you, That Elias is indeed come, and they have done unto him whatsoever they listed, as it is written of him." Now if John is the Elias, concerning whom this was written, as the Lord says here, the declaration of Malichi is already fulfilled. For there is nothing more said concerning the coming of Elias. The declaration which the Lord made a little before: " Elias verily cometh first, and restoreth all things," may be fairly interpreted, as if the Lord had been speaking of his office in this way: Yes, I know well that Elias must first come, and restore all things; but he has already come and done this.

This view of the subject is required by the circumstance, that immediately after speaking of the coming and office of Elias, he speaks of his own sufferings: "It is written of the Son of Man, that he must suffer many things, and be set at naught." Now if this was to take place after the coming of Elias, he must surely have already come. I know nothing more in regard to the coming of Elias, unless it might be that his spirit, that is, the Word of God, will be brought forth again, as it now seems to appear. For I have no longer any doubt, that the Pope with the Turks is Antichrist;— no matter what you may believe about it.

---

[*] A. I hang between heaven and earth, and much rather hesitate as to whether he will come bodily, &c.

[†] A. Nor shall I contend strenuously about this; let him that will, believe it, or believe it not.

Now, in returning to Christ, we assert, that it is necessary firmly to believe that Christ is true God and true man, and that the Scriptures and Christ himself sometimes speak in regard to the divine nature of Christ, and at other times in reference to his human nature. As, for instance, the declaration, John 8, 58, "Before Abraham was, I am," has reference to his divinity; but the declaration, Matt. 20, 23, "To sit on my right hand, and on my left, is not mine to give," is made in regard to his humanity, which could not help itself on the cross; although some wished to show great skill here by their abstruse interpretations, for the purpose of opposing the heretics. Thus, too, the passage, where it is said,[*] Mark 13, 32, "Of that day and that hour knoweth no man, no, not the angels which are in heaven, neither the Son, but the Father," has reference to the *man* Christ.

The explanation, *the Son knew not*, that is, he did not choose to reveal, is unnecessary here. Of what advantage could such a gloss be? The humanity of Christ, even like any other, holy, natural man, did not always consider, speak, desire, and observe all things. Some make out of him an almighty man, unwisely blending together the two natures, and their works. As he did not always see, hear, and feel all things; so, in like manner, he did not always contemplate all things in his heart, but as God moved him, and brought them before him. He was full of grace and wisdom, so that he was able to judge and to teach all that came before him, because the Godhead which alone sees and knows all things, was personally present in him. And, finally, all that is said about the humiliation and exaltation of Christ, must be applied to the man; for the divine nature can neither be humiliated nor exalted.

"Whom he hath appointed heir of all things."

---

[*] A. " My Father is greater than I," John 14, 28. Again, Matt. 23, 37: " How often would I have gathered thy children together, even as a hen gathereth her chickens under her wings. It.

This is spoken in regard to his humanity. For we must believe that Christ is over all things, not only according to his divinity, but also according to his humanity; so that all creatures are subservient and subject to the man Christ. As God he creates all things; but as man he creates nothing, and yet all are subject to him, as David, Ps. 8, 6, says:— "Thou hast put all things under his feet."

Thus, Christ is our Lord and God. As God he creates us; as Lord we serve him, and he rules over us. Thus, it is the object of the Apostle to speak of him, in this Epistle, as true God, and Lord over all things. For although the natures are different, yet they constitute one person; so that all that Christ does or suffers, God has certainly done and suffered; notwithstanding only the one nature is effected.

For illustration, when I speak of a wounded limb of a man, I say, the man is wounded,—although his soul, or his entire body is not wounded, but only a part of his body,—because his body and soul constitute one person. Now, as I must speak differently concerning body and soul; so, too, must I speak concerning Christ. Again, it is not improper to say, I do not know the sun, in the night, when at the same time I know it well in my understanding, but not by my eyes. Thus Christ knows nothing about the last day, and yet he knows it well.

"By whom also he made the worlds."

This is the Son, you will observe, who is appointed heir of all things, according to his humanity, and yet by him, as God, all the worlds were made. He has only one person, but two natures, and two kinds of works. There is only one Christ, but in him there are two natures. In reference to him the highest terms are employed.

It is evident, indeed, that the Apostle speaks concerning the Son, who is appointed heir, and by him all the world is made. If, then, every thing is made by him, he himself could not have been made. Hence, it follows clearly, indeed, that he is true God.

For, all that is not made, and still is something, must be God. Again, all that is made, must be a creature, and cannot be God; for it does not derive its existence from itself, but from him, who created it. But now all things are made by Christ, and he is made by nothing; hence, he has his existence from and in himself, and not from any created thing, nor from any creator.

If then, moreover, he is a Son, he cannot exist alone; he must have a Father; and if by him God made the world, that God who made the world by him, must not be he, by whom he made it. Thus it follows, that there must be two distinct persons, the Father and the Son, and yet* the divine nature is only one, and there cannot be more than one God. Hence it is conclusive, that Christ with the Father is true God, in one divine essence, Creator and Maker of the world, and there is no difference, except that one is the Son, and the other the Father; neither is he created by the Father, like the world was, but must be begotten in eternity; nor is he less than the Father, but like him in every way and respect, except that he is begotten of the Father, and not the Father of him.

Now, if we cannot comprehend this by our reason, we must submit to these and similar Scriptural declarations, and believe. For if we could comprehend it by our reason, there would be no necessity for believing it. It is evident that these words speak of two, when it is said: "By whom also he made the worlds." Nor is it less clear, that he, who is not made, but by whom all things are made, must be God, but how this may be, the Scriptures neither say, nor express; it must be believed.

Now, this manner of speaking is employed in the Scriptures: *The world is created by Christ, of the Father, in the Holy Spirit*, and for this there is good reason, although not very clear or comprehesible. But for the purpose of a mere intimation, this manner of speaking is employed, in order to indicate that the Father does not de-

---
* A. because.

rive his divine essence from the Son, but the Son from the Father, and that he is the first, original person in the Godhead. For this reason, it is not said that Christ made the world by the Father, but that the Father made it by Christ, that the Father may be regarded as the first person, and from him, yet by Christ, all things have their existence. In this manner John also speaks, John 1, 2: "All things were made by him;" and Col. 1, 16: "All things were created by him, and for him;" and Rom. 11, 36: "For of him, and through him, and to him, are all things."

You perceive now, how appropriate the language is in which Christ is called an heir, according to his humanity. For who should be more entitled to inherit all the estate of God, than he who is Son? He together with the Father created all this or all creatures; but he is now also man, and Son, and because he is Son, he inherits these, and he is a Son now in both natures. But whence this mode of speaking is derived, we shall hear in the Gospel.

"Who being the brightness of his glory and the express image of his person."

He expresses here, by several similes, as clearly as possible, that Christ is a distinct person from the Father, and yet he is real, true God. But the German and Latin words are not entirely equivalent to the Greek terms employed by the Apostle. He styles him such a brightness as proceeds from the glory of the Father; like the aurora rising from the sun, which has with and by itself the whole sun, and is not a part of the brightness, but the whole brightness of the whole sun, shining from the sun, and remaining on it. So that, in this way, by a single word, the birth, the unity of the nature, and the distinction of the persons are understood. For Christ, without intermission, is eternally begotten of the Father, ever proceeding, like the sun in the morning, not at midday or in the evening. Nor is he the Father according to the person; like the brightness is not the sun; and yet he is with the Father and in the Father, neither before nor after him; but co-eternal with him and in him as the brightness is at the same time with and in and on the sun.

He also calls the brightness of the the Father, *Doxa*, which properly implies honor or glory; because the divine nature is pure glory and honor, as that which derives all from itself, and not from another, and may boast of, and glory in itself. Now, he says Christ is an entire light, a full brightness of his honor; that is, he also has in himself the whole Godhead, and can boast of, and glory in all that the Father can; except that he derives it from the Father, and not the Father from him. He is the brightness proceeding from the paternal honor; that is, he is God begotten, and not God begetting, yet he is God complete and perfect, as the Father is.

The Scriptures you will observe, do not employ this mode of speaking in regard to the Saints, who are also an honor to God: that is, they were made and created for the honor of God. But here, when he says, Christ is the brightness of the paternal honor, the words force the conclusion, that the paternal honor is in the brightness itself, otherwise it would not be the brightness of his honor. And what shall I say? These words may be better understood with the heart, than expressed by the tongue or the pen. They are clearer in themselves, than any of the glosses render them, and the more they are glossed, the more obscure they become. This is the sum of the matter: the whole Godhead is in Christ, and to him, as to God, all honor is due; yet he does not derive this from himself, but from the Father. This is equivalent to two persons, one God. For in this place he does not speak concerning the Holy Ghost, in whom it is easy to believe, when we have advanced so far as to be able to regard two persons as one God.

In regard to the other simile, in which he styles him an image or sign of the being or essence God, I shall still claim the privilege of speaking plainly and clearly. When an image is made according to the likeness of a person, it is not an image of the essence or nature of the person. For it is not a person, but it is stone or wood; and it is an image formed out of the substance of stone or wood, in the likeness of the man. But if I could take the essence of the man, as the potter takes clay, and make an image out of it, which would at the same time be the image of the man, and also entirely include in itself his essence or nature, it would, you perceive, be an essential image, or an image of the human substance. Such an image is a creature; for all images that are made, are formed out of a substance and nature different from that of which they are images.

But here the Son is an image of the paternal essence, of such a character, that the paternal essence is the image itself; and, were it admissible so to speak, the image is made out of the paternal essence, so that it is not only like, and one with the Father, but it also contains in itself his entire essence and nature; as it may be said in reference to the brightness of his glory, that the brightness is made out of the glory, and that it is not only like it, but contains it in itself wholly and naturally, so that the brightness and the glory are one thing.

Now observe, as I say concerning the image of a man: This is a wooden image, or image formed out of stone; so I say: Christ is a divine image, so that, as true as the former image is wood, so true is the latter image God. St. Paul, therefore, calls Christ the image of the living and invisible God.

Now, in the wooden image this perfection is wanting. For, although it is indeed a wooden image, it is still not an image of the wood, but of the individual; nor does it represent the wood but the individual. If the individual, moreover, is really fashioned in the wood, yet he is still not wood, and his essence is something different from the substance, in which his image is formed; and in regard to all creatures, the image is a different substance from that of him, whose image it is; nor can any image be found, that is his essence or substance. But here the image and he, whose image it is, are one essence, except that the Father is not an image. For he is not fashioned from the Son, but the Son from the Father and according to the Father, in one simple, real, divine essence.

Such perfection is also wanting in regard to the brightness of the sun. The sun has its own splendor, and the brightness, its own; but the brightness derives its splendor from the sun. But here the brightness is the splendor in such a way, that out of the splendor, (so to speak,) the brightness is made or constituted, and the splendor is entirely and essentially the brightness itself, except that the brightness is not thus constituted out of itself, but out of the paternal splendor.

Observe, these words are still clearer in themselves, than this explanation. His declaration, The image of his person, the brightness of his glory, is clear enough. Here the tongue should be silent, and let the heart reflect. The Hebrew mode of speaking is thus: *Pauperes sanctorum, i. pauperes sancti. Virtus Dei, i. virtus Deus. Sic, character substantiae, i. character substantia, subsistens et ipsemet Deus. Sic, splendor gloriae, i. splendor gloria ipsa.* Latinists may well comprehend this, but for the Germans, and the common people, it is enough to call that, which is made out of gold, an image of gold. Thus, they should also call Christ an image of God, because he is entirely constituted out of God, and besides him there is no God; except that he has this Godhead and image from the Father, as the first person; and the two are one God. This is not the case with creatures. For the golden image does not represent its golden nature, but a different nature, that of the individual. Therefore, although it is a golden image, yet it is not an image of the gold's own essence. For gold must be represented by another image, as by a golden color, or by something that is not gold.

But here the image is also the essence itself of that, of which it is an image, and no other image is needed but its own.* Here faith, and not

* A. Essence.

sharp speculation, is needed. The words are sufficiently clear, indubitable, and forcible. Whoever will not recognize the divinity of Christ in these words, will not recognize it in any other way. Nor is Christ called an ordinary, common image here, but *Character;* that is, an express image, so that nothing else, as a portrait, is like it. Thus, too, he is not an ordinary image, but *Apaugasma*, a real brightness, which is like nothing else, but the glory, from which it proceeds.

"And upholding all things by the word of his power."

This is the third instance here, in which Christ is represented as God. In the first place, it is said that the worlds were made by him; in the second place, that he is the brightness and image of God, and here, that he upholds all things. If he upholds all things, he is not held up, but is rather above all things; hence he must be God. But to uphold all things is, to support and maintain all things: so that, all things are not only made by him, as already said, but are also perpetuated and preserved by him; as St. Paul, Col. 1, 17, says: " By him all things consist." The word, *upholding,* is well selected. He uses neither coercion nor restraint, but he gently upholds, and permits all creatures to enjoy his gentle goodness; as it is written in the Wisdom of Solomon, 8, 1: " Wisdom reacheth from one end to another mightily; and sweetly doth she order all things."

But I have not made up my mind with certainty, in regard to what is intended by the phrase, " By the word of his power." Were a man thus to speak, I would conclude that he had fallen into error, because Christ himself is the Lord, and he has no word, by which he operates. Were it spoken in reference to the person of the Father, it would fully accord with the Scriptures; for the Father made all things through his Word, and upholds all things in the Word; as it is said, Ps. 33, 6: " By the word of the Lord were the heavens made."

Here I shall withdraw my view, giving place for another and better one, and simply state my opinion.

He may, perhaps, speak thus, for the purpose of blending the persons in one Divinity or Godhead, since they are one God, and that is said in reference to the person of the Father, since whatever God does, each person does. Thus God upholds all things by his Word. Christ and this Word are really that God.

There are other portions in the Scriptures, in which the persons are suddenly changed. As for instance, in the second Psalm, ver. 6, 7: " Yet have I set my King upon my holy hill of Zion. I will declare the decree; the Lord hath said unto me, Thou art my Son," &c. Here the first part is spoken in the person of the Father concerning the Son, and the other, in the person of the Son in regard to the Father. Here in a single passage the persons are changed, because both are one God. This may be the case in the declaration of the text, that, when it is said, he is the image of God, the reference is to Christ, and when it is said, He upholds all things by his word, it is to the Father, without making any distinction, because both persons are one God, without distinction.

If this is not satisfactory, we might look at the matter in this light. By the term, *word,* something like an act or history might be understood, as it is said in the Gospel, Luke 2, 15, concerning the shepherds: " Let us now go even unto Bethlehem, and see this thing," word, history, " which is come to pass;" that is the history or the act which is come to pass there. This might be the meaning here, Christ upholds all things by the word of his power; that is by the act of his power. For by the operation of his power, all things are preserved, and all that has existence and power, derives these, not from itself, but from the active power of God. And here, moreover, the power and the word should not be separated, but the word and the power are one thing, as if we should say relative to an efficacious, or efficient word, that the power is the nature and essence of the word, which operates in all things. Now let each one adopt whatever view may be deemed most proper.

"When he had by himself purged our sins."

Here he properly touches the Gospel. Whatever may be said concerning Christ, is no benefit to us, till we learn that it is spoken for our use and benefit. What advantage would preaching be, were it designed for Christ's sake alone? Now, it wholly and entirely concerns us and our salvation. Let us, therefore, listen with joy. The language is lovely beyond measure. That Christ,—who is so great, who is heir of all things, the brightness of God's glory, the image of his person, who upholds all things, not by extraneous power or assistance, but by his own act and power, in a word, who is all in all,—has come to our service, poured out his love for us, and prepared a purification for our sins.

He says, Our, our sins not his sins, not the sins of unbelievers. This purification is of no advantage, nor is it adapted to him who does not believe it. Nor did he effect this purification through our free-will, reason, power, works contrition, or repentance —these all are nothing in the sight of God,—but through himself. How, through himself? By taking our sins upon himself on the holy cross, as Isaiah, 53,6, says.

But even this is still not enough. He has effected it *through himself*, so that, when we believe in him, that he has effected it for us, he himself dwells in us through and on account of such faith, and daily purifies us through his own work; so that nothing but Christ himself contributes anything towards purifying our sins. Now he neither dwells in us, nor does he work in us such purification through himself in any other way, but in and through faith.

Hearken then, ye deceivers of the world and blind leaders of the blind, ye Pope, bishops, priests, monks, learned, and idle talkers, who teach that sins are purged by human performances and satisfactions made by men for sins, issuing indulgences, and vending devised purifications for sins. Listen here: purification for sins is effected not by human efforts, but by Christ alone and through Christ himself. Now Christ is communicated to us, not through any work, but through faith alone, as St. Paul, Eph. 3, 17, says: "Christ * dwells in your hearts by faith." Hence it is clearly evident that purification for sins, is faith, and he that believes that Christ has purged his sins, is most assuredly purified through that faith, and in no other way. Hence, St. Peter, Acts 15, 9, appropriately says: "Purifying their hearts by faith."

Now, when we are in possession of this faith, and this purification is effected in us by Christ himself, we should perform good works, hating and repenting of our sins; then our works are really good; but before the existence of this faith, they avail nothing, inducing false confidence and trust. For our sins are an evil so heinous, and their purification cost a price so enormous, that a personage so exalted, as Christ is here represented, had to intervene, and purge them himself.— What could our weak, ineffectual performances,–performances of creatures, sinful, weak, and corrupt,—accomplish in matters of such magnitude? They would be like an individual, who would presume to burn heaven and earth with an extinguished brand. Our sins require a price equal with God, who is offended by our sins.

"Sat down on the right hand of the Majesty on high; being made so much better than the angels, as he hath by inheritance obtained a more excellent name than they."

This declaration has reference to the human nature of Christ, in which he effected a purification for our sins; yet it is true, however, that the Son of God effected it. Nor should the person be separated for the sake of distinguishing the natures. Hence it is also true that the Son of God sits on the right hand of the Majesty; although this occurs according to his humanity alone; for according to his divinity, he, too, himself is the only Majesty with the Father on whose right hand he sits. We shall now, however, cease this manner of speaking, as it is obscure, and adhere to the language of the text, which is clearer.

To sit on the right hand of the Majesty, is certainly to be like the Majesty. Therefore, where Christ is represented as sitting on the right hand of God, there it is established fundamentally, that he is true God. Since no one, but God himself, is like God. The fact, therefore, that the man Christ, is said to sit on the right hand of God, is equivalent to saying that he is true God. It is said, Ps. 110, 1 : *The Lord said unto my Lord, sit thou at my right hand;"* that is, he said to Christ who is man, Be like me; that is, Thou shalt be recognized, not simply as as man, but as God; as the Apostle here adduces this passage from this Psalm.

Again, Ps. 8, 7, it is said; "Thou hast put all things under his feet;" that is, Thou hast made him equal with thyself; not because he then first began to be God, but because the man was not previously God and equal with God. For as soon as he began to be man, he began to be God. The Scriptures speak so much more appropriately concerning Christ, than we do, enveloping the person so deeply in the nature, and again separating the natures, that few properly comprehend it. I have frequently fallen into error myself, in regard to these and similar passages, attributing to the nature what belongs to the person, and *vice versa*. Thus Phil. 2, 6, 7, it is said : " Who being in the form of God, thought it not robbery to be equal with God : but made himself of no reputation, and took upon him the form of a servant, and was made in the likeness of men : and being found in fashion as a man." This passage, however, is obscure.

Now in returning to our text we should observe that the Apostle begins to adduce his principles of Scripture from the Old Testament, showing that Christ is God. For, hitherto, he expresses his views and language as derived from the Scriptures, saying that Christ is so much better than the angels; for he has become God, and has by inheritance obtained a more excellent name than they. All this is designed to indicate that the man Christ has began to be God, and is glorified, and recognized as God. " For unto which of the angels said he at any time, Thou art my Son, this day have I begotten thee ?"

This declaration appears in the second Psalm. For the purpose of rendering it still more clear that he is speaking of Christ, we shall adduce the entire Psalm, which reads as follows: " Why do the heathen rage, and the people imagine a vain thing ? The kings of the earth set themselves, and the rulers take counsel together, against the Lord, and against his anointed, saying, Let us break their bands asunder, and cast away their cords from us. He that sitteth in the heavens shall laugh: the Lord shall have them in derision. Then shall he speak unto them in his wrath, and vex them in his sore displeasure. Yet have I set my king upon my holy hill of Zion. I will declare the decree: the Lord hath said unto me, Thou art my Son; this day have I begotten thee. Ask of me, and I shall give thee the heathen for thine inheritance, and the uttermost parts of the earth for thy possession. Thou shalt break them with a rod of iron ; thou shalt dash them in pieces like a potter's vessel. Be wise now, therefore, O ye kings: be instructed, ye judges of the earth. Serve the Lord with fear, and rejoice with trembling. Kiss the Son, lest he be angry, and ye perish from the way, when his wrath is kindled but a little. Blessed are all they that put their trust in him."

Here we clearly perceive that Christ, against whom the Jews together with Pilate, Herod, and the chief priests, raged, is intended. To him, he says, "Thou art my Son," &c.

This passage the Jews endeavor to evade by the introduction of wild interpretations; and because they are unable to deny that this Psalm has reference to an individual who is to be a king, and Christ, which implies anointed, they assert that it has reference to David, who also was a Christ. For they style all kings messiahs or christs, that is, anointed ones. But, their position will not hold. For David never inherited the heathen, nor did his kingdom extend to the uttermost parts of the earth, as the Psalm asserts in regard to this king. Nor is there a single declaration in the Scriptures, in which it is said to any man, Thou art my Son.

But even if they admit that this Psalm speaks of the Messiah, they resort to other subterfuges. They maintain that the Messiah is yet to come, and that this Jesus Christ is not the Messiah; and, besides, that, even if he is called the Son of God, he is not, therefore, God. For it is written and said concerning all the children of God, Ps. 82, 6: "I have said, Ye are gods; and all of you are children of the Most High." And in many places in the Scriptures, the saints are called the children of God: as, Gen. 6, 2, Ps. 89, 27, Matt. 5, 45, 1 John 3, 2; and, in various places, Paul calls us children of God, and, therefore, we also call him Father, saying, "Our Father," &c.

How shall we reply to this? Shall we leave the Apostle in this difficulty, as if he had not adduced good and clear grounds from the Scriptures? This would be injustice. In the first place, experience shows that this Jesus is the one, of whom the Psalm speaks; for in Christ it is fulfilled. He was persecuted by kings and rulers. They sought to exterminate him and, by their effort, brought derision on themselves. They were destroyed, as it is here said. He is recognized as Lord throughout the whole world; so that no king, either before him, or since him, ruled or rules as far and wide as he does. Now, if in him this Psalm is fulfilled, it cannot be construed as referring to any one else.

Although saints are called gods and the children of God, the reasoning of the Apostle, based on the fact that it is nowhere said in reference to any angel, much less to any man,— Thou art my Son, is sufficient to show that Christ is God. Hence, he must be a peculiar Son, above all men and angels. Now, since he does not call him a son in common with others, but singles him out, he must be higher than all others. Now, he cannot be higher than angels, unless he be true God, since angels are the highest order of beings.

He begets, moreover, all other children through means, as St. James, 1, 18, says: "Of his own will begat he us with the word of truth." Angels are not begotten, but created. This Son, however, he did not create, but begat him through himself, saying, I, I myself, by myself, I have begotten thee, this day. Such language is not used in regard to any one else. This single, personal bringing forth includes a natural birth. It is true, he says, 1 Chron. 22, 10, relative to Solomon:— "He shall be my son;" but still he does not say specially to him, Thou art my Son, I have begotten thee. David begat him. But this one was begotten by no one except God.

He also says, *This day*, that is, in eternity. It is not possible to effect a natural birth in a day. This we see in the human species, and in all animals. But for the purpose of distinguishing this birth, he adds, This day; since God begets his Son at once, eternally, and this begetting and bringing forth of a Son are simultaneous. He does not say, I begat thee a year ago, but even now, Thou art my Son, I have begotten thee. This must, therefore, be a transcendental birth of an exalted character, which no one can comprehend.

It is written, Hos. 11, 1, that God says: "I called my Son out of Egypt." This, like this Psalm, indicates a Son. The Jews, however, assert that this has reference to the people of Israel. But St. Matthew refers it to Christ. Let this be as it may, we find no declaration of Scripture, in which it is said, in regard to any man, not even to a king, or a great king, Thou art my Son; and, much less do we find any place where it is said, relative to any man, I myself have begotten thee, This day have I begotten. Hence it is clear and evident from this Psalm, that Jesus is the Christ, and the true, natural Son of God.

We should observe here, moreover, with special care, that the Apostle attributes such authority to the Scriptures, that we are under no obligation to accept anything that is not asserted in them. Were this not the case, his declaration, "Unto which of the angels said he at any time," &c., would not be conclusive. The Jews might say, If he did not assert it in the Scriptures, it may nevertheless have been asserted; since not everything that occurred, is contained in the Scriptures. Now, if it is his design, that we are not under obligation to accept anything that is not presented in the Scriptures, we should also reject all doctrines not taught in them.

This operates against the presumption of the Pope and the papists, who shamelessly assert that we must accept more than the Scriptures contain; and that, when it is said, "It is not in the Scriptures; therefore, it is not authentic," it is not conclusive. In this way, they impair the position of the Apostle more than the Jews do, introducing their *Concilia*, teachers, and high Schools. Beware of this; be certain that all you accept is in the Scriptures. But, relative to whatever is not in them, you should exclaim, as the Apostle does here, "When did God ever assert it?"

"And again, I will be to him a Father, and he shall be to me a Son!"

They have also impaired the force of this passage. It seems that the object of their being teachers is to weaken the force of the Scriptures. They assert that this passage has two meanings: In the first place, it should be understood in reference to Solomon, as a figure of Christ; in the second, in reference to Christ. But, if it were admitted that the Scriptures do not present an indubitable sense, they already cease to be conclusive. The Jews might maintain that it has reference to Solomon. Hence the Apostle would apparently be cast in the sand, and establish nothing. We should, therefore, firmly maintain that it is spoken concerning Christ alone, even as the previous passage describes a peculiar Son, above all other sons, so that this was not said to angels, much less to Solomon; as the Apostle says here, that he has obtained a more excellent name than the angels; so that the reference can in no way be to Solomon.

Now it is not enough for us simply to believe the Apostle; we are under obligation to show that he conclusively establishes with clear grounds the position which he occupies. It is necessary, therefore, to know that this passage is adduced from 2 Sam. 7, 14, and Psalms, Ps. 89, 23, 28, which are prophetic books. In these passages the reference is to Christ alone, and not to Solomon. But in 1 Chron. 22, 10, which is a historical book, the reference is to Solomon alone: "He shall be my son, and I will be his father." Now it is admitted even by the Jews that the 89th Psalm, v. 26, 27, where it is said, "He shall cry unto me, Thou art my Father, my God, and the Rock of my salvation. Also, I will make him my first-born, higher than the kings of the earth," has reference to the true Christ. Again, v. 6, "Who among the sons of the mighty can be likened unto the Lord?" That is, among the sons of God, there is one, who is God, and no one is like unto the Lord?"

Now, although the passages, 2 Sam. 7, and 1 Chron. 22, accord, yet the circumstances, 1 Sam. 7, are of such a nature, that it cannot be understood concerning Solomon; so that the declaration must have been made twice to David: once concerning Christ, and once concerning Solomon. In the first place, 2 Sam. 7, 12, God says to David: "When thy days be fulfilled, and thou shalt sleep with thy fathers, I will set up thy seed after thee, which shall proceed out of thy bowels."

Now, Solomon was not set up as a king after the death of David, nor subsequent to him, but whilst he was yet alive, 1 Kings 1, 30, sqq. David, also, well knew that this declaration was made concerning Christ; and hence it is that he rendered God such cordial praise, 2 Sam. 7, 19, saying: "O Lord God; but thou hast spoken also of thy servant's house for a great while to come." But whilst he was yet alive, David ordained Solomon as his successor, saying, 1 Chron. 22, 9: God said unto me, "A son shall be born to thee, who shall be a man of rest. * * * He shall build an house

DR. LUTHER'S CHURCH-POSTIL.

SERMONS ON THE EPISTLES.

HEB. I, 1-12.

for my name," not thou, who "hast shed blood abundantly." In 2 Sam. 7, there is nothing said about the shedding of blood. There God says, He will build a house for David. The fact that, in 2 Sam. 7, he so freely, without any addition, promises,—saying, "If he commit iniquity, I will chasten him with the rod of men, and with the stripes of the children of men: but my mercy shall not depart away from him,"—his grace in regard to those things which are so bitterly bewailed in the 88th Psalm, is still more favorable to this view.

This promise is not made in regard to Solomon, as the 132d Psalm shows, except with the addition: "If thy children will keep my covenant," &c., as David also indicates, 1 Kings 2, 4, and as God himself says to Solomon, 1 Kings 3, 14. The passage, 2 Sam. 7, not the passage, 1 Chrom. 22, should, therefore, be understood specially concerning Christ. This is clear and conclusive.

"And again, when he bringeth in the first-begotten into the world, he saith, And let all the angels of God worship him."

This is the third passage of the Scriptures adduced from the 97th Ps., v. 7, which clearly speaks of the kingdom of God, concerning which Christ also preaches in the Gospel. In this kingdom Christ reigns, and is Lord. It commenced after his ascension, and is completed through the preaching of the Gospel. For it clearly speaks of preaching, and reads thus:

"The Lord reigneth; let the earth rejoice; let the multitude of isles be glad thereof. Clouds and darkness are round about him,' (that is, he reigns in faith concealed,) 'righteousness and judgment are the habitation of his throne. A fire goeth before him, and burneth up his enemies round about. His lightnings enlightened the world;" (these are his miracles.) "the earth saw, and trembled. The hills," (the great chiefs and the proud,) "melted like wax at the presence of the Lord, at the presence of the Lord of the whole earth. The heavens," (the Apostles,) 'declare his righteousness," (faith,) "and all the people see his glory;" (for the Gospel is everywhere preached). "Confounded be all they that serve graven images, that boast themselves of idols; worship him, all ye Gods."*

Experience and its fulfillment explain this Psalm. For all this was fulfilled in Christ. He is preached in all the world, and reigns in the kingdom of God. This was not the case with any other king. Hence, the Apostle introduces a preface, saying, "And again when he bringeth in the first-begotten into the world;" as if he should say, Here, in the Psalm, the Spirit speaks of the second coming into the world, through the Gospel. For, previously, he once came bodily into the world and, through his crucifiers, he was driven out in death : but afterwards, in his resurrection, and through the Word, he entered again, and now properly reigns. He will never die any more, nor be driven out. Of this entrance the Psalm speaks.

I admit, says he, God has more sons; but this is the first-born son, whom he brings in, and constitutes king, so that the angels worship him,

---
* In the edition A, the whole of the 97th Ps. appears.

D

—a thing which they neither would do, nor would they be commanded to do it, were he not true God.

We read, it is true, that David and many others were worshiped; but no angel ever yet worshiped any one, except God alone. This passage, therefore, shows conclusively that he, whom angels worship, must be God. For since men, even on earth, worship that alone, which is superior to them, and since nothing but God alone, is superior to angels, that king, who is heard and brought into the world through the ministers, and worshiped by the angels, must be God. The fact that the Apostle does not adduce every word from the Psalm, is a matter of no consequence. The language in the Psalm is: "Worship him, all ye Gods;" and that of the Apostle: "Let all the angels of God worship him." The meaning, however, is the same, the object being in the future, the angels should worship him. But, if they worship him, he must be God. The angels also are his, although he is also man. It should be observed, however, that, in the Hebrew, the passage reads thus: Worship him, all ye *Eloim*, that is, all ye gods. The angels and all the saints are thus styled, because they are the children of God.

"And of the angels he saith, Who maketh his angels spirits, and his ministers a flame of fire."

His design, here, is to show that such titles are not ascribed to angels, in the Scriptures, as render it admissible to say to any one of them, Thou art my Son, he shall be my Son, all the angels shall worship him. They are simply constituted messengers, whom he sends forth into the world; and, although much is committed to the angels, yet he does not constitute any of them Lord, but they are wind and a flame of fire. He calls them wind or spirits, and a flame of fire, because when they are sent, they assume such form, flying lightly and swiftly, like the wind, and shining like lightning and flame, as is evident in many portions of the Scriptures. But, in consequence of this, no one of them becomes Lord of the world, and is preached everywhere, as this King is proclaimed Lord over all things. This even the Jews must confess.

"But unto the Son he saith. Thy throne, O God, is for ever and ever : a sceptre of righteousness is the sceptre of thy kingdom : Thou hast loved righteousness, and hated iniquity : therefore God, even thy God, hath anointed thee with the oil of gladness above thy fellows."

This is the fourth passage; it is quoted from the 45th Psalm v. 6, 7. In my view, it shows in the clearest and most forcible manner, that Christ is God. In opposition to this, even the Jews can bring no objections. Let us examine the matter. In the first place, it is acknowledged by all, that this Psalm has reference to Christ, even if he is yet to come, as the Jews erroneously presume. In the second place, the first part, in which it is said, "Thy throne, O God, is for ever and ever," must be spoken in regard to the real, true God, who has a throne and the government; for although the title, God, is sometimes ascribed to saints, as we have already heard, Ps. 82, 1; yet the government and the throne belong to no one but the real, true, and natural God. Is not this clear and certain? Well, thus we have that God, who has the throne, and eternally reigns.

Now, the following language is employed, in regard to that same God: "Thou hast loved righteousness, * * therefore God, even thy God, hath anointed thee * * above thy fellows." What does this imply? That God, who has an everlasting throne, and reigns eternally, is anointed by his God above all his fellows. He that anoints here, must indeed be the real God; so, too, he who is anointed, is real God, because he has the throne, and reigns eternally. Now, God does not anoint himself—but he that is anointed, is under his anointer. Since, to anoint here implies, to infuse the Holy Spirit with his graces, as is evident,—a thing which is applicable only to a creature.

Observe, then, it is beyond all contradiction that, according to the first part of this passage, this king is true God; and that, according to the last part, he is true man: for, according to his humanity, he has fellows—since he is the head of all believers, who are partakers of his Spirit, which he so abundantly possesses above all others. But, according to his divinity, he has no fellows; for there is only one God, and yet not one person only. This passage forces the conclusion that there are two persons; one who reigns, and another who anoints him, and who, according to his divinity, cannot be anointed. Hence, we must conclude, that he is the Son of God; for, such title is ascribed to him, because he is God. He has an everlasting throne, which is the kingdom that was introduced after the ascension of Christ: and yet he has fellows, is anointed, and loves righteousness, by which he deserved to be anointed. This is altogether applicable to real man.

The rod or sceptre of his kingdom is the Gospel, which is a sceptre of righteousness, because it proceeds upon the principles of justice and righteousness. This declaration stands in opposition to human doctrines, which abound with intricacies and perplexities, and still contribute nothing to salvation. Thus, we are again reminded of the fact here, that we shall accept nothing in Christendom, but this sceptre of his kingdom. He desires his kingdom to be ruled by no other sceptre, but this righteous sceptre of the Gospel.

I was compelled to use the word God, God thy God, twice in the latter part of this passage, because we have only one word that implies God. The Hebrew tongue has many, and hence these two, *Eloim, Elohe,* appear.

In the Old Testament, there are many other similar passages, so mysteriously employed, and so incontrovertibly conclusive, in regard to this matter; as Gen. 19, 24: "The Lord rained upon Sodom and upon Gomorrah brimstone and fire from the Lord out of heaven." What can this mean, God from God, except that two persons are indicated here—the Father and the Son? Again, Zach. 3, 2:— "The Lord said unto Satan, The Lord rebuke thee, O Satan." Observe here, God speaks of another; and Ps. 68, 18, where much is said concerning God, it is stated : "Thou hast ascended on high, thou hast led captivity captive." This ascension, however, has reference only to the man Christ. Again, in the same Psalm: "Thy God hath commanded thy strength," &c. Moreover: God commandeth the powers of God. There are many other similar passages.

"And, Thou, Lord, in the beginning hast laid the foundation of the earth; and the heavens are the works of thine hands: They shall perish; but thou remainest: and they all shall wax old as doth a garment; And as a vesture shalt thou fold them up, and they shall be changed: but thou art the same, and thy years shall not fail."

The manner, in which this declaration may be employed in rendering this matter clear, does not yet appear. To take it as it stands, it may be readily explained as having reference to God, as one person. We must, therefore, take into consideration the entire Psalm, which also speaks of the future kingdom of God, the regulation of which is assigned to Christ, in the Scriptures, as in the following, and other passages:

This Psalm, 102, 12, 13, 14, 15, 16, speaks thus, concerning this kingdom: "But thou, O Lord, shalt endure for ever; and thy remembrance unto all generations. Thou shalt arise, and have mercy upon Zion; for the time to favor her, yea, the set time is come. For thy servants,' (the Apostles,) 'take pleasure in her stones, and favor the dust thereof' (through the Gospel;— this is said concerning Christ, whose servants the Apostles are, bringing the stones of Zion, the elect, to grace, through their preaching. Such servants no king ever had.) 'So the heathen shall fear the name of the Lord; and all the kings of the earth thy glory. When the Lord shall build up Zion, he shall appear in his glory," &c.

Then, lastly, follows this passage : "And thou, Lord, in the beginning hast laid the foundation of the earth." Hence, he concludes, that the king, whose servants have favored the stones of Zion, and who is proclaimed in all the world, so that the heathen, and all the kings of the earth fear him, is the God, who created the earth, and who is always the same in himself. Now, no king has ever been proclaimed among all heathens, as Christ has. Hence, it follows, that he is true God and man. Whatever else may be deemed necessary to be said on this subject, I leave for higher spirits.*

Thus we perceive that this whole Epistle is pure armor, maintaining clearly the article of faith, that *Christ is God, and Lord over all things even according to his humanity.* We see with astonishment how clear the Scriptures are, in themselves, and that the defect, that we perceive not, is in us; so that Luke, ch. 24, v. 32, well says, Christ opened the understanding of the disciples, so that they understood the Scriptures. He did not open the Scriptures, but the understanding;—the Scriptures are open, but our eyes are partly closed.

mous words against this holy place, and the law:

For we have heard him say, that this Jesus of Nazareth shall destroy this place, and shall change the Customs which Moses delivered to us.

When they heard these things, they were cut to the heart, and they gnashed on him with their teeth.

But he, being full of the Holy Ghost, looked up steadfastly into heaven, and saw the glory of God, and Jesus standing on the right hand of God,

And said, Behold, I see the heavens opened, and the Son of man standing on the right hand of God.

Then they cried out with a loud voice, and stopped their ears, and ran upon him with one accord,

And cast him out of the city, and stoned him: and the witnesses laid down their clothes at a young man's feet, whose name was Saul.

And they stoned Stephen, calling upon God, and saying, Lord Jesus, receive my spirit.

And he kneeled down and cried with a loud voice, Lord, lay not this sin to their charge. And when he had said this, he fell asleep.

ST. STEPHEN'S DAY.

EPISTLE, ACTS 6, 8-14, and 7, 54-60.† A B.

And Stephen, full of faith and power, did great wonders and miracles among the people.

Then there arose certain of the synagogue, which is called the synagogue of the Libertines, and Cyrenians, and Alexandrians, and of them of Cilicia, and of Asia, disputing with Stephen.

And they were not able to resist the wisdom and the spirit by which he spake.

Then they suborned men, which said, We have heard him speak blasphemous words against Moses, and against God.

And they stirred up the people, and the elders, and the scribes, and came upon him, and caught him, and brought him to the council,

And set up false witnesses, which said, This man ceaseth not to speak blasphe-

* A. I can do no more.

† A. B. Here, in consequence of its length, a whole chapter, in which St. Stephen replied to their complaints, is omitted. The individual who regulated, and thus arranged this Epistle, passed over the better portion, and then added the following part of the seventh chapter.

IN ORDER THAT the text of this Epistle, or lesson, may be understood, it is necessary to introduce, to some extent, that which is omitted, and to present the matter in connection with the causes which gave rise to it. The dispute arose from the fact, that Stephen asserted that whatever does not proceed from faith, is unprofitable, and that men cannot serve God, by the erection of churches, or works, independent of faith in Jesus Christ. This faith alone renders us pious, and builds the temple of God, which is believing hearts. In opposition to this, the Jews brought up the law of Moses, and the temple at Jerusalem, concerning which it is frequently said in the Bible, that God has chosen that city, that his eyes shall always be directed towards it, and that it is called the house of God. In this way they presumed to carry the point.

On the other hand, St. Stephen adduces, in opposition to them, the declaration, Isa. 66, 1, 2: "The heaven is my throne, and the earth is my footstool: where is the house that ye built unto me? and where is the place of my rest? For all those things hath mine hand made, and all those things have been, saith the Lord." This declaration is so clear and forcible that no one can gainsay it. It shows that God does not dwell in houses made with hands, since all that is necessary for these, has been previously created by him, and already belongs to him. If, moreover, neither the heaven nor the earth contain him, as he here asserts, The heaven is not my house, but my throne, and the earth is not my habitation, but my foot-stool, why should he dwell in a house made by men? To this effect Solomon also speaks, 1 Kings. 8, 27, although he built that house.

Being confounded by the power of this declaration, and similar passages, which they were unable to gainsay, they proceeded to construe his language, as if he had asserted, that Jesus would destroy the temple, and change the customs of Moses; notwithstanding Stephen intended to make no such impression, but simply asserted that we are saved, not by the law, or the temple, but by faith in Jesus Christ, and that, when faith exists, we may properly observe the law, whether we have a temple or no temple. He merely desired to remove the false confidence, which they had in their works and in the temple.

So too, at the present time, when the papists hear that it is asserted that works are ineffectual, and that faith in Christ must first accomplish all, they exclaim: Good works are prohibited and the commandments of God are blasphemed. Were St. Stephen to preach now, it is true, he might not be stoned, but he would be burnt with fire, or torn to pieces with tongs, by the enraged papists.

To their false accusation Stephen replies, and beginning with Abraham, and going through the Scriptures, he shows that, previous to the time of Solomon, who built a house for God, neither Abraham nor any of the patriarchs ever built a house for him, and still they were not, on that account, regarded as inferior in the sight of God. He then concludes with the declaration, Isaiah, saying: "But Solomon built him an house. Howbeit the Most High dwelleth not in temples made with hands; as saith the prophet, Heaven is my throne, and earth is my footstool: what house will ye build me? saith the Lord: or what is the place of my rest? Hath not my hand made all these things?"

After the introduction of this language, St. Stephen rebukes them, saying: "Ye stiffnecked and uncircumcised in heart and ears, ye do always resist the Holy Ghost; as your fathers did, so do ye. Which of the prophets have not your fathers persecuted? and they have slain them which shewed before the coming of the Just One; of whom ye have been now the betrayers and murderers: who have received the law by the disposition of angels, and have not kept it."

After his declaration of these words, follows the latter part of this Epistle, in which it is said: "When they heard these things, they were cut to the heart, and they gnashed on him with their teeth," &c. Hence, it is evident that the dispute was in regard to faith and good works. But what will the papists do, who have not the least shadow of ground for their position, except their own human laws and doctrines? If they could bring forth a shadow of grounds, like the Jews had, namely, that God gave the law of Moses, and chose the temple at Jerusalem, they would instantly raise a cry, *de jure divino*, as did also, indeed, the Jews, their forefathers.*

There seems to be no difficulty connected with this Epistle; it is plain. *An example of the faith of Christ, in St. Stephen, is presented.* Very few glosses are required. We shall proceed to examine it briefly. The first principle it teaches, is, that we cannot secure the favor of God by the erection of churches and institutions. This St. Stephen clearly shows, here, from Isaiah. But, if we assume this position and maintain it, we will have to risk the same thing, which St. Ste-

---
Luther's Works 7r Bd.
* B. The doctrine of this Epistle.

phen did. In consequence of such a position,* the bulls of the Pope, the clouds of indulgences, the laws of the ecclesiastics, and the incessant preaching about churches, altars, institutions, cloisters, chalices, bells, tables, candles, and apparel, would disappear. This would, not unreasonably, offend the holiness of the Pope, and his adherents. For, in this way, the luxuries of the kitchen and the cellar, and all temporal possessions would be diminished. In the course of time, idleness, voluptuousness, and ease, would be changed for labor, poverty, and disquietude; they would have to study and pray, or support themselves, as other people do. This would not be so agreeable to them. The holy Christian Church would be despised, as Christ and the Apostles were. They could no longer live in such royal pomp, waging wars, plundering, and shedding blood, under the pretext of honoring God and elevating the holy Church, as hitherto the most holy fathers in God have done, and still do.

We must not come to the conclusion, however, from this view, that it is wrong to build and establish churches; but, it is wrong to go to such an extreme as to forfeit faith and love in consequence of it, presuming in this way to accomplish good works, by which we may merit the favor of God. From this, such abuses result as preclude all moderation. Every nook and corner is filled with churches and cloisters, regardless of the object for which churches are built.

For there is no other reason, if, indeed, this be a reason, to build churches, except to afford a place in which Christians may assemble to pray, to hear the Gospel, and to receive the Sacraments. Wherever such occasion ceases, the churches should be pulled down, as we do other buildings when they cease to be useful. But now, every one, in all the world, desires to establish his own chapel or altar, even his own mass, with a view of securing salvation and purchasing heaven.

Is it not a miserable, a lamentable

---

* B. On that account, the bulls of the Pope must.

error and delusion, to teach poor people to depend so much on their works, to the great disparagement of their Christian faith? It would be better to destroy all the churches and cathedrals in the world, and to burn them to ashes,—it were a less sin, were some one to do it through malice,— than to let one single soul be misled and lost by such error. God has given no special command in regard to the building of churches, but he has issued his commands in reference to our souls, which are his real, peculiar churches, concerning which St. Paul speaks, 1 Cor. 3, 16, 17: "Ye are the temple," church, "of God. * * If any man defile the temple," church, "of God, him shall God destroy."

But, observe the holiness of the papists. The souls, in all the world, are disturbed in their foundation by such error, and the real church of God cast into ruins. This does not interrupt them, yea, they contribute to it. They effect nothing else by their preaching of works, but the destruction of that church everywhere. Then they come along and, in place of it, build churches out of wood and stones, reducing the conscience to such straits, as to believe that whoever defaces with a knife these stones and this wood, a little, has profaned the whole church. Here the expense and trouble of reconsecration must be incurred. Are not such persons, as have no conscientious scruples about the destruction of the real church, yes, convert that great sin into eternal merit, but are very conscientious about the vain juggling of their own churches, raving and raging, foolish and fanatical, yes, frantic and infuriated.

I assert still, that, for the purpose of exterminating such error, it were well at once to overthrow all the churches in the whole world, and to preach, pray, baptize, and perform all Christian duties in common houses, or beneath the heavens; especially, since the reason they assign for building churches, is so unfounded. Christ preached upwards of three years, and still he preached only three days in the temple at Jerusalem. The remainder of the time, he preached in the synagogues, in the wilderness, on the mountains, in ships, at table, and in private houses. John the Baptist never entered the temple, but preached at Jordan and other places.

The Apostles preached in the market-place and in the streets, at Jerusalem, on the day of Pentecost. Philip preached to the eunuch on the chariot. St. Paul preached on the riverside, and in the jail at Philippi, and at various places in private houses; Christ also commanded, Matt. 10, 12, them to preach in private dwellings. These preachers, I presume, were equally as good as those of the present day. But, thus it must be: costly houses with great arches must be supported for these erroneous preachers and devilish teachers. But the word of God must find an inn in all Bethlehem, in which it may be born.

Is it not time then for us to exclaim with St. Stephen, in regard to these irrational creatures, Ye stiffnecked, and uncircumcised in heart and ears, ye do always reject the Holy Ghost; ye are betrayers and murderers of innocent, harmless Christian souls? Ye have received the commandments from the Apostles, but have observed none of them. I presume their hearts would burst, and they would gnash their teeth,* saying: He has blasphemed against God, and spoken against the holy place; he has profaned all the churches. O, God, what blind leaders and murderers of souls rule under the accursed popery!

Here you may perceive some reason why lightning strikes those churches more frequently than any other buildings. The wrath of God seems to rest upon them more than upon other buildings, because greater sins, greater blasphemies, greater destruction of souls and churches, occur in these, than in brothels and dens of thieves. For, where the pure Gospel is not preached, the keeper of a public brothel is a much less sinner, than such a preacher, and the brothel is not as bad as such a church; even if the keeper of the brothel would prostitute virgins and pious wives and nuns every day,—a thing which is dreadful and abominable,—he would still not be worse and more disadvantageous than such papistical preachers.

If this is astonishing to you, remember that such a preacher does nothing else, by his preaching, but daily derange and violate souls newly born in Baptism—young Christians, tender souls, who are the pure, consecrated virgins and brides of Christ. But since this does not occur bodily, but spiritually, it affects no one; but God is displeased with it beyond measure, and, in his wrath, he exclaims through the prophets, in unmistakable terms, Thou harlot, thou openest thy feet to every one that passes by. So little can he tolerate such preaching. Of this, Jeremiah also complains, Lamentations, 5, 11, in his prayer: "They ravished the women in Zion, and the maids in the cities of Juda." Now, indeed, the spiritual virginity, the Christian faith, is immeasurably better than the bodily, since it alone gains heaven.

Such doctrines and works are destructive not only of faith, but also of Christian love. The fool may always be known by his cap. Many a one has a poor neighbor, who has a sick daughter, child, or wife, or is otherwise needy. Him he passes, without making an effort to administer to his wants; he proceeds to contribute to some church; or else endeavors to heap up treasures during his health, and when he is thrown upon his deathbed, he makes a will, and bequeaths his estate to some institution or other. Him will the priests and the monks surround; they will extol his deed, absolve this pious man, administer the Sacrament to him, and bury him in the midst of honors, proclaiming his name from the pulpit and during mass, exclaiming, Ay, this is a precious thing! He has made ample provision for his soul; many blessings shall hereafter be conferred upon him —yes, alas, hereafter, but eternally too late!

But, no one warns him of the sins he committed during his life, by not administering to the wants of his

* B. Bite together.

neighbor, when it lay in his power, passing him, and leaving him, as the rich man did Lazarus, in the Gospel. Nor does he think of them himself;—hence, they must go unconfessed, unrepented, and unabsolved, no matter how many bulls, indulgences, and spiritual fathers may have been present. This is the very sin that will be referred to on the day of judgment, concerning which Christ will say: "I was naked, and ye clothed me not," Matt. 25, 43. This pious fellow will then say, I heaped up treasures to establish an institution for thee, and have in this way satisfied a decree of the Pope, and hence I have been absolved from all my sins by him. What else should such person expect to hear, but this sentence: "Depart from me, ye cursed, into everlasting fire?" Because, by their works, they destroy the Christian faith, and for the sake of wood and stones despise Christian love.

Let us be wise, therefore, beloved friends; it is necessary: let us learn indeed that we are saved through faith alone in Christ, as has been already sufficiently shown; so that no one may rely upon his works. During our lives, let us engage in such works alone as are profitable to our neighbors, letting testament be testament, and institution, institution, and directing our efforts so as to contribute to the welfare of our neighbors, during the whole course of our lives.

I will here relate an example of a pious female, St. Elizabeth. She once entered a cloister, and seeing on the wall a fine painting, representing the sufferings of our Lord, she exclaimed: The cost of this you should have saved for the sustenance of the body; the sufferings of Christ should be painted in your hearts. What a striking, pious, forcible sentence this is against such things as are generally regarded as precious. If she would thus speak at the present time, the papists would assuredly burn her, as one who had blasphemed against the sufferings of Christ, and spoken against good works: she would be denounced as a heretic, even if she were worth more than ten saints.

Secondly, it teaches that the commandments of God are not fulfilled by works.

For St. Stephen here rejects not only their views in regard to churches and the building of churches, but also all their works, saying: Ye "have received the law by the disposition of angels, and have not kept it." Hence, they too, in return, reproved him not only as one who had spoken against the temple, but, also, as one who had blasphemed against the law of Moses, desiring to teach works, to which they were not accustomed. Indeed, Stephen could not have charged them with not having observed the law, so far as their external works were concerned. For they were circumcised, and observed meats, apparel, and festivals, and whatever Moses had commanded. Hence, they stoned him, on account of the law.

But St. Stephen spoke from the same spirit, from which St. Paul spoke, Rom. 2 and 3, saying, *That by the deeds of the law no one is justified in the sight of God, but through faith alone.* Because, where the Holy Spirit does not exist, and grant grace, the heart of man cannot be friendly towards the law of God, but it would rather there were no law; as each one feels in himself that he is dull and disinclined to do that which is good, but ready and inclined to perform that which is evil; as Moses, Gen. 6, 5, and 8, 21, says: "The imagination of man's heart is evil from his youth."

Now, since such unwillingness exists in man, he takes no real delight in performing the deeds of the law. Destitute of proper motives, he is rather constrained to perform them, through the fear of punishment, shame, and hell, or else through the love of gain and hope of salvation, and not through love and honor to God. Hence, all such works are sheer hypocrisy and, in the sight of God, are not regarded as good. The Holy Spirit is, therefore, promised and given to all who believe in Christ. This Spirit, through his grace, produces in the heart a willingness and a desire for that which is good; so that the individual freely, and without any expectation of reward, performs these works in honor to God. For, through faith and the Spirit, he is already justified and in a state of salvation,—a position which he never could have attained by any works. According to this principle, we may freely conclude that all who are destitute of faith and grace, fail to observe the law, even if they torture themselves to death with the works of the law.

Now, by his declaration, in which he asserts that the Jews always resist the Holy Ghost, St. Stephen designs to convey the idea that, in consequence of their works, they become presumptuous, have no disposition to accept the assistance of the Spirit, and are unwilling that their works should be rejected as insufficient; ever working and working at the law, without observing any part of it, they remain hypocrites as long as they live; they are unwilling to accept the faith, through which they might be able to accomplish good works, and the grace of the Spirit, through which they might secure a love and desire for the law, and thus they obscure it to a free, spontaneous heart. For, such doers and observers of the law, and no others, God desires.

Hence he also calls them, "Stiffnecked uncircumcised in heart and ears," because they will neither listen nor understand—ever crying out, Good works, good works, law, law, without doing any of these themselves; precisely as our papists do, as their forefathers did, and as their descendants and the whole mass of this generation still do, persecuting the righteous, and then boast that they do it for the sake of God and his law. Thus we have the substance of this Epistle. Let us now examine it a little further.*

In the first place, here we perceive in the conduct of St. Stephen an example of love towards God and man. He manifests his love towards God, by censuring the Jews so earnestly and severely, calling them betrayers, murderers, and transgressors of the whole law, yea, stiffnecked, resisting the law and its fulfillment, as well as the Holy Ghost himself. He styles them, moreover, "uncircumcised in heart and ears." How could he have censured them more highly and severely? He so completely strips them of everything good, that it seems as if he were actuated by impatience and wrath.

But what individual, who should thus attempt now to censure the papists, would the world tolerate? But his love for God constrained and impelled him thus to act. No one in possession of such love, can silently and calmly allow the commandments of God to be rejected; he cannot dissemble; he must censure and rebuke any one that acts in opposition to God. This he cannot allow, even at the risk of his life. Such love the Scriptures call *zelum Dei*, a holy indignation, because such conduct affects the love of God, and disparages in an intolerable manner, the honor and obedience due him,—an honor and obedience, which an individual of such zeal ardently seeks and desires. This we perceive in the prophet Elijah, who was so remarkable for his holy indignation in opposition to the false prophets.

From this example, we may learn, that all who silently pass over sins and the transgressions of God's commandments, are destitute of love for him. Where, then, will hypocrites appear, who rather applaud such transgressions? Where calumniators, and such as delight in, laugh at, and speak of the faults of others.

Nor is the fact that the Pope, in his nonsensical laws, commands and teaches the papists not to censure and reprove governors, a sufficient excuse for any to abstain from the administration of proper reproof. Whom does St. Stephen censure here? Is it not the governors of Jerusalem? and still he was nothing more than a mere ordinary man, neither ordained, nor clothed with the priestly office. Yea, his example teaches us, that every Christian has the right to administer proper reproof in regard to the Pope and governors; yes, he is rather under obligation to do it; let no one, then, presume that he has no such

---

* B. An example of Godly zeal and Christian love.

right and power; and, especially, should spiritual sins be rebuked. St. Stephen administered his reproofs not in regard to gross sins, but in regard to hypocrisy, because they believed not, and resisted the Holy Spirit.— For, in this way, they did the greater injury, misleading themselves and the multitude by their laws and works.

Thus, the Pope, the bishops, and all papists, deserve public censure, as stiffnecked and uncircumcised hypocrites, resisting the Holy Ghost and keeping none of the commandments of God, betraying and murdering Christian souls, and thus becoming the betrayers and murderers of Christ who bought them with his own blood.

Now, since we have occasion to state that St. Stephen was a layman, or an ordinary individual, and not a priest, and since the papists claim that he was a Levite, constituting out of his office the office of the priest who reads the Epistle or the Gospel at the altar during the communion service, perverting, indeed, the whole matter, it becomes necessary to know that St. Luke, Acts 4 and 5, writes, that the Christians, in their commencement at Jerusalem, gave all their goods to the congregation, when the Apostles distributed to each one whatever he needed. But it happened that the widows of Grecians were not provided for like the widows of the Hebrews. Hence there arose a murmuring among them. The Apostles, perceiving that these duties would so overburden them, as to require them to relinquish, to some extent, their praying and preaching, assembled the multitude of the disciples, and said, "It is not reason that we should leave the word of God, and serve tables. Wherefore, brethren, look ye out among you seven men of honest report, full of the Holy Ghost and wisdom, whom we may appoint over this business. But we will give ourselves continually to prayer, and the ministry of the word." Thus St. Stephen, together with six others, was chosen and appointed to distribute these goods. Hence is derived the word *Diaconus*, servant, minister, because they served the congregation, ministering to their wants in a temporal point of view.

Hence, it is clear, that St. Stephen was a steward, or an administrator and guardian of the Christians; whose duty it was to minister in temporal goods to those who were in need. But in the course of time his office was perverted into the office of a priest who reads the Epistles and Gospels; so that there is scarcely a trace of St. Stephen's office left, except a slight resemblance which appears in the office of the provosts of the nuns, and in that of the administrators of hospitals and guardians of the poor.— Such should be these readers of Epistles and Gospels, not the consecrated, the shorn, the bearers of dalmatics, and those who mind the flies at the altar, but common laymen of piety, who keep registers of the needy, and have control of the common purse, to distribute wherever it may be necessary. This is the real, the proper office of St. Stephen, who never dreamed about reading Epistles and Gospels, or about bald pates or dalmatics. These are all human devices.

Hence, a question may arise here: Whether a layman, or an ordinary individual, should be allowed to preach. Since St. Stephen was not appointed to preach, (an office which the Apostles reserved to themselves, as already stated,) but, to perform the duties of steward, and yet, when he went to the market-place and mingled among the people, he immediately created a stir by the performance of signs and wonders, as the Epistle says, and even censured rulers. Had the Pope and the papists been there, they certainly would have made inquiry in regard to his credentials and *character*, and had he been found without a bald pate and a prayer-book, he would undoubtedly have been committed to the flames as a heretic, since he was neither a priest nor a clergyman. For, the title, priest or clergyman, which the Scriptures attribute to all Christians, they have assumed to themselves, calling all others laity. They even call themselves the Church, as if the laity do not belong to the Church. Still these refined, noble people, perform not a single office or work of a priest, a clergyman, or of the Church, but dupe the world by their human devices.

The precedent of St. Stephen, however, stands firm. By his example, he gives every one authority to preach wherever the people desire to hear, no matter whether it be in a house or at the market-place. He does not confine the word of God to bald pates and long gowns; yet he does not, in this way, interfere with the preaching of the Apostles. He attends to his office, and is ready to be silent where the Apostles themselves preach.

It is true, order must be maintained, so that all do not speak at once, but, as St. Paul, 1 Cor. 14, writes, Let one or two speak, and if anything be revealed to another, let the first hold his peace. This is, also, evident from Acts 15, where it is said, that St. Peter, after the discourses of certain Pharisees, having ceased preaching, Barnabas and Paul preached, and, lastly, St. James; they all spoke, one after another. Slight traces of this custom still exist in the disputations of the high schools. But now, only one babbles along about Dietrich of Bern, or whatever he may have dreamed.

A regular sermon should be conducted like a subject is treated, at a collation, at table. Hence, Christ instituted the Sacrament, in order that we might, on that occasion, sit at table, and treat of his word. But every thing is perverted, and mere human order has taken the place of divine order.

Now, let this suffice in regard to this matter. In the second place, St. Stephen gives us a beautiful manifestation of love for his fellow-men, in the circumstance that he entertains no malice or ill-will towards even his murderers. However severely he may have rebuked them, for the purpose of maintaining the honor of God, still he is so kindly disposed towards them, that in the very agonies of death, having commended his own spirit, and made provision for himself, he is unmindful of his own concerns, and is wholly concerned about them, and under the influence of that love, he yields up his spirit. Not without reason, did St. Luke locate the words employed by St. Stephen, in his prayer for his murderers, in the last place. Moreover, whilst he was praying in behalf of himself, and commending his spirit, he stood erect, but finally, when he prayed for his murderers, he knelt down. Besides, in the latter case, he cried with a loud voice,—a thing, which he did not do in the former.

O, how much more fervent was his prayer for his enemies than was that for himself; how must his heart have burned, his eyes over-flowed, and his whole body been moved and agitated, by the wretchedness of his enemies, which he beheld. It is the opinion of St. Augustine that St. Paul was saved by this prayer; nor is it unreasonable to believe, that it was certainly heard of God, and from eternity, he foresaw that something great would result from this dispensation. Of this we have a manifestation in the person of St. Paul. This prayer could not be denied, although all of them may not have been saved.

He arranges his words very appropriately, saying: "Lay not this sin to their charge;" that is, cause it not to be immovably fixed, like a pillar or a foundation. In this way he makes confession, repents, and renders satisfaction for them. As if he should say, Beloved Lord, it is true, it is a sin, it is wrong; this cannot be denied; as it is customary to say in repentance and confession, simply deploring and confessing the guilt. He then prays, and offers himself up, as a satisfaction for the requirements of sin.

Behold, here we perceive how great an enemy and how great a friend, true love can be at the same time: how severe its censures, how sweet its assistance. It is like a nut with a hard shell, but a sweet kernel; bitter it is to our old Adamic nature, but exceedingly sweet to our new man.

This Epistle not only inculcates this forcible doctrine and example of faith and love, but it also affords us consolation and encouragement. It not only teaches, but it incites and impels. It styles death, which is a terror to all the world, a sleep. Luke says, "He fell asleep;" that is, in an easy death which he felt not, thence departing, like a person when he goes to sleep, not knowing how it occurs—falling unconsciously asleep.

The position, that the death of the Christian is a sleep, an easy death, may be safely based on the declaration of the Spirit; it will not deceive us. This is the result of the grace and power of Christ. The bitterness of our death has been far removed, by his death, when we believe in him, as he says, John 8, 51: "If a man keep my saying, he shall never see death." Why shall he not see it? Because the soul, embraced in his living word, and filled with its life, cannot feel death. The word lives, and does not feel death; so too, the soul that believes and lives in that word, does not taste death. For this reason the words of Christ are styled the *words of life*, and they are the words of life; and he that hangs upon, and believes in them, must live.

This consolation and encouragement are heightened the more, by his declaration; "I see the heavens opened, and the Son of man standing on the right hand of God." This circumstance shows how closely, ardently, and diligently Christ watches over us, and how ready he is to lend us his aid, if we but believe in him, and cheerfully risk our lives for his sake. This manifestation was designed not simply for the benefit of St. Stephen, nor was it left upon record merely for his advantage, but for our consolation, so as to remove every doubt, that we, too, shall enjoy the same happy results, if our conduct is like that of St. Stephen.

That the heavens are standing open affords us the highest consolation, and removes every terror of death. What should not stand open and be ready, when the heavens, the highest works of creation, stand open, waiting for us, and rejoicing at our approach?— Yea, you might desire them to stand thus visibly open to you, too. But, should this occur to every one, what would become of faith? It is enough, that it once occurred, for the consolation of all Christians, for the strengthening of their faith, and for the removal of every terror of death. For, as we believe, so it will be with us, although we do not see it.

What angel, moreover, what creature, would not feel ready and prepared, when the Lord himself stands ready and prepared to help? It is a remarkable fact, that he saw neither an angel, nor God himself, but the man, Christ, who is the most lovely and delightful to nature, and affords man the highest consolation. For a man would rather see a man, than an angel, or any other creature, especially when he is in need.

Here our subtile teachers, who measure the works of God by their reason, and the seas with a spoon, ask; How could St. Stephen look into the heavens, when we are unable with our eyes to see a bird when it has flown but a short distance up in the atmosphere; how could he see Christ so accurately as to know with certainty that it was Christ, and no one else? When we look at a man on a high steeple, he appears to us like a child; nor do we recognize him.— Hence they endeavor to mend the matter, by saying: St. Stephen's vision must have been sharpened in a supernatural manner, so as to enable him to see accurately at a distance so great. But how, if St. Stephen had been in a house, or under a vault? Away with such human babble.— Surely St. Paul heard the voice of Christ from heaven, near Damascus, and yet his hearing was not sharpened. The Apostles on Mount Tabor, John the Baptist, Luke 3, 22, and the people, John 12, 29, heard the voice of the Father, and still their hearing was not sharpened. Is it not more difficult to hear a voice from on high at a great distance, than it is to see an object at an equal distance? Our eyes have a range immeasurably wider, than our ears have.

Whenever God desires to reveal himself, heaven and all things are near. No matter whether he was under a roof, or in the open air, heaven was near to St. Stephen; it was not necessary for him to be able to see a great distance. God is everywhere; there is no need for his coming down from heaven. Hence, it is easy for such a sight, as his being really in heaven, and still observed in narrowest range, to appear, without sharpening or perverting the senses.

It matters not whether we fully comprehend, or not, how this can be effected. The wonders of God, are not designed to be brought within our grasp and comprehension, but to induce us to believe and confide. Illustrate to me, ye that presume to be so wise, how a large apple, pear, or a cherry, and things less mysterious, can be nourished through a stem so small. Let God work; believe, and presume not to bring God within your grasp and comprehension.

Who can estimate all the virtues contained in this example? In it loom up all the fruits of the Spirit. In it we find love, faith, patience, benevolence, peace, meekness, wisdom, truth, simplicity, strength, consolation, and philanthropy; here we perceive aversions and censures for every species of evil; here we discover a disposition not to value the advantages of this life, or to dread the terrors of death; here we find liberty, tranquillity, and all the noble graces and virtues. There is no virtue, of which this is not an example; no vice which it is not ready to rebuke; so that the Evangelist may well say, Stephen was full of faith and power.* Power here implies activity or action, as if he should say, He has a great faith, and therefore he did much, and was mighty in deed. For where faith properly exists, there its fruits must follow; and the greater the faith, the more abundant will be its fruits.

True faith is a very strong, efficacious, active principle. Nothing is impossible for it. It neither rests nor hesitates. Hence St. Stephen, in consequence of the superior activity of his faith, performed not simply common, ordinary works, but wonders and signs, publicly, among the people; yes, great wonders and signs, as Luke says. This was intended as an evidence, that he who is inactive, is destitute of faith, and has no right to boast about it. There was an object in placing the word *faith* first, and then the word *power*. It was designed to show, that our actions are evidences of our faith, and that nothing good can be accomplished without it. It must be foremost in every action. In this may God assist us. Amen.

ST. JOHN'S DAY.

EPISTLE, ECCLESIASTICUS 15, 1-6.

HE that feareth the Lord will do good; and he that hath the knowledge of the law shall obtain her.

And as a mother shall she meet him, and receive him as a wife married of a virgin.

With the bread of understanding shall she feed him, and give him the water of wisdom to drink.

He shall be stayed upon her, and shall not be moved; and shall rely upon her, and shall not be confounded.

She shall exalt him above his neighbors, and in the midst of the congregation shall she open his mouth.

He shall find joy and a crown of gladness, and she shall cause him to inherit an everlasting name.

TEACHING does not seem to be the design of this Epistle or lesson. It is rather occupied in presenting the praise or advantages resulting from a proper course of conduct. It does not state the things that should be performed, and the manner of performing them, but the advantages re-

---

* A. Our text reads thus, Stephen was full of grace and power; but St. Luke, who wrote in Greek, says, Stephen was full of faith and virtue, power.

sulting to those who pursue a proper course of conduct. Hence, its object is to incite and admonish us to perform those duties, with which we are already acquainted. St. Paul, Rom. 12, 7, 8, divides all discourses into two parts: the one, *doctrine*—the other, *admonition*. Doctrine presents that which we do not already know and possess. Admonition incites, impels, and urges us to act according to the doctrine; and encourages us to patience and perseverance. Whilst this feature of a discourse, therefore, is less difficult than the former, it is no less useful and beneficial.

Now, whoever desires to incite, arouse, encourage, and admonish a person to action, must present appropriate reason to induce him to act. This he may do by referring to the great advantages, the benefits, the beauties, and honors, which must result from such action, or to the injuries and disgrace that must follow its neglect. This is the course that is pursued in this Epistle. *It points out many advantages and honors, which result to those who fear God, and love righteousness.* This we shall now consider:

What is meant by righteousness and the fear of God is not mentioned here. We have frequently stated, however, that to fear God, is not to depend upon ourselves or upon anything that is in us, or to rely upon our honor, power, wealth, strength, advantages, or skill—no, not even upon our good works and piety. But, we should be careful in regard to all these, so as not to commit sin; we should fear, yes, we know, that if God should earnestly deal with us according to his justice, we should be lost a thousand times. Therefore, we should not exalt ourselves in any way above the most insignificant individual on earth; we should be humble and mild in the whole course of our conduct and in all our designs; we should manifest no arrogance towards any one, but be mild and affable. The influences of humility will render all our works good. St. Peter, 1 Pet. 5, 5, says: "God resisteth the proud, and giveth grace to the humble." Whatever, then, is done in that grace, is all well done.

Thus, righteousness, as we have heard, is nothing else but faith. This is effected in the following manner. In the first place, no one can stand before the judgment of God; every one in all his efforts and operations must be filled with fear. This fear impels him to seek and to find something independent of himself, upon which he may rely, stand, and rest. This is nothing else but the pure mercy of God, promised and set forth in Christ. This reliance, faith, and confidence render us just and pious before God, as St. Paul, Rom. 1, 17, says: "the just shall live by faith."

Now, in proportion as a person distrusts himself and his own ability, and feels himself a sinner before the judgment of God, in all things; so, in the same proportion, will he console himself with the extraneous grace of God, and in consequence of it become righteous in all things. So, these two, judgment and grace, fear and confidence, must exist simultaneously.— Judgment produces fear; grace produces trust and confidence. Thus, through judgment, fear divests us of ourselves and all that we have. But confidence invests us in God, and in all that belongs to God; so that not our merits, but the blessings of God are praised and extolled. This accords with Ps. 147, 11: "The Lord taketh pleasure in them that fear him, in those that hope in his mercy."

Now, if his faith is right, he will also conduct himself properly towards his neighbor, as he believes, that God has acted and still acts towards him. This he will do through pure grace, forgiving him, bearing with and tolerating him, endeavoring to relieve him from his wretched condition, administering to his wants, allowing him to enjoy his hospitalities, denying him nothing, risking his body, life, property, and honor for him, in all respects, as God has acted towards him. For, he believes, that God thus acted towards him through pure grace, regardless of his demerits, and that he certainly will do towards him, as he believes. Therefore, as God pours out his blessings upon him, regardless of his demerits; so he will confer his favors upon his neighbor, notwithstanding he may be his enemy, and destitute of all merit. He also feels satisfied, that this will not impoverish him; for, the more favors he confers, the more blessings will God pour out upon him, and the more he fills his neighbors with favors, the more will God fill him with blessings.

This, you will perceive, is the true, the real faith, which renders us just before God; it is the Christian righteousness, which receives blessings from above, and issues them below,— a beautiful illustration of which, we find, Judges 1, 13, 15, in the piece of land, given by Caleb, the holy father, to his daughter, Achsah, from which issued beautiful fountains of water; that is, it was watered by springs above and springs below. Hence, it was very fertile and valuable. This is the faith, as already said, concerning which we cannot say too much.

Achsah implies ornaments or jewels of shoes, and is the lovely Maggie in scarlet shoes, the little daughter of God, the believing soul, which glides along in beautiful, scarlet, gilted shoes; concerning which St. Paul, Eph. 6, 5, says, "Your feet shod,' with what? "with the preparation of the gospel." Here, you perceive, that when the heart proceeds in the gospel, and lives in that word, through faith, it is Achsah, Maggie in her beautiful shoes, concerning whom Solomon, Song of Solomon 7, 1, speaks in regard to the bride: "How beautiful are thy feet with shoes, O prince's daughter! Now let us take into consideration the reasons which should invite and urge us to fear God and to love righteousness.

The First is:

"DO GOOD."

The whole world talks about doing good. But, if you wish to know how to do good, hearken, do not act as fools do, who examine the various works, desiring to select such as they conceive to be good, and reject such as they conceive to be bad, making a distinction among works. Act not thus; leave the works as they are, regard one like another; but fear God, and be just, (as we have already said,) and then perform whatever presents itself, and all will be well done, no matter if it be the duties of a hostler or a teamster.

The text is unchangeable: "He that feareth the Lord will do good," no matter what he may do. His works are good; not in consequence of the character of the works, but on account of the fear that gives rise to them. Here you will perceive a great consolation, and how quickly you are covered with good works, so that your whole life is good, if you fear God;—your eating, drinking, walking, standing, seeing, hearing, sleeping, and waking, all are good works. Who should not be incited by such advantages, to fear God? Behold, these are the lambs of God, in whom everything is useful.

But, the separators of works, the courtly saints, on the other hand, with their choice and selected works, really perform no good works. Why? Because they do not fear God; and highly esteeming their own efforts, they do not trust in him; hence, their works, also, which they regard as the very best, are evil. For, this truth is immovable: The works of him, that fears God, are good, and the works of him, that does not fear God, are evil.

The Second:

"HAVE THE KNOWLEDGE OF THE LAW."

Thus, he says: "He that hath the knowledge,' (apprehends righteousness,) 'of the law, shall obtain her." This is the same in meaning as the former, only it is expressed in different words. To have the knowledge of the law, to adhere to righteousness, is to persevere and continue in faith. Where this is the case, the individual will apprehend righteousness, so as to make it his own. Hence, all his actions and his life will be right, having attained such a position as enables him to dwell in it, as in a heritage. Whoever, therefore, desires to do right and to live in righteousness, must believe, and persevere in faith, and then perform, without any distinction, such works as present themselves to him.

Thus, he is endowed with such prerogative as renders it unnecessary for him to ask and ascertain how such works become right. They are already right, because they are performed, and the righteousness is already apprehended, without any selecting and choosing, since he perseveres in faith.

But, in all their works, righteousness will flee from the unbelieving, who neglect it. They may even snap after it, as a dog snaps at flies, still it will elude them. St. Paul, Rom. 9, 31, says, in regard to the Jews: "Israel, which followed after the law of righteousness, hath not attained the law of righteousness." Like these, are those unbelieving persons, who run after their shadows, desiring to obtain righteousness by their works; but it flees from them, and they cannot apprehend it, because they did not first allow themselves to be apprehended in faith, and then adhere to righteousness; here then they would have been apprehended in all works, and the shadow would have followed of itself.

The Third:

"AS A MOTHER SHALL SHE MEET HIM."

What does this imply? It is spoken according to the custom of the Hebrews, who are in the habit of saying: A child of wisdom, a child of wickedness, a child of wrath, a child of condemnation; thus, here, too, children of righteousness. Now, whoever is a child of sin, or of unrighteousness, has a mother of disgrace, of whom he must be ashamed, and in whom he cannot rejoice. Whoever is a child of righteousness, has a mother of honor, of whom he may boast, and in whom he can rejoice. For, even a natural mother, who is a reputable woman, is an honor, a glory, and a consolation to her child; on the other hand, if she is disreputable, she is a disgrace to her child; so that scarcely any reproach is more stinging to any one, than to mention the disgrace of his mother, and to censure him of being illegitimate or ill-bred.

Now the wise man wishes to show, that righteousness meets her child in the most affectionate manner, as a mother meets her child, as she approaches it; that is, she is always ready to do for it, all that lies in her whole heart and power. In this way he designs to show the great security, consolation, peace, joy, and glory, which result to the heart, before God, through faith. For, a natural mother caresses, kisses, carries, and supports her child, always desiring to meet and oblige it. There is no greater kindness than the kindness of a mother for her child. Thus, too, righteousness embraces, carries and supports man, approaching and meeting him in every way, so that he may bask in security and in the peace of his heart. To such great honor he is entitled, of which he may boast before God; for he has a mother of honor.

The Fourth:

"AND RECEIVE HIM AS A WIFE MARRIED OF A VIRGIN."

What does this imply? Its import, expressed in other words, is similar to that of the preceding phrase. The object is to show the anxious care manifested by righteousness for her child. He compares her feelings or affections to those of a new bride, who never has been a wife before. He says:—Precisely as a virgin, who is now for the first time become a wife, feels towards her bridegroom, so are the feelings of righteousness towards her child. The affections or feelings of such a bride, I shall leave for those who have experience in that direction, to describe. It is a well-established fact, however, that there is no greater desire, love, or concern, than that of a young bride for her bridegroom. The Scriptures abound with instances of the love of brides. Here he styles her a wife married of a virgin, because she recently became a wife, and never before had any experience in regard to the love of a husband. For a widow, who had before been a wife, has no such feeling towards her second bridegroom.

Observe, how carefully and deeply the wise man seeks out his admonition. Is it not a forcible, a vivid incitation to faith and piety? How could he have introduced a simile more expressive of affection, than that of a virtuous mother's affection for her child, and a new bride's love towards her bridegroom? A woman is naturally more inclined to love and affection than a man is. Now, such affection, love, and care of righteousness for us, we cannot obtain by works.— It must be all conceived in the heart. Here, in faith, the conscience feels all the security, desire, and love in righteousness, that a child can find in its mother, and a man in his new bride.

The Fifth:
"WITH THE BREAD OF (life and) UNDERSTANDING SHALL SHE FEED HIM."

This is equivalent to saying, she shall feed him with life and understanding. This is effected in the following manner: Precisely as natural bread not only supports the body, but also nourishes and fills it, so that it grows and increases, and becomes hale and robust, strong and capable of labor; so, too, righteousness nourishes an individual, so that he daily increases in spirit, and continually gains more information in regard to things, divine and human. This we learn from experience; and without experience the passage would not be intelligible. Such an individual improves his mind by everything that comes under his observation, growing in knowledge, and still increasing in life and wisdom, especially when he contemplates the Scriptures.

Thus Solomon had learned many things, as his Proverbs and Canticles show. He places the word, *life,* before the word, *understanding*; because, without life, understanding would be of little use. It is not the knowledge derived from heathens and natural reason, concerning temporal things, that is to be regarded, but the knowledge which is derived from faith, concerning spiritual and divine things, and which makes the soul alive before God. This teaches all that is necessary to be known in reference to salvation.

The Sixth:
"AND GIVE HIM THE WATER OF WISDOM TO DRINK."

The import of this phrase is similar to that of the foregoing, and it has reference to the increase of the spirit; and especially does it refer to saving knowledge, for the purpose of excluding the knowledge of the world and of men, which is not salutary. This drinking takes place like the eating. Man draws wisdom from everything that comes under his observation.— Everything, in heaven and on earth, affords him pasture; but especially the Scriptures, from which he derives meat and drink, through a real, saving knowledge.

The Seventh:
"HE SHALL BE STAYED UPON HER."

Hitherto he has been enumerating the blessings and advantages which we derive from righteousness, and enjoy in ourselves, in times of peace.— Now, he enumerates her advantages in times of conflict, and contentions against enemies, saying: He shall be stayed upon her; that is, she will throw around us such protections as will enable us not only to receive these former blessings, but also to guard and protect them against every attempt to wrest them from us. By this, however, he acknowledges that, whoever fears God and desires to be pious, must encounter difficulties, conflicts, and misfortunes. Crosses will not stay away from him; as St. Paul, Acts 14, 22, says: "We must through much tribulation enter into the kingdom of God."

In this way he meets the timid and faint-hearted, who would readily accept these great inducements and benefits, were it not for their fears that, in consequence of it, they would have to risk their property, honor, bodies, lives, and all that they have. This he does not deny, nor does he make any effort to relieve their minds in that respect, or to give them flimsy consolation. But, he strengthens their minds, and admonishes them against such views, affording them the consolation, that righteousness, if they cleave to it, will give them sufficient courage, firmness, and stability to endure all these things.

The Eighth:
"AND SHALL NOT BE MOVED."

This is equivalent to being stayed

D2

upon her. What more do you want, if you are able to overcome all things? This ability the self-righteous do not possess; they do not stand securely; they have no firmness—all is yielding and vacillation, because they hang upon their own efforts. These may be easily taken away, and they, with them. But with the Christian, the believing righteousness hangs upon the mercy of God, which no one can take away; hence, those who hang upon it cannot be moved, even if they are deprived of everything else.

The Ninth:
"AND SHALL RELY UPON HER."

That is, she shall sustain his honor. Here the wise man acknowledges that a pious believer must suffer not only many evils, but must also endure shame and scandal. The special sufferings of a Christian consist not in enduring evils only, like other persons, but shame and scandal also, as the worst evil-doers, precisely as Christ suffered. These are also called sufferings of Christ, or of the cross. These have reference not so much to temporal honor, but to the honor which should be in the conscience and before God. Thus all the martyrs were put to death, not as if they had committed a temporal crime, but as if they were the greatest enemies and blasphemers of God. Now, lest any one should be deterred by this, he introduces this declaration as a comfort and encouragement to all believers, to assure them that they shall be preserved, and maintain their honor before God and the world.

The Tenth:
"AND SHALL NOT BE CONFOUNDED."

The import of this is similar to that of the former, only it is expressed in other and clearer terms. She may, it is true, permit him to be overtaken by shame and disgrace, in order that her power may be tested and proved,* as the Wisdom of Solomon, 10, 12, says: "In a sure conflict she gave him the victory; that he might know that godliness is stronger than all." The heart indeed must be tempted; it cannot exist without incurring shame; it will be so touched and affected by it, that it will even tremble and waver as if God would leave it in its shame. But here it finds such assistance as enables it to maintain a firm confidence; and thus sustained, it walks or triumphs over shame or scandal,—a thing which hypocrites cannot, by any means, accomplish.

The Eleventh:
"SHE SHALL EXALT HIM ABOVE HIS NEIGHBORS."

That is, such temptations and conflicts only elevate and distinguish him in the minds of the people. Paul, Cor. 11, 19, says: By heresies the approved Christians are made manifest. Such conflicts so distinguish him and raise him in the admiration of all, that he attains a high degree of eminence and honor. The self-righteous, on the other hand, pass along, unheeded, inexperienced, untried, dwelling in their own element, and destitute of information in regard to the blessings and operations of God.

The Twelfth:
"AND IN THE MIDST OF THE CONGREGATION SHALL SHE OPEN HIS MOUTH."

That is, in this way he becomes a good preacher and teacher. For through faith he rightly understands everything, and through conflict he feels and experiences it, so as to gain the fullest assurance; and hence he may speak with the utmost confidence, giving every one instruction. So that Taulerus may well say, Such a person is able to judge and teach the whole world. Without such conflicts or trials, no one will ever become a successful preacher; he must remain a mere babbler, not knowing what or when to speak, as St. Paul, 1 Tim. 1, 7, says: "Desiring to be teachers of the law; understanding neither what they say, nor whereof they affirm;" useless babblers are they, says he.

The Thirteenth:
And shall fill him with the spirit of wisdom and understanding.

He has already said, With the bread of understanding shall she feed him, and give him the water of wisdom to drink. This has reference to an individual who has simply received

---
* A. But she does not leave him in or under it, if he only cleaves to her.

the gifts of God, and has not as yet been exposed to temptations and trials. But, after he shall have experienced temptations, and been tried and proved, he shall be filled not only with the gifts of wisdom and understanding, but also with the giver of these gifts, the Holy Spirit himself, and be rendered wholly perfect.

Not because the Holy Spirit did not previously exist in him; for where his gifts are, there is he also, most assuredly: but because the individual, not yet exposed to temptations, has not as yet attained that degree, in which he perceives and experiences the presence of the Holy Spirit,—a position which he will not reach until he is tried and proved. Then he who was previously filled with gifts, will be full of the Spirit; so that he will be useful not only to himself, in consequence of these gifts, as he was previous to his having experienced temptations, but will, from that period, render himself useful to others; so that through him they also may attain the same grace. Now, he was, previously, useful in a temporal point of view, in consequence of his distribution of favors to his neighbors.—(as already stated,) an act, which he was induced to perform, in consequence of his faith and the gifts which he had received; in this way, however, he was useful, not in a spiritual, but simply in a temporal point of view.

So, after experiencing temptations, the Spirit enters, and causes him not only to be fed with the bread of wisdom and understanding, as was the case before, but to open his mouth, and feed others with the bread of wisdom and understanding, rendering them spiritual service. Thus, previous to the sufferings of Christ, the Apostles were merely guests of the Lord, eating and drinking of his wisdom and understanding, and leading pious lives; but they, themselves, alone were affected by this. After his resurrection, however, they became hosts, feeding others, and rendering them pious, through the spirit of wisdom and understanding, of which, after having experienced temptations, they were full.

The Fourteenth:
With a garment of honor shall she clothe him.
That is, she will give him great reputation and a great name, far and wide, as God said, in regard to David, I have made thy name great. In this way he will be so adorned, that all the world will esteem and declare him honorable, on account of his wisdom and knowledge. For honor, which attains distinction and secures a great and glorious name among the people, is glory. This he calls a garment:—for it adorns more than ornaments and jewels.

The Fifteenth:
"He shall find joy and a crown of gladness."
Hitherto he mentioned the blessings or advantages which he should enjoy in this life. Here he draws his conclusion now in regard to the blessings which are held in reserve for him in the life which is to come; namely, eternal joy and gladness. This is the treasure which she has in reserve for him, and which has no end.

The Sixteenth:
"And she shall cause him to inherit an everlasting name."
That is, after his death, and not merely during his life, will the remembrance of his name be perpetuated and held in honor. After this all the self-righteous strive, but in vain. For they neither fear God, nor hang upon the righteousness of faith.

Behold, then, these great fruits and blessings, which are so well calculated to afford us consolation and to admonish us to continue in faith and in the fear of God. I have hastily passed over this matter, treating it in the briefest manner; otherwise, a special, a long sermon might have been drawn from each point, by expatiating upon it, in the Scriptures.

We must not infer, however, from this, that we should fear God or believe in him simply for the purpose of securing these blessings. This would be deceptive. It is not written in order to induce us to seek or desire such advantages, but in order that we may know that such blessings will assuredly result to those who fear God:—

and even those alone, who do not seek them, shall find them; that is, those who fear God, without seeking their own honor, and continue to hang upon the grace of God. To these, such blessings unsought must result. These, the self-righteous, with all their pretences, can not reach.

This Epistle or Lesson beautifully accords with the Gospel. Here it is said, Righteousness receives an individual, like a reputable mother, her child, and like a bride, her bridegroom. Thus, too, Christ took John upon his breast, and regarded him as the beloved disciple. In both, faith is commended and present, in regard to its character.

SUNDAY AFTER CHRISTMAS.

EPISTLE, GALATIANS 4, 1-7.

NOW I say, That the heir, as long as he is a child, differeth nothing from a servant, though he be lord of all;
But is under tutors and governors until the time appointed of the father.
Even so we, when we were children, were in bondage under the elements of the world:
But when the fullness of the time was come, God sent forth his Son, made of a woman, made under the law,
To redeem them that were under the law, that we might receive the adoption of sons.
And because ye are sons, God hath sent forth the Spirit of his Son into your hearts, crying, Abba, Father.
Wherefore thou art no more a servant, but a son; and if a son, then an heir of God through Christ.

THIS EPISTLE, or lesson, is very characteristic of the Apostle Paul; and hence, it is not generally understood: not on account of any difficulty or obscurity in it, but because the doctrine in regard to faith, which it is so necessary to understand, in order to comprehend St. Paul, whose mind, with all his zeal and energy, is occupied with the subject of faith, in all his Epistles, is almost extinct in the world. For the purpose, therefore, of rendering it clear, a lengthy exposition will be required; and, in order that we may have space to treat it in the clearest manner possible, we shall let this suffice as a preface and as an introduction.*

It is necessary to know, that it is one thing to treat of good works, and another to treat of justification; precisely as the essence or person of an individual is one thing, and his actions or works are another. Now, justification has reference to the person, and not to his works. For the person, and not the works, is declared just and is saved, or is sentenced and condemned. It is, therefore, also conclusive that no one is justified by works, but must first be justified, without any works, through some other means.

Thus, Moses, Gen. 4, 4, 5, says:— "The Lord had respect unto Abel, and to his offering." First, he had respect to Abel, the person, and then, to his offering, because he was already pious, just, and acceptable, as to his person; and hence, his offering was also acceptable, on account of the person, and not the person on account of the offering. "But unto Cain, and to his offering, he had not respect." Thus, in the first place, he had not respect unto Cain, the person, and hence, too, he had not respect afterwards to his offering. From this text we may conclude, that it is impossible for any work to be good in the sight of God, unless the person [performing it] first be good and acceptable. On the other hand, it is impossible for any work to be evil in the sight of God, unless the person [performing it] be first evil and unacceptable. Now, let this be sufficiently conclusive for the present, that there are two kinds of good works:— some precede, and others follow after justification. Those which precede, merely *seem* to be good and effectual; but those which follow *are* really good.

Behold, this is the contention between God and presumptive saints;

* B. Concerning the Justification of man.

pt] nature contends, and
1st the Holy Spirit. In re-
his the Scriptures every-
:. In them God concludes
s works of an individual
his justification, are evil
tual; he requires the per-
be just and good. In the
:e, he concludes, that all
1ilst in a state of nature,
o their natural birth, are
evil, as it is said, Ps. 116,
1en are liars;" and Gen. 6,
1magination of the thoughts
was only evil continually."
an individual can perform
ork, and whatever he may
way, is nothing more than
that of Cain.
dam Hulda steps in with
d nose, nature, and dares
ct her God, and to charge
alsehood. She hangs on
pery, straw-armor, natural
1n, free-will, natural pow-
cing heathenish books and
trines, and begins to harp
saying, Good works also
tification, and they are not
of Cain, as God says, but
good, that by them a per-
ed. For, Aristotle taught,
er does much good, will
:ome good. To this she
es, perverting the Scrip-
>resuming that God must
:spect to the works and
e person. Such devilish
gns at this time in all the
s, institutions, and clois-
uch persons are nothing
1ke Cain, whom God does

:ond place, since she bases
simply on works, and at-
little importance to the
justification, she proceeds
, and attributes all merit
hest righteousness to the
1 follow justification, say-
without works is dead,"
s, James 2, 26, says. Now,
oes not understand this
she attaches very little
to faith, and thus she con-
here to works, presuming
God to allow the person

to be acceptable on account of works.
Thus, these two continually strive
against each other: God has respect
to the person; Cain to the works.—
God rewards the works on account of
the person; Cain would have the person crowned on account of the works.
God will not yield his position, so just
and righteous, and Cain, the young
nobleman, will never allow himself to
be convinced of his error. We must
not reject his works, slightly regard
his reason, or look upon his free-will
as impotent, else he will become angry with God, and slay his brother,
Abel, as all history abundantly teaches.

But, if you ask: What then must I
do? How shall I first become good
and acceptable in regard to my person? How shall I secure that justification? The Gospel replies: You
must hear Christ and believe in him,
wholly despairing of yourself, and
resting assured that you will be
changed from [the character of] Cain
to [that of] Abel, and then you may
offer your offering. This faith, as it
is proclaimed without any of your
merit, is also given independent of
your works and without any of your
merits, through pure grace. Behold,
this justifies the individual, and it is
even justification itself. On account
of this, God remits and forgives all
sins, as well as the old Adam and
Cain, for the sake of Christ, his beloved Son, whose name is in this faith.
He grants, moreover, his Holy Spirit,
who alters the individual and changes
him into a new creature, who then has
different reason and a different will,
inclined to that which is good. Such
a person, wherever he may be, performs purely good works, and whatever he does is good, as already stated in the foregoing Epistle.

Nothing else, therefore, but to hear
Jesus Christ, and to believe in him as
the Savior, is necessary to justification. But this is not the work of nature, but of grace; and whoever presumes to attain it by works, throws
obstacles in the way of the Gospel,
faith, grace, Christ, God, and all
good. On the other hand, nothing
else, but justification, is necessary for

good works, [for, whoever is justified, and no one else, does good, and all that he does in a state of justification is good, without any distinction of works,] so that the beginning, the sequel, and order of man's salvation, is, in the first place, to hear the Word of God above all things,* and then to act, and thus to be saved. Whoever changes or perverts this order is certainly not from God.

This order is described by St. Paul, Rom. 10, 13, where he says: "Whosoever shall call upon the name of the Lord shall be saved. How then shall they call on him in whom they have not believed? and how shall they believe in him of whom they have not heard? and how shall they hear without a preacher? And how shall they preach, except they be sent?" Therefore, Christ teaches us to pray the Lord of the harvest to send laborers into his harvest; that is, faithful preachers. When they come, they preach the true word of God. When we hear this, we are enabled to believe; and this faith justifies us and renders us pious; then we call on God, and do all that is good. In this way we are saved. That is, whoever believes shall be saved; but, whoever works without faith, shall be damned; as Christ, Mark 16, 16, says: "He that believeth not shall be damned;" here, works avail nothing.

Now, observe the common course pursued and the language employed by the people, who are accustomed to say: Aye! I expect to become pious; aye! we must become pious, &c. But if they are asked, what course we must pursue in order to become pious, they begin and say, Aye! we must pray, fast, go to church, abstain from sin, &c. One will enter a monastery, and another some other order; one will become a priest, and another will put on a hair-garment; one will punish himself in one way, and another in some other way. These are like Cain, and do the works of Cain. As to their persons, they are like they were before; they are destitute of justification; they assume only an external change and alteration of works, clothing, condition, and habits; they are real apes, who assume the habits of saints; still they are unholy; they do not think of faith, but rush along with their good works towards heaven, (as they imagine,) torturing themselves.

Relative to these, Christ says, in the Gospel, Luke 13, 24: "Strive to enter in at the strait gate: for many, I say unto you, will seek to enter in, and shall not be able." Aye, why not? Because they do not know which is the strait gate. It is faith. This humbles an individual, yes, brings him down to nothing, so that he must despair of all his good works, and cleave only to the grace of God, forsaking all else, on account of it. But saints like Cain, imagine that good works are the strait gate. Hence, they neither humble themselves, nor despair of their good works; no, they gather them in large bags, and throwing these over themselves, desire to pass through; and they will pass through, like a camel with his great hump on his back passes through the eye of a needle.

Now, if any one speaks to them about faith, they scoff and laugh, saying, Are we regarded as Turks or heathens, that it is necessary for us first to learn what faith is? Can there be so many monks, nuns, and priests, without knowing what faith is? Who does not know what is to be believed, when even open sinners know? Hence, as if they had already accomplished everything in regard to faith, they imagine that they must henceforth be occupied with works, regarding faith as of very little importance, as already said. For they neither understand, nor know, that by it alone, we are justified.

To hold as true, whatever they hear about Christ, they style faith. This kind of faith the devils also have, and yet they are not thereby rendered pious. This, however, is not Christian faith; no, it is an illusion, rather than faith. In the preceding postils we have already heard that, in order to be a Christian, it is not enough for an individual simply to believe that all that is said about Christ is true,—

---

* A. Then to believe.
Luther's Works, 7r Bd.

such a faith saints like Cain possess, —but, he must, without any doubt or vacillation, believe that he, himself, is one of those to whom such grace and mercy are given, and that he has really secured them through Baptism or the Sacrament. Now, when he believes this, he may freely say in regard to himself; I am holy, pious, just, and a child of God, assured, without the slightest doubt, of salvation; not in consequence of anything in me, or in my merits or works, but through the pure mercy of God in Christ, poured out upon me. This he will prize so highly, as it really is so valuable, that he cannot doubt that it renders him holy, and constitutes him a child of God. But if he doubts this, he disparages, in the highest degree, his Baptism and the Sacrament, and censures, with falsehood, the Word of God, and his grace in the Sacraments.

For here he should entertain neither fear nor doubt, that he is pious and a child of God through grace, but he should rather entertain fear and anxiety relative to the manner, in which he may remain steadfast until the end; here lie all the fear and anxiety. For, here, he is assuredly in possession of the whole salvation, but there may be some doubt and anxiety as to whether he will continue steadfast, and retain it. Here we must walk in fear; for such faith does not hang upon works or itself, but only upon God and his grace. This cannot forsake the individual, as long as this reliance continues. But he knows not how long it will continue. If temptation should force him away from it, so that this reliance ceases, the grace will also cease.*

When these *Cain-ites* hear this faith, [doctrine] they bless themselves, making the sign of the cross with their hands and their feet, and exclaim:—

Aye! God forbid: How could I say that I am holy and pious? How could I be so high-minded and presumptuous? No, no, I am a poor sinner. In this way, you perceive, they render this faith useless to themselves, and all such doctrine must be regarded as heresy. In this way, then, the whole Gospel is exterminated. These are the persons, who deny the Christian faith, and drive it out of the world, and concerning whom St. Paul prophesied, when he said, 1 Tim. 4, 1: "In the latter times some shall depart from the faith." For this faith is now silenced in all the world; yes, condemned and banished, with all who teach and hold it, as the worst heresy; the Pope, the bishop, the foundation, the cloister, the high-schools, stood unanimously in opposition to it for nearly four hundred years, and did nothing else but drive all the world, with violence, into hell;—this is the real, the last persecution of Antichrist.

But, if you say to them: Yes, but the prophet, Ps. 86, 2, says,: "Preserve my soul; for I am holy;" and St. Paul, Rom. 8, 16: "The Spirit itself beareth witness with our spirit, that we are the children of God:" they reply: Yes, the Prophet and the Apostle did not make these declarations to establish a doctrine or an example, but because they were enlightened, and it was revealed to them that were holy. In this way they construe every passage that speaks concerning this matter, as if it were designed, not as a doctrine, but as a special wonder and prerogative, not intended for every believer. This gloss is a mere figment of their own mind. For, because they do not believe, or taste of the Spirit, they imagine that no one else should thus believe, or taste. By this, as their own fruits, they may be clearly known as thorns and thistles, not as Christians, but as enemies and destroyers of all Christians, and persecutors of the Christian faith.

But, on the other hand, their faith is of such a character as leads them to believe that they are rendered pious and holy through their works·

---

* A. This is the view of Solomon, Ecc. 9, 1: "The righteous, and the wise, and their works, are in the hand of God: no man knoweth either love or hatred by all that is before them,"—so that he knows not whether he is worthy of grace or displeasure. He does not say it is uncertain in regard to the present, but to the future. Because the person does not know whether he will be able to stand against the assaults of temptation.

and that in consequence of these, God must save them. Behold, in their opinion, to become pious through works, is Christianity; but to become pious through the grace of God, is heresy. Their works seem to be of greater importance and of more value than the grace of God: their faith can hang upon works, but not upon the grace of God. And since, building upon the sand, they reject the rock, it is but serving them right, that they must fall into their works, and torture themselves to death, to the honor of the devil, because they will not adhere to the grace of God, and render him a reasonable service.

For all who are in possession of such Christian faith, must consequently be happy and secure in God and his grace.—They will even delight in good works. The prayers and apparel observed by these Cain-ites, are not good works; but such works only as are useful and beneficial to our neighbor, are good, as already stated in the Gospel lesson.—Yes, they will be ready and willing to suffer all things; for they doubt not that God is with them, and that they are in his grace. These are the persons that honor God, and are useful to man.

These Cain-ites, moreover, are useless to God, to the world, and to themselves. Yes, they are a mere useless burden to the earth, injurious to themselves and to everybody else. For, since they are not in possession of this faith, they neither serve nor honor God. They perform none of those works, from which their neighbor can derive any benefit in regard to his body, property, honor, or soul. For their works are of a peculiar character, consisting in gestures, apparel, situations, times, and meats.

Tell me, what does it benefit me for you to wear a large bald pate, or a gray cowl? Who profits by your fasting on one day, and observing another as a holy-day; by your abstaining from certain meats, and secluding yourself in a certain place, reading and muttering every day? In this way you do nothing else but murder yourself for the devil, and leave a bad, a pernicious example for every one to follow such life and conduct, as if it were good and consistent with the principles of Christianity. For, you do not believe in a Christian manner, and, hence, you cannot pray in that manner; and, hence, your fasting is not a mortification of the body, as it should be, but it is performed as a good work; so that such a life is nothing else but the idolatry of Baal and Moloch, formerly practiced among the Jews, who tortured, murdered, and burnt their children in honor to the devil.*

You may, perhaps, say, if it is true, that we are justified, not by works, but by hearing and believing Christ, as the being who is given to us as our own, of what use or advantage, then, are the commandments? Answer:—Here, we now come to the Epistle lesson which tells us the object for which the commandments were given. The Galatians first learned the Christian faith from St. Paul, and were afterwards so perverted by certain false preachers, as to turn back again to their works, and imagine that they must become pious through the works of the law. Here, St. Paul recalls them again from these works to faith, and in a multiplicity of terms, points out to them the two kinds of works of the law, drawing the conclusion that the works which precede justification or faith, are useless, and merely constitute us servants; but faith makes us children or sons of God; and hence really good works then follow.

But, we must make ourselves acquainted with the language employed by the Apostle, in which he distinguishes between a servant and a child. The self-righteous he calls a servant, concerning whom much has already been said. The believer in Christ he styles a child, who is justified by faith alone, without works.—This distinction results from the fact that the self-righteous does not render his services in the same spirit that actuates the child and the heir, in his services, relative to his own inheritance, but he renders them in the disposition of a day-laborer, upon the possessions of some one else. Al-

* B. THE USE AND NECESSITY OF THE LAW.

though the works performed by both may be precisely of the same character, yet the disposition, the conscience, and faith make a distinction. The child has a conscience, and expects to continue an heir to the inheritance.— The servant feels that he must ultimately leave, and hence he does not await the inheritance; as Christ, John 8, 35, says: "The servant abideth not in the house forever: but the son abideth ever."

Thus, these Cain-like saints, because they have not this Christian faith, (as they themselves confess,) which would enable them to regard themselves as the children of God with certainty,—but separate themselves from it, as an enormous, heretical presumption, by making the sign of the cross,—continue to hang in doubt. It occurs to them as they believe; they are not, nor will they ever be, the chidren of God, and become happy, in that way; although they may perform the deeds of the law, and diligently attend to its practical exercises. This will constitute them servants; they will continue to be servants, and in this way they will secure nothing more than a temporal reward, a competency on earth, quietude, honor, and pleasant days.— This we now perceive in the spiritual orders, in which all the wealth, power, pleasure, honor, and favors in the world, are enjoyed. This is their reward; they are servants and not children; and hence, in the hour of death, they will all be cast out from the eternal inheritance, in which they would never believe, and which, in this life, they would never receive through faith. Thus you will perceive that there is scarcely a difference between the works. The faith, however, and the disposition, make the distinction.

Now, it is the design of the Apostle to show, and it is really true, that without this faith, the law, with all its works, constitutes us nothing but servants; for this faith alone makes us children. Neither the law, then, nor its works, nor our own nature can produce this faith in us: but the Gospel alone brings it with itself,—when we hear the Gospel, the word of grace, accompanied by the Holy Ghost, wherever it is quietly preached. This is clear from the example of Cornelius and his family, Acts 10, 44, who received the Holy Ghost, simply by hearing St. Peter.

Thus, too, the law was given for no other purpose, but to enable man to perceive how graceless, how destitute of filial affection, and how servile he is, serving God without faith and confidence, as well as without a free, spontaneous spirit. For, these saints themselves confess that they are destitute of such confidence; and, if they would confess still further, they would have to admit that they would rather there were no law, and that they do not submit to it from choice. Thus, faithless as they are, their whole course of conduct is regulated by restraints; and they must acknowledge that, by the law, they can attain no higher degree of perfection. This they should learn from the law, and perceive that they are servants and not children, with a view to emerge from their state of servitude to the position of a child, regarding their own efforts as ineffectual; so, through faith and the grace of God, they may attain the proper position in life.

This is a correct view and a proper use of the law, since it contemplates nothing else but to convict and vanquish all who presume to fulfill it without faith, because they are servants, and, hence, engage in its requirements without a free, spontaneous spirit, and without reliance upon grace. It designs them to come in conflict with it, to try themselves, and to learn how unwilling and destitute of faith they are, and, consequently, to seek help in some other direction, not presuming by their own strength to fulfill it. For it must be fulfilled from a free, spontaneous spirit, and by children alone. It is an enemy to the unwilling, and to servants.

Now, they go on and acknowledge that they are destitute of faith; yes, they reject that faith which would constitute them children; they sensibly perceive their unwillingness, and prefer being from under the law; and yet they presume by their own works to render themselves pious, desiring to remain servants, and not to become children,—still cleaving to the inheritance, perverting everything. The law, (in conflict with which they should come, and from which they should learn that they are servants without a free, spontaneous spirit, so that they might despair of their own efforts, and cleave to faith, which would afford grace, and constitute them children,) they so pervert as to enter upon its demands through their works, presuming in this way to fulfill it. Thus, they obstruct the object and end of the law, even striving against faith and grace, to which the law directs, impels, and urges them. Thus, they remain a blind, perverse, laborious, and servile people, forever.

This is the design and intention of St. Paul, Rom. 3, 20, and 7, 7, where he fearlessly says: "By the deeds of the law there shall no flesh be justified in his sight." Why not? He answers and says, Because, by the law, nothing more is effected than the knowledge or perception of sin. Beloved, how is this accomplished?— Place before you an individual like Cain, and you will see. In the first place, it is with great toil and labor that he performs his works, according to the law; and yet he readily confesses that he does not believe that he is holy and a child of God; yes, he condemns that faith, as an abominable presumption and heresy, as already stated; he continues in doubt, and expects to become a child through his own works.

Behold, here you may clearly perceive that the person is neither good nor righteous, since he is destitute of faith; yes, he is an enemy to faith;— and hence, too, an enemy to righteousness; and, consequently, his works are not good, no matter how beautifully they may appear, according to the law. Thus, you will perceive that St. Paul speaks correctly, when he says: "By the deeds of the law there shall no flesh be justified in his sight." For, in the sight of God, the person must be good before his works are good. By works, it is true, he may be justified by men, who judge according to the works, and not according to humility or the heart. Men judge persons according to their works; God judges the works according to the persons.

Now, the first commandment in the law requires and orders us to love and to honor God; that is, to trust in him, to confide in him, and to rely upon him. This is the true faith, which constitutes us the children of God. Thus, you may perceive, and clearly understand from this law, the sin that dwells in a person like Cain, namely, his unbelief. From it, too, you can feel in yourself whether you believe or not,—a thing which no one could feel or know without such law. This, observe, St. Paul styles knowing sin by the law.

Now, from this unbelief you cannot extricate yourself, nor can the law extricate you. All your works, therefore, by which you intend to fulfill the law, are nothing but works of the law, and cannot justify you in the sight of God, who regards as just, only those who believe in him and are children; for these, only, fulfill this commandment, and hold him as true God. For, although you may torture yourself to death with works, yet, from that source, your heart cannot secure such a faith as this commandment requires; yes, works neither comprehend nor tolerate that faith, as already said; nor do they know that it is required by the law. An individual entertaining such views must continue, therefore, a martyr of the devil, and a persecutor of faith and the law, even through the works of the law in which he trusts, until he comes to himself, understands himself, and despairs of himself and of his works, giving God the honor, perceiving his nothingness, and sighing after pure grace, to which God has driven him by the law. Here faith and grace come, and fill the empty and feed the hungry; here, then, really good works follow. These are not works of the law, but works of the spirit of grace, and are styled, in the Scriptures, the works of God, which he produces in us. For, all that God does not produce in us by grace, or all that we perform of ourselves, without grace, is really a work of the law, availing nothing in justification, and is rather evil and in opposition to God, in consequence of the unbelief in which it is performed.

In the second place, a person like Cain never performs his duty willingly and from a free, spontaneous spirit, unless he is first hired, and allowed to use his own pleasure, and to have whatever he desires; precisely as a servant, who does not do his duty unless he is driven, or allowed to have his own way. Now, such servants as must be driven or praised and begged, are very disagreeable. So, too, all persons like Cain are disagreeable, and by no means acceptable in the sight of God, because they perform no work of the law, unless driven and impelled by the fear of hell and punishment, or, indeed, by being begged, and allowed to have their own way, or in order to secure a full competency from God, and to use it as they desire.

Thus you perceive, moreover, that they are not actuated by cordial love for the law, but by the expectation of reward, or the fear of punishment, so that it is evident that, as they are enemies to the law from the bottom of their hearts, they would rather there were no law. Hence, if the person performing the work is evil, the work is also evil, because it is extorted by fear only, or by granting the individual the privilege of exercising his own will and pleasure in the matter, precisely as when a person is induced by entreaty and persuasion to act.

The law teaches us to see and feel the unwilling and perverse state of our mind. This is altogether sinful in the sight of God. What kind of holiness is it to perform required duties with our hands, when, at the same time, our hearts are unfriendly towards the law and the law-giver? Yea, it is sinful, indeed, to be unfriendly towards the law.

This, you will perceive, is what St. Paul here calls knowing sin by the law, to come in conflict with it, to feel and experience this perverseness of our hearts, to shudder in consequence of it, to despair of ourselves, to strive with haste and thirst after grace,— which removes from us this disinclination, and produces in us a willing, a cheerful spirit, which renders us, from the bottom of our hearts, friendly to the law, and enables us, from a free, spontaneous disposition, to perform our duties, without constraint —regardless of any motive except pure delight in righteousness and the law, without the expectation of reward or the fear of punishment. Thus, out of a slave a child is made, and out of a servant an heir,—a spirit which nothing but the faith of Christ alone can bring and produce, as we have already sufficiently stated. Now, let us take into consideration the Epistle.

"The heir, as long as he is a child, differeth nothing from a servant, though he be lord of all."

He introduces a simile, derived from human customs. We see that a minor, a child, or an heir, to whom an estate has been left or bequeathed by parents, is reared and restrained like a servant, in regard to its estate. It has no power to use it according to its own will and pleasures; but it is kept in fear and discipline, so as to derive from it only its food and raiment, although the estate really belongs to it. Hence, it is like a stranger and a servant, so far as its property is concerned.

So, too, in *spiritual* matters, God made a testament, when he promised Abraham, Gen. 22, 18: "In thy seed shall all the nations of the earth be blessed." This testament was afterwards established by the death of Christ, and, after his resurrection it was distributed through the Gospel, which is nothing else but a revelation and manifestation of this testament— in which it is declared to all the world that, in Christ, the seed of Abraham, grace and a blessing are assigned and given to all men, which may be received by all who believe it.

Now, before this testament was opened and proclaimed, the children of God were under the law, and encumbered and constrained by the works of the law; although they were not justified in this way, but their works were servile and unprofitable; yet, however, since they were pre-determined in regard to the faith which was to come and constitute them children, they were assuredly heirs of that grace and blessing, although they were not in possession of them, nor did they use them, but like other faithless individuals, they were servile and occupied with works.— Precisely as it is the case now, and always has been, that many persons believe, and acknowledge the faith, who were, previously, drowned in works, and knowing nothing concerning faith, were engaged in the performance of works, like other hypocrites. But, now, since they apprehend the faith, and receive the inheritance, they were certainly heirs before, and pre-determined by God, although at that time they knew nothing about it, and were servants, self-righteous, and *Cain-ites*.

Thus, at this time, some are still occupied with works, maintain a holiness like that of Cain, and are servants like he was, yet they are heirs and children in regard to the future, because they will yet believe; by this they will be enabled to lay aside their servile disposition, to surrender their works, and secure the great blessing and inheritance of justification, by which they become righteous and happy, without works. Then will they, from a free, spontaneous spirit, perform all their works, to the honor of God and the benefit of their neighbors, without any expectation or design to secure a reward or righteousness. For they already have, in the inheritance and blessing, that which Christ has bequeathed to them in his testament, and caused to be opened, read, proclaimed, and distributed, through the Gospel, from pure grace and mercy.

Abraham and all the patriarchs, you will observe, recognized the testament of God; nor was it any less given and administered to them, than it is to us; although it was not, at that time, read and proclaimed throughout the world, as it was after the ascension of Christ; still, however, they secured the very same thing that we and all the children of God secure, through the very same faith. The grace, the blessing, the testament, the faith, is the same; as the Father is one, and one God of us all.

Thus, you will perceive, here, that St. Paul everywhere teaches that justification results, not from works, but from faith alone, without any works, not at intervals, but at once. For the testament includes all in itself, justification, salvation, the inheritance, and the great good. Through faith, it is wholly enjoyed at once, not at intervals. So that it is clear, indeed, that faith, only, affords such blessings of God, that is, justification and salvation,—at once, not at intervals, (as would be the case with works,) and constitutes us children and heirs, who, from a free, spontaneous spirit, perform all their duties, without presuming to become pious and meritorious by a servile disposition. Here, merit is unnecessary; here, faith alone presents all, and more than any one can merit. Here, they will perform all their works from a free spirit; being already in possession of all that these *Cain-ites* seek through works, and never find, namely, justification and divine inheritance, or grace.

"But is under tutors and governors until the time appointed of the father."

These are the individuals who rear the heir, and keep him on his father's possessions, so that he does not grow wild and become a vagabond. And, notwithstanding they do not give him control of the inheritance, they are still profitable and advantageous to him, in various ways. In the first place, as already said, they keep him at home at his estate, in order that he may be better prepared to enjoy the inheritance. In the second place, a greater desire for the inheritance is produced in him, by seeing how assiduously and closely he is kept. For, when he arrives at the years of discretion, he will begin to desire freedom, and feel unwilling to continue under the control of others.

This is, and must be, the case with every one who is still engaged in works, under the law, and is a servant. The law is his tutor and governor, under whose control he is, as under the constraint of another; and this is designed, in the first place, to rear him up and keep him in proper limits, so as to secure him externally, through the fear of punishment, against the perpetration of evil works; so that he may not become entirely dissolute, endangering everything, and shutting himself out entirely from God and his salvation, as those do who give themselves over entirely to sin.

It is intended, in the second place, to learn him to know himself, and to bring him to his reason, so that he may see how unwillingly he is under the law, and that he performs no work willingly, as a child, but through constraint, as a servant. In this way he learns, by experience, where his defects lie; namely, in not having a free, renewed, and willing disposition, which the law and his works can not give him; yes, the more he works, the more unwilling is he, and the more arduous is it, to work, when under the influence of such a defective disposition.

When he discovers this, in himself, he perceives that he observes the law only externally, by his works; but, internally, in his heart, he is an enemy to it, and opposed to it, so far as his willingness and disposition are concerned. Hence, he is really, without intermission, *internally*, a sinner against the law, and, *externally*, a saint according to the law; that is, he is a real *Cain*, and an egregious hypocrite. It is manifest to him, that his works are works of the law; but his heart is a heart of sin. For his heart is not disposed to the law; hence, it is disposed to sin, and his hands are merely constrained to observe the requirements of the law.

St. Paul has, therefore, very properly styled such works, works of the law. For, the law forces them out, and they are nothing but mere results of compulsion. Now, the law demands the heart also, and desires a willing obedience, which may be said to be, not only a work of the law, but a heart of the law; not only the hands of the law, but the will, disposition, and powers of the law, as Ps. 1, 1, 2, says: Blessed is the man, whose delight is in the law of the Lord.* Such a disposition the law demands, but it does not produce it; nor is nature able of itself to produce it. Hence, the law presses it, and condemns it to hell, as disobedient to the commandments of God. Here anguish and distress of conscience follow, and yet there is no help.

Here is the time appointed of the Father; here it will desire grace and help; here it will confess its wretchedness, inability, and guilt; here it will let its security in its works fall, and despise itself. For it perceives that between it and public sinners there is no difference, except in regard to the external conduct. In its heart, it is as much opposed to the law as any other sinner is. Yes, it may be that its heart is more embittered against the law, than that of any other sinner. Since the sinner, in the accomplishment of sins, may find less desire for sinning, and become somewhat inimical to sin, in consequence of the displeasure and the injuries which result from it, and which he meets in it. The former, since the law and the tutor lie in its way, and restrain it, may really burn and rage in its desires and lusts for sin, and yet, it dare not commit the deed.— Thus, in regard to its works, it may be more pious, but in regard to its heart, more wicked, than the latter.

Now every one may easily perceive that it is a very unequal division, to give our hands to the law, and our whole heart to sin. Since the whole heart is immensely more than the works or the hands. What else is this, but giving the chaff to the law, and the grain to sin, the shell to God, and the kernel to the devil? Thus, it is that, as it is said in the Gospel, the sin of the public sinner is only a mote, and that of the other, a great beam.

Now, when the circumstances are of such character that *Cain* does not see this beam, and in this way learn to know himself according to

* B. And meditates in his law day and night.

the law; but continues obdurate and blinded in his works, disregarding his inward abominations, he goes on very unceremoniously to judge all the world in a malicious manner, despising sinners, as did the Pharisee, in the Gospel,—considering himself unlike other persons, and presuming himself pious. If any one attempts to rebuke him, and to condemn his course of conduct, as it should be, he rages and raves, and kills Abel, persecuting everybody, and saying that he does it for the sake of good works and righteousness, to the praise of God—expecting to merit much in that way, as a persecutor of blasphemers, heretics, errorists, and wicked persons, who wish to lead him astray, and draw him away from good works.

Behold, here, everything that the Scriptures say in reference to these venomous spirits, presents itself.— These, Christ calls a generation of serpents and vipers. These are like Cain, and will continue like him; they are servants, and will continue to be servants. But those who are, prospectively, like Abel and children, learn to know themselves by the law, how little cordial delight they have for the law, cease to hang upon their presumption, let their hands and feet sink, and are completely undone in their own eyes, by this perception. Here, the Gospel appears; here, God gives grace to the humble. These comprehend the testament, and believe. With, and in this faith, they receive the Holy Spirit; he gives to them a new heart, that delights in the law, and hates sin, acting uprightly from a willing and free disposition. Here there are no longer works of the law, but hearts of the law. This is the time appointed of the father for the heir, no longer to be a servant, or under the tutor. This is what St. Paul means by the following words:

"Even so we, when we were children, were in bondage under the elements of the world."

* Here the Apostle uses the same word, *elements*, which we employ.— Here we must not understand by the

* A. Here we must bear in mind that the Apostle means by elements of the world, the, &c.

term elements of the world, the four natural elements, fire, air, water, and earth. The Scriptures do not employ the word elements to express the four creatures just mentioned. This use of the term elements originated from heathen philosophy; and it would be entirely inadmissible to use it in that sense in the Scriptures. But he calls the writing, or letters of the law, elements. For, both the Latin and the Greek languages call the letters elements.

Thus, Heb. 5, 12, he says: "When for the time ye ought to be teachers, ye have need that one teach you again which be the first principles, [elements,] of the oracles of God;" and Col. 2, 8: "Beware lest any man spoil you through philosophy and vain deceit, after the tradition of men, after the rudiments [elements] of the world, and not after Christ;" and Gal. 4, 9, 10: "How turn ye again to the weak and beggarly elements, whereunto ye desire again to be in bondage? Ye observe days, and months, and times, and years."

It is rather with contempt that he calls the law, elements or letter, which is weak and beggarly, because it can afford no relief. It renders us, also, weak and beggarly. It requires the heart and the mind, and yet these are absent. Hence, the conscience grows weak and beggarly, seeing that it neither has nor can have what it should have. This view he expresses, thus, 2 Cor. 3, 6: "The letter killeth, but the spirit giveth life."

By the word, elements, some understand, not the letter or the law, but the ceremonies and external gestures which are used in worship and in leading a pious life, and with which we begin to exercise children; so that elements implies the first, rude, childish manners employed in worship.

But, he calls them elements of the world, because the self-righteous, who attempt to do the works of the law, do not observe it, except in regard to external, temporal, worldly matters, as days, meats, apparel, places, persons, vessels, and the like. These are all creatures of this world, and this is about the extent of works of the law.*

But faith, apart from the world, hangs upon God, his word, and his mercy, and justifies us, not through works or any worldly thing, but through the eternal, invisible grace of God. To the Christian, one day is like another, all meats, all places, apparel, and all worldly things are alike. These neither help him nor hinder him in his salvation and justification, like they do Cain and the self-righteous. Hence he pays no attention to the elements of this world, but regards the plentitude of the eternal blessings.

In like manner, although he acts in an external, temporal point of view, yet he knows nothing of worldly matters. In regard to such things he is free to act. All are alike to him: persons, places, days, meats, apparel, &c. He does not single out any thing in particular. He does whatever presents itself, and is unconcerned about that which does not. His external course of conduct does not consist in anything select and peculiar.

But persons like Cain pursue a different course. They must have some distinction and peculiarity.— They eat no meat, wear nothing black, pray not in houses, observe days; one is bound to one thing, and another to another; and yet, these are all temporal, worldly, transitory things.— They are all servants of the elements of this world; and still these things are styled holy orders, good morals, and real ways to salvation.

In reference to this, he says, Col. 2, 20, 21, 22; "Wherefore if ye be dead with Christ from the rudiments, [elements] of the world, why, as though living in the world, are ye subject to ordinances, (Touch not; taste not; handle not; which all are to perish with the using;) after the commandments and doctrines of men? Which things have indeed a show of wisdom in will worship, and humility," &c.

From this, and the preceding statements, it is clear that all the orders, institutions, and cloisters, which are now styled ecclesiastical positions, are

* B. Therefore we have rendered it elements of the world.

directly opposed to the Gospel and the freedom of Christian life, and that all who are confined to such things are in greater danger than worldlings are. Since all these, their devices, are mere elements of this world, confined to apparel, persons, situations, meats, vessels, times, and gestures, all of which are nothing but mere worldly, temporal things. And since they adhere to these, with a view of becoming pious and spiritual, faith is excluded, and they are not Christians. Their whole course of conduct is nothing but sin and corruption.

It is more necessary, therefore, for them, than for any other persons, to guard against these, their dazzling devices, and to adhere firmly and steadfastly to the faith, the righteousness of which is beyond the world and worldly things. For, such glitter and appearances tear them away from the faith with greater violence, than do gross, open sins, and make them like those, concerning whom St. Paul here says: "We, when we were children, were in bondage under the elements of the world;" that is, when we were ignorant of the faith, and were occupied with the works of the law, we performed, unwillingly however, as servants, such works as consisted in temporal things, presuming to become pious and happy in that way. This impression was false and rendered us children and servants. Such works would have resulted in no injury, had not an impression existed, which excluded faith, and the doctrine that we become pious through grace only, and had all temporal things been left optional.

"But when the fulness of the time was come, God sent forth his Son, made of a woman, made under the law, To redeem them that were under the law, that we might receive the adoption of sons."

Since the law cannot produce justification and faith, and, since nature with all its works cannot merit them, St. Paul introduces him, who merited such faith, in our room and stead, and who is a master of justification,—justification was not secured for naught; it cost much, namely, the Son of God, himself,—saying: "When the fulness of the time was come;" that is, when the time in which we were children and servants, terminated, or ended. St. Paul here speaks according to the manner employed in the Scriptures, in which it is customary to say, The time is fulfilled, when it has terminated or ended, as in Acts 2, 1: "When the day of Pentecost was [fulfilled] fully come;" that is, when it was completed; and in Ex. 23: "The number of thy days I will fulfil;" that is, I will not shorten them, but will give them their full measure.*

Now, as that time was fulfilled for the Jews, by the bodily advent of Christ; so, it is still daily fulfilled, when a person is enlightened through faith, so that his state of servitude and his legal works terminate, or end. For, the bodily advent of Christ would be useless, if it would not produce such a spiritual advent of faith. He made his bodily appearance, for the purpose of establishing this spiritual advent. For, to all those who previously and subsequently believed in his bodily advent, he came. Therefore, in consequence of this faith, he was always present with the ancient fathers; and still he has not yet come to the Jews of the present day, in consequence of their unbelief.

Everything, from the beginning of the world to its end, must depend on that bodily advent, through which dependence the state of servitude is terminated, when, and where, and in whom such dependence exists. Therefore, the time of each one is fulfilled, when he begins to believe in Christ, as in him who was to come, and is now come.†

But, this declaration is so rich and copious, that I scarcely know whether I shall be able to explain it according to its merits. It is not enough to believe that Christ is come, but we must believe that he has come, as St. Paul here states; namely, that he is sent of God, and is the Son of God;—again, that he is true man;—again, that his mother was a virgin; again, that he alone has fulfilled the law;—again, that he did this, not for himself, but for our good, and to secure grace for us. These points we shall examine in regular order.

On the *first*, the whole gospel of St. John insists, as already said in our remarks on Christmas. He continually shows that Christ is the Son of God, and that he is sent by the Father.—For, he who does not believe that he is true God, is already lost, as it is said, John 8, 24: "For if ye believe not that I am he, ye shall die in your sins." Again, John 1, 4: "In him was life; and the life was the light of men." Again, John 14, 6: "I am the way, and the truth, and the life." And this is the reason:

The soul neither can nor should be contented with anything but the Highest Good, which created it, and which is the fountain of its life and salvation: therefore, God, himself, chose to be the one, on whom it should hang and believe. No one, but God, deserves the honor of being believed in by the creature. Therefore, God himself came, became man, and gave himself for man, drawing him unto himself, and inviting him to believe in him. For, God had no need, so far as he was concerned, to come, and become man; but, it was necessary for us, and for our benefit. Now, if Christ were not true God, and we would not cleave to him by faith, God would be robbed of the honor due him, and we of our lives and salvation. For, it is our duty to believe on God only—who is the Truth himself;—for, without God, we cannot live or be saved.

The Apostle says, God sent his Son. If he was to send him, he must have previously existed; hence, he existed before he came, and became man. And, if he is a Son, then he is more than an angel. If he is

---

* A. Luke, 1, 57: "Now Elizabeth's full time came that she should be delivered," &c. Here the high-minded doctor committed an error, in construing this declaration of Paul in the following manner: The time of the fulfilment is the time of grace, which came after the birth of Christ: directly in opposition to the Apostle, who does not say, The time of the fulfillment, but the fulfillment of the time, and means the previous time, appointed by the Father for the heir, during which he should be under the tutor.

† B. What and how we are to hold concerning Christ.

DR. LUTHER'S CHURCH-POSTIL.

SERMONS ON THE EPISTLES.

more than man, and angels, which are the highest creatures, he must be true God. For, to be the Son of God, is more than to be an angel, as it is said in the Epistle for Christmas-day. If, moreover, he is sent by God and is his Son, he must be a different person. Thus, St. Paul teaches here, that there is one God, but two persons, Father and Son. We shall also speak of the Holy Spirit.

In the second place, we must likewise believe that he is true, natural man and the Son of man, as St. Paul says here, He was born of a woman, or made of a woman. But that which is born or made of a woman, is real, natural man. According to her nature and kind, a woman bears nothing but true man. Thus, too, John 6, 53, Christ says: "Except ye eat the flesh of the Son of man, and drink his blood, ye have no life in you." This eating and drinking is nothing else, but believing that he is the Son of God, and that he really has flesh and blood, like another man.

This is also the testament of God, where he says to Abraham, Gen. 18, 18, c. 22, 18: "In thy seed shall all the nations of the earth be blessed." If he was to be the seed of Abraham, surely he must have Abraham's flesh and blood, and must be his natural child.

No one must presume, therefore, by his own devotion or efforts, to institute a way of his own, to approach God. It avails nothing to call on God, like the Jews and Turks do.— You must approach him through the seed of Abraham, and be blessed through that seed, according to the testament of God. He will not recognize a way of your own; nor will he for the sake of your services disannul his testament. You must abandon your own efforts, and cleave to that seed, to that flesh and blood, or you will be lost with all the skill and wisdom which you have gained in regard to God. For thus says Christ, John 14, 6: "No man cometh unto the Father, but by me."

The divine nature being so exalted and incomprehensible, God has for our good presented himself in our own nature, with which we are more thoroughly acquainted. Here he awaits us; here, and nowhere else, may he be found; whoever calls on him here, will be heard immediately: here is the throne of grace; here no one that comes to him, is excluded. But those who regard him as vainly dwelling in this position, and, in some other aspect, presume to serve and call upon God who created heaven and earth, may see their sentence already pronounced in Ps. 18, 42, where it is said concerning such: "They cried, but there was none to save them: even unto the Lord, but he answered them not."

In the third place, we must believe, that his mother was a virgin. This the Apostle clearly indicates, where he says, the Son of God was made of a woman, that is, not of a man, like other children; he only among all others, is born of a woman alone.— The Apostle did not feel disposed to say, of a virgin, because that is neither a name nor a state in nature. But woman is a name and a state in nature, which is naturally adapted to bearing fruit and bringing forth children. Thus the mother of Christ is a

E

neal, natural woman, who brought forth that fruit; yet from herself alone, not from a man; hence she is a virgin woman, and not simply a virgin.

The Apostle attaches more importance to the birth of Christ, than to the virginity of Mary. For this reason he passes in silence her virginity, which is only a peculiar, personal ornament, beneficial to her only, pointing out her woman-hood, which is beneficial not only to her, but also to her fruit. To Christ, her virginity is not so important, as is her woman-hood. Nor was she selected as a virgin for her sake, but for the sake of Christ, because he desired such a woman to be his mother, so that he might be born without sin,—a thing which could not occur, without a virgin woman, who could conceive and bring forth without the interposition of man.

The testament of God seems to force this conclusion, where it is said, All the nations of the earth shall be blessed in the seed of Abraham. If they are to be blessed, it is evident that they must be under a curse, in consequence of their physical birth, which takes place in sin, resulting from Adam. If this seed of Abraham is to be a blessing to all, it cannot be under a curse itself; and consequently the Savior could not issue from Adam's birth, which is wholly under the curse.

He must be the natural child, flesh and blood, of Abraham, moreover, in order that the testament of God, who cannot falsify himself, may hold. But what must be the result of this course of reasoning? He is to be a natural child, born of flesh and blood, and still he is not to be a child of carnal birth. The difficulty is removed by the fact, that a woman alone, not a man, was chosen for this purpose; so that a real, natural child, truly the seed of Abraham, might be born of a woman, without sin, but full of blessings, in order that, in him, all who are, in consequence of their own birth, under the curse, may be blessed. In this way the requirements of God's testament are fully met, the idea of a carnal birth and the inordinate desire of Adam, is avoided, and a physical birth is really effected, in a spiritual manner.

If, therefore, on account of her virginity, Mary, the holy virgin, is entitled to high honors, she is entitled to infinitely higher ones, on account of her woman-hood; because the organs of her sex were called into action, in order that the testament of God might be fulfilled, and the blessed seed of Abraham might be the blessed fruit of her sex; for the accomplishment of which her virginity alone would have been insufficient, yes, entirely useless.

In the fourth place, we must believe, that Christ alone has fulfilled the law; as he says, Matt. 5, 17:— "Think not that I am come to destroy the law, * * but to fulfill." This, too, is the meaning of the testament, where it is said: All the world is condemned, "and in thy seed [Abraham's] shall all the nations of the earth be blessed," Gen. 22, 18. Now, if every one is condemned, the person cannot be good, is destitute of blessing, and like Cain; nor, can the works be good, as already stated: and, hence, God does not regard the works, but the persons, Abel and Cain. Nor do the works of the law render any one pious or just.

Since Christ rejects all works of the law, demanding in the first place the blessing and goodness of the person, it may seem, as if he rejects good works, and intends to destroy all the law, when, at the same time, he really teaches us to perform good works. It is for this reason that he speaks in opposition to such erroneous views. Matt. 5, 17: "Think not that I am come to destroy the law," because I reject the works of the law; I rather design to fulfill it, through the faith that is in me, which first renders the person good, and then enables him to do really good works.

In like manner, St. Paul says, where he rejects all works of the law, and extols faith alone: "Do we then make void the law through faith? God forbid: yea, we establish the law,"— Rom. 3, 31. So, too, it is said at the present time, in reference to us, that we forbid good works, when we condemn the course of conduct in the cathedrals and cloisters, in the performance of works; when, at the same time, we really desire the people to entertain true faith first,—through which their persons may become good, and be blessed in Christ, the seed of Abraham, so that they may perform good works, which contribute to the mortification of the body and to the good of mankind. To this end, however, the works performed in the cathedrals and cloisters contribute nothing; as we have already stated.

But we must observe, that no one is able to fulfill the law, unless he is first liberated from it. It is necessary, for this reason, to pay particular attention to the peculiar phraseology of Paul, when he speaks of being under the law, in order that we may ascertain who is really under the law and who is not under it. All who perform good works, simply because they are commanded, and in consequence of the fear of punishment, or the expectation of reward, are under the law. Their piety and good deeds result from constraint, and not from a willing spirit. Hence, the law is their master and driver, and they are its servants in a state of bondage. This is the disposition of all men, apart from Christ, the blessed seed of Abraham. Our experience and conscience teach us this. Were it not for the restraints of the law, the fear of punishment, or the expectation of reward, and were each one allowed to act according to his own inclinations, in regard to doing good or evil, uninfluenced by the fear of punishment, or the expectation of reward, he would do evil, neglecting that which is good, especially under the influence of temptation and alluring circumstances. But when the law interposes with its threatenings and promises, he abstains from evil, and endeavors to do that which is good: not through love for the good, and hatred towards the evil, but through the fear of punishment, or the expectation of reward. For this reason they are under the law, and are controlled by it, like servants. These are saints like Cain.

Those, however, who are liberated from the law, do good, and avoid evil, regardless of the threatenings and promises of the law, or of the fear of punishment, or the expectation of reward; they do it from a free, spontaneous spirit,—from love for the good and hatred to the evil,—delighting in the law of God. Even if there were no law given, their disposition would still be the same; they would do good, and abstain from evil. Such persons are really children. Nature cannot produce this disposition; it arises from the seed of Abraham; by his blessing, Christ makes persons of such disposition, through his grace, and the influences of the Holy Spirit.

Wherefore, to be liberated from the law, is not equivalent to being at liberty to do evil, and to avoid good, according to our inclination. But it is equivalent to doing good and avoiding evil, not in consequence of fear, or the restraints and requirements of the law, but from pure love and a cheerful spirit; as if, were there no law, our course of conduct would still flow along in this direction freely and spontaneously. Precisely as the body eats, drinks, digests, discharges, sleeps, moves, stands, sits, and performs its natural functions. It needs no law, no driving. It acts of itself at the proper times and occasions, without fearing punishment or expecting reward; so that it may be properly said, indeed, that the body is not under any law, and still it performs its functions freely and spontaneously.

Observe, a willingness must dwell in us, so free and spontaneous, as to incline to good, and recoil from evil. This is spiritual liberation and redemption from the law. This is the meaning of St. Paul, 1 Tim. 1, 9: "The law is not made for a righteous man:" that is, from his own impulses, he inclines to good, and abstains from evil, without the fear of punishment or the expectation of reward. Again, Rom. 6, 15: "We are not under the law, but under grace;" that is, we are children, not servants; we incline to good from a free spirit, without compulsion or restraint. Again, Rom. 8, 15: "Ye have not received the spirit of bondage again to fear; but ye have received the spirit of adoption, whereby we cry, Abba, Father." The law produces a fearful, servile, Cain-like spirit, but grace, a free, filial, Abel-like disposition, through Christ, the seed of Abraham, in regard to which it is said, Ps. 51, 10 : "Renew a right spirit within me, O God."* Again, in Ps. 110, 3, it is said concerning the people of Christ : Thy people shall be willing, * * in the beauties of holiness.

Thus Christ has fulfilled the law, freely and willingly, not through any compulsion or restraint of the law.— And besides him, there never was any one, nor will there ever be any one, who will thus fulfill it, unless he do it through him. For this reason St. Paul says here: He was "made under the law, to redeem them that were under the law."

In the fifth place, we should believe that Christ did this for our benefit, in order that he might make children out of us servants. What is implied by the declaration, "To redeem them that were under the law?" Doubtless, to redeem us from under the law.— But how does he redeem us from under the law? As already stated, not by the threatenings or rewards of the law, but through the gift of a free, spontaneous spirit, that acts without compulsion or restraint, regardless of the terrors or rewards of the law; precisely as if there were no law, and everything would still proceed from a natural impulse, as did Adam and Eve, pevious to the fall.

But how is the fact, that he gives us such a spirit, and redeems us from under the law, accomplished? In no other way, but through faith. He that believes that Christ came for that purpose, and that he has accomplished all this, for the purpose of redeeming us, is really redeemed. As he believes, so it shall be with him. This faith carries with itself the spirit which renders us children, as the Apostle here explains himself, saying : Christ has redeemed us from under the law,

---

* B. "Create in me a clean heart, O God : and renew a right spirit within me."

---

that we might receive the adoption of sons. All this must be accomplished through faith, as we have stated.— Thus we have these five points in this text.*

The question, however, still arises, here : How can Christ be under the law, if to do good through the restraints and compulsion of the law, is to be under the law, and if no one who is under it, can fulfill it ? God requires free and spontaneous action in conformity with the law. The Apostle, however, seems to make a distinction here, when he says : Christ was put or made under the law; that is, he voluntarily put himself under it; so, too, by his voluntary consent the Father put him under it, when at the same time he was not really under it. We, however, were put under it, contrary to our inclinations. We, as he says, were naturally and essentially under it, in opposition to our will. Whilst Christ was, not naturally, but freely and willingly under the law, we were naturally, not freely and willingly, under it.

There is a marked difference between being put under the law, and being under the law; precisely as there is a difference between will and nature. There is a very material difference between that which is done according to the pleasures of the will and that which is done from the impulses of nature. That which is done according to the pleasures of the will, may be omitted, as there is no compulsion. But whatever is done from the impulses of nature, must be done, because it is not optional. An individual may go to the Rhine, or he may not go. But he must eat, drink, sleep, grow, digest, and advance in years, regardless of his will. Christ put himself under the law willingly, when he had it in his power not to do so. But we had naturally to be under it; there was no other alternative; we could not spontaneously observe and endure the law, as if there were no law requiring us so to do, as already stated. But Christ, independent of any obligation to do the

---

* B. How Christ was made, or put under the law.

law, observed and kept it freely and willingly, as if there were no such requisition.

Take for illustration the circumstance of St. Peter, the Apostle, Acts 12, 6, 7, who lay captive in the prison of Herod, bound with two chains, between two soldiers, whilst the keepers stood at the door. The angel of God entered the prison with a great light, and awoke Peter, leading him out through all the keepers and the door, and leaving the chains in the prison. By this event we may learn how Christ liberates us from under the law. Let us take it into consideration.

Peter was an inmate of the prison, not by the consent of his will; he was kept there by force; he knew not how to extricate himself. The angel also entered the prison, but willingly; he was not compelled to be there; he was not there for his own sake, but for the sake of Peter; he knew how to extricate himself. Now when Peter followed, adhering to him, he was liberated.

This prison is the law, in and under which our conscience is unwillingly held captive. For no one willingly does the good required by the law, or omits the evil forbidden by it. He does it through the fear of punishment, or the expectation of reward. This fear or threatening and this reward or expectation of reward, are the two chains, which keep us in prison under the law. The keepers are the teachers of the law, who make known to us the law. In this way we go, yes, we lie unwillingly in the law. Christ is the angel who willingly approaches us in this prison under the law, even willingly doing the works which we unwillingly perform. This he does for our benefit, in order that he may attach us to himself and extricate us. He well knows how to liberate. For he is already free and independent in regard to his will. Behold then, if we cleave to him and follow, we too shall be extricated.

But how is this effected? We cleave to Christ and follow him, when we believe that he accomplishes all this for our benefit. This faith introduces the Spirit. Then we, too, shall do all these things freely, unfettered, and liberated from the prison of the law. The two chains, the fear of punishment and the expectation of reward, will no longer restrain us; all our actions will flow out freely from pure love and a free disposition.

But for the purpose of perceiving more clearly how Christ was put under the law, we must observe, that he put himself under the law in a twofold manner. In the first place, he put himself under the works of the law. He permitted himself to be circumcised, and to be presented and purified in the Temple. He was subservient to his father and mother, &c., when at the same time there was no obligation requiring it. For he was Lord over all laws. But he did it freely, independent of any fear of punishment or expectation of reward, that might result to him. But, when we take into consideration the mere external works, we perceive very little difference between him and others who are actuated by compulsion and restraint. Hence, his liberty and willingness were concealed from the people; precisely as the prison and unwillingness of others were concealed. Thus he proceeds under the law, and still he is not under it. He acts like those who are under it, and yet he is not thus under it. In regard to his will, he is free, and for this reason he is not under the law. In regard to its works, which he observes freely, he is under it. But we, both in regard to our will and the works of the law, are under it. For we engage in these through the restraints of our will.

In the second place, he willingly put himself under the penalty and punishment of the law. He not only performed the works of the law, which he was under no obligation to do, but he also willingly and innocently suffered the penalty which the law threatens and adjudges to all who do not observe it. Now, the law adjudges all, who do not keep it, to death, condemnation, and damnation, as St. Paul, Gal. 3, 10, quotes from Deut. 27, 26: "Cursed is every one that continueth not in all things which are written in the book of the law to do them."

It is sufficiently evident from the remarks which we have already made, that no person who is out of Christ, is able to keep the law, and all such are under it, like servants, fettered and constrained. Hence it follows, that whoever does not observe the law, deserves its judgments and penalty. For this reason, whoever is under the law, according to the first manner, according to its works, must also be under it according to the second manner, according to its punishment; so that, according to the first mode, all our works are sinful, because they are not performed from a willing disposition, but in opposition to our will; and according to the second mode, we are adjudged and condemned to death and condemnation.

Here Christ intervenes, before the sentence is executed upon us; he interposes, and approaches us under the sentence; he suffers the penalty, death, the curse, and condemnation; precisely as if he had violated the whole law himself, and deserved the whole penalty that rests upon the transgressor; when at the same time he has not really broken it, but fulfilled it, without being under obligation so to do; so that his innocence is of a twofold character. First, he was under no obligation to suffer, even if he had observed no law, as he had a right not to do. Second, because he kept it from a superabundant good will, and because he was consequently under no obligation to suffer its penalty. So, on the other hand, our guilt is twofold. First, because we were under obligation to keep it, and failed so to do; and consequently we should justly suffer all its calamities. Second, because, if we had observed it, we should reasonably suffer whatever God designs.

Behold, this is putting the Son of God under the law, that he redeemed those who were under the law. For us, for our good, he accomplished all this, not for himself. He desired to manifest towards us nothing but love and goodness and mercy; as St. Paul, Gal. 3, 13, says: "Christ hath redeemed us from the curse of the law, being made a curse for us." As if he should say, For us he put himself under the law and complied with its demands; so that all who believe that he did this, might be redeemed from under the law and its curse.

Observe then, the abundant treasure with which the believing Christian is blessed. To him all the works and sufferings of Christ are attributed as his own; so that he may rely upon these as if they were his own, and as if he had accomplished them himself. For, as already said, Christ did all these, not for himself, but for us. He needs none of them; he accumulated the treasure, so that on it we might hang, rely, and rest. This faith, moreover, is accompanied by the Holy Spirit.

What more should God do? How can the heart help being free, joyful, cheerful, and willing in God and Christ? What work or suffering can it meet, which it will not endure, singing, and leaping with love and praise for God? Where this is not the case, there is assuredly some defect about our faith. For the greater our faith, the greater our liberty and joy; the less our faith, the less our joy. This, observe, is the Christian redemption and freedom from under the law and its curse; that is, from sin and death; not that the law or death shall be removed, but because both, the law and death, shall become as if they were not. The law shall not lead us to sin, nor death to shame; but faith shall lead us through into righteousness and eternal life.*

---

* A. Here we might take occasion to admonish our poor Cain-like saints, the ecclesiastics, if it were possible to admonish them in their condition. If they would observe their orders, laws, ceremonies, prayers, masses, apparel, meats, &c., like Christ did the law, they might be retained; namely, if they would assign to Christian faith its proper sphere, giving to it the regulating control of the heart, and acknowledging that they do not become pious and happy through their orders, conditions, or works, but alone through faith in Christ, and if they would then observe them, with the understanding that they are optional, and useful merely for the mortification of the body, and the benefit of our neighbor. But, when they observe them under the

CONCERNING THE PEOPLE OF THE LAW AND GRACE.

Let this suffice in regard to the text. We were compelled to treat this subject elaborately, from the fact that there is so little known concerning the doctrine of faith, without a knowledge of which, we cannot properly understand Paul. Follows:

"And because ye are sons, God hath sent forth the Spirit of his Son into your hearts, crying, Abba, Father."

Here we perceive that the Holy Spirit is communicated, not through works, but through faith; for he says here that the Spirit is given to them because they are children, and not servants. Children believe; servants work; children are free from the law; servants are under it. All this we may clearly perceive from our previous illustrations. It may be necessary, however, for us to pay some attention to the sense, in which St. Paul uses the words, child and servant, free and bond. Works performed through compulsion are the works of servants, and works performed through the freedom of choice, are the works of children.

Why does he say the Holy Spirit was given to them, because they were children, since the Holy Spirit makes children out of servants, and must be essentially present before they become children? Answer: He is speaking in the same sense, in which he spoke in the third verse, where it is said: Before the time was fulfilled, we were under the elements, &c. They were children prospectively, in the sight of God. For this reason the Holy Spirit was sent to them, to make them children, as they were designed to be.

He calls the Spirit, the Spirit of the Son of God. Why not, the Spirit of God? Simply, because he wishes to adhere closely to the point. They are styled children of God, and for this reason God sends them even the Spirit that Christ has, who is also a child, so that with him they may cry, "Abba, Father!" As if he should say, God sends you his Spirit, who dwells in his Son, so that you may be brethren and heirs with him, crying as he does, "Abba, Father." In this way the unspeakable goodness and grace of God are extolled, because, through faith, we occupy with Christ the undivided blessings, and have all that he has and is, even his Spirit.

By these words, moreover, the doctrine of the third person, the Holy Ghost, in the Trinity, is established, because he not only dwells in Christ, as in an individual, but he also is his, deriving his divine essence from him, as he derives it from the Father. Otherwise the language of Paul would be false, where he says: "The Spirit of his Son." No creature can say, nor can any creature say in reference to himself, that the Holy Spirit is his spirit.—He is the Spirit of God only. Creatures belong to the Holy Spirit. —It is true, one might say, My Holy Spirit, in the same sense, in which we say, My God, my Lord, &c.—Hence, the Son is God, because the Spirit of God is his Spirit.

Here every one should be careful to ascertain whether he feels the Holy Spirit, and perceives his voice. St. Paul says, When the Holy Spirit is in the heart, he cries, "Abba, Father;" so, too, he says, Rom. 8, 15: "Ye have received the Spirit of adoption, whereby we cry, "Abba, Father." This crying we perceive, when without doubt or vacillation the conscience is firmly persuaded and fully satisfied, that its sins are forgiven, and that it is a child of God, and when thus assured of salvation, it may with a joyful and undoubting heart approach God and call him its beloved Father. Of this it must be so certain, that its own life is not more certain, and that it would rather suffer death in all its forms, yes, hell in all its pangs, than

---

impression that they are essential and must be observed, in order to become pious and happy, they are delusive and sinful, leading people to hell, and meriting its everlasting tortures: because they militate against the free, filial faith, through their servile and compulsory works. Faith cannot exist beside such stupid works. It alone renders us pious and happy, and constitutes us children. Then all works are optional; we may freely observe and endure all that God directs, and all that contributes to the welfare of our neighbor. These, and no other, are the works of faith; it seeks not after numerous masses, appointed fasts, and peculiar apparel, special meats, and selected positions, persons, or works; yea, it rejects all these as obstructions to its liberty.

be deprived of the Spirit, or doubt in reference to him. It would be doubting the abundant achievements and sufferings of Christ, too much, not to believe that he has superabundantly accomplished all these for us, and not to let them incite and strengthen us in this confidence, with as much force, as sin or temptation terrifies us from it.

It is true, a conflict may arise here. An individual may feel and fear that he is not a child of God; he may feel and imagine that God is a judge over him, angry and austere. This was the case with Job, as well as with others. But in this conflict, this filial confidence must achieve the victory, although it may tremble and quake; or else all will be lost. But when a person like Cain hears this, he will bless himself, crossing his hands and feet, exclaiming with great humility: Ay, guard me, O God, against such abominable heresy and presumption! Shall I, a poor sinner, be so presumptuous as to say, I am a child of God? No, no, I will humbly confess that I am a poor sinner, &c. Let such a person go, guard against him as against the worst enemy to Christian faith and to your salvation.

We know full well, too, that we are poor sinners; but it is of no advantage to contemplate what we are and accomplish. We should rather take into consideration what Christ is and what he has accomplished, and still accomplishes for us. We are not speaking about our nature, but about the grace of God, which is as much above us, as "the heaven is high above the earth," and as far, "as the east is from the west," Ps. 103, 11, 12. If you regard it as a great thing to be a child of God, think it not a small thing, that the Son of God came, was born of a woman, and made under the law, so that you might be such a child.

The works of God are great and important; they fill us with joy, courage, and fortitude, so as to know no fear, and to be able to endure whatever may befall us. But the principles of those like Cain, are narrow and contracted, producing nothing but trembling, quaking hearts, altogether unable to endure and act, starting at the shaking of a leaf; as it is said, Lev. 26, 36. Let us, therefore, adhere closely to the text. The crying of the Spirit in your heart, you must perceive. For, it is indeed the cry of your heart; why then should you not perceive it?

St. Paul introduces the word, *crying*, when he might as easily have said, the Spirit whispers, or speaks, or sings. The former is more forcible. He calls and cries with full power;— that is, with a full heart, because everything lives and moves in such confidence; as it is said, Rom. 8, 26:— "The Spirit itself maketh intercessions for us with groanings which can not be uttered;" again, Rom. 8, 16:— "The Spirit itself beareth witness with our spirit, that we are the children of God." Why, then, should our hearts not perceive this crying, intercession, and bearing of witness?

O, how precious temptations and afflictions are in this direction. They drive us to these cries, waking up the spirit. But we fear and start at the cross. For this reason we never perceive the Spirit, but continue in the condition of Cain. Now, if you do not perceive this crying, reflect, cease not your petitions till God hears you: you are like Cain; your condition is perilous. You must not expect, however, that nothing but such crying alone will exist purely in you; the cry of murder will rise up there, so as to drive you to, and exercise you in such crying. This was the case with all others.

Your sins will also cry; that is, they will produce in your conscience strong tendencies to despair. But the Spirit of Christ shall and must out-cry that cry; that is, he will produce in you a confidence stronger than the tendencies of that despair; as St. John, 1 John 3, 19-22, says:— "Hereby we know that we are of the truth, and shall assure our hearts before him. If our heart condemn us, God is greater than our heart, and knoweth all things. Beloved if our heart condemn us not, then have we confidence towards God. And whatsoever we ask, we receive of him, because we keep his commandments, and do those things that are pleasing in his sight."

Now, this crying and calling of the Spirit is nothing else but a strong, powerful, indubitable confidence arising from our hearts, as from loving children, towards God, as a beloved Father.

Here you may perceive how highly the life of a Christian is exalted above nature. Nature is incapable of such a cry, and of such confidence in God. It merely starts, and cries the cry of murder, upon itself, exclaiming, O wo, O wo, thou austere and intolerable judge; like Cain cried to God, Gen. 4, 13: "My punishment is greater than I can bear. Behold, thou hast driven me out this day from the face of the earth; and from thy face shall I be hid;* and it shall come to pass, that every one that findeth me shall slay me." Such exclamations are and must exist in all saints like Cain. Why? Because they depend upon themselves and their works, and not upon God and his Son. who was sent, born of a woman, and made under the law; nor do they believe that this was designed for them; nor are they concerned about it; they are occupied merely with their own works, endeavoring thus to help themselves, and to secure the grace of God.

Yes, in persecuting this faith, and in defaming and condemning it as heresy and presumption, they act like their father, Cain, did towards his brother, Abel. In this way they slay in themselves Christ, their brother. This innocent blood will not cease crying towards heaven, against them;— like the blood of Abel did against Cain. God will inquire after this Abel, and demand of each one of them; Where is Christ, your brother? Then Cain, deranged as it were, will proceed, and, presuming to know nothing about him, will say: What do I know about him; am I my brother's keeper? This is equivalent to saying:— Shall I be so presumptuous as to regard myself pious and holy, and a child of God, merely through Christ?

* B. "and I shall be a fugitive and a vagabond in the earth."

No, no, I will work till I become pious myself without him. Behold, thus the crying blood of Abel continued on Cain, and the crying blood of Christ will continue on all unbelievers, and still cry for vengeance and wrath. But, in regard to believers, it will cry for pure grace and reconciliation, through his Spirit.

The Apostle introduces a Hebrew word and a Greek word in apposition. *Abba, Pater.* In the Hebrew, Abba means father, and hence the prelates in certain cloisters are called Abbots. In former times the holy hermits called their chiefs *Abba Pater.* These terms were introduced also in the Latin and German languages. Abba, Pater is equivalent to father, father: or in full German, Mein Vater, mein Vater; or lieber Vater, lieber Vater.

But why does he duplicate the word and cry of the Spirit? Allow me to give my opinion. In the first place, he does it, to show the force and greatness of the cry. When a person cries very earnestly, he frequently repeats his cries. Thus the cry and confidence of the heart must be so strong and great as not to be suppressed by sin and the cries of Cain.

In the second place, it seems to be characteristic of the Scriptures, to indicate, by a duplication of words or phrases, certainty and assurance. Joseph, Gen. 41, 32, says to king Pharaoh, that in this way God indicates the certainty of a thing, which will assuredly come to pass, as the words say. Thus here too, the spirit cries Father twice in order that we may be certain and sure that God is and will be our Father; so that, indeed, our confidence may not only be great, but also certain.

In the third place, it may have been his design to show, that it is to remain steadfast. The first Abba indicates its commencement. But here a great conflict will arise. The devil will assail it without intermission. For this reason it is necessary for us to persevere, and employ the other *Pater* too; that is, we must not cease; as we have begun to cry, we should ever continue so to do. From this process an experience of this confidence will result, which must fill us with the utmost assurance and certainty. It may, perhaps, have also been the design of St. Paul, when he introduced the word Abba,—a Hebrew word, rather strange and not generally understood,—and when he afterwards introduced the word Pater,—a native, Greek term, well understood,—(he was writing in the Greek, and speaking to Greeks,)—to show that a person is not accustomed to and familiar with this confidence in its incipiency. But after he shall have properly used and exercised it, he becomes as familiar with it, as it were part of his nature, and as if he were at home with God, his Father.

"Wherefore thou art no more a servant, but a son: and if a son, then an heir of God, through Christ."

No more, (says he,) Christ having come and being known, art thou a servant. There is a remarkable difference between a child and a servant, as already stated. Their dispositions are entirely dissimilar. A child is free and willing; a servant constrained and unwilling. The child is subject to faith; the servant, to works.

From this we may perceive that, in the sight of God, no one can accomplish any thing in regard to his salvation, through works; it must be secured and enjoyed, previous to the accomplishment of works, so that these may follow freely and spontaneously, to the honor of God, and the benefit of our neighbor, uninfluenced by the fear of punishment or the expectation of reward. This is implied in the words:

"If a son, then an heir of God."

It is sufficiently apparent from what we have already said, that faith alone, independent of all works, constitutes us children. If it constitutes us children, it constitutes us heirs. A child is an heir. If the inheritance already exists, can it be secured in the first instance through works? It is inconsistent, to conclude, that the inheritance, bequeathed through pure grace, is already present, and that it must still be sought and secured through works and merits, as if it were not bequeathed and in existence. The inheritance is nothing else but eternal salvation. We have frequently asserted, that through his baptism and faith, a Christian is already in possession of everything, and that it is given to him all at once; but he does not yet perceive it openly; he possesses it simply in faith, in consequence of the fact, that, in this life, he could not bear the open manifestation of such blessings.

Thus says St. Paul, Rom. 8, 24: We are already saved, but in hope; we do not yet see it, but we wait for it. Again, St. Peter, 1 Pet. 1, 4: Your salvation is reserved and ready in heaven, to be revealed in the last time.

For this reason, the efforts of a Christian ought not to be influenced, like those of a servant, by a disposition to secure advantages, but by a desire to aid and benefit others; so that he may live and act, indeed, not for himself, but for his neighbor here on earth. In this way, he lives and works most assuredly also for God. Through his faith, he has enough already for himself; he is rich, full, and happy.

He adds, "Through Christ," lest some one might conclude that this inheritance is given without any merit and cost. Although it cost us nothing, and although it is given without our merit, yet it has placed Christ under great obligations; on account of it, he was made under the law, for us, in order to secure and merit it for all who believe in him. When we confer a favor upon our neighbor, without his merit, it costs him nothing; yet, that which we bestow on him freely and through pure goodness, like Christ bestowed and still bestows his blessing upon us, costs us our labor and substance.

The fact, that St. Paul says, that servants no longer exist, but children, and that, notwithstanding, few believe in Christ and are children, and the world is full of heretics and persons like Cain, may somewhat confuse illiterate persons. But we must bear in mind that he makes this assertion on account of the doctrine inculcated; as if he said: Before Christ came, and before the Gospel was preached, through which children exist, nothing but the law was preached, which makes nothing but servants through its works. The Gospel being preached now, we have no need for the servant-maker, the law; all who were previously servants like Cain, through the law and its works, become pious and happy, through faith, without works. For this reason, to say, servants no longer exist, but children, is equivalent to saying that no servile doctrine is to be preached and inculcated now; so that we may become, children, not servants. That is, nothing but faith and the Gospel are to be preached and to be our doctrine. This imparts the Spirit, teaches us to confide in God, and to serve our neighbor. In this way all the law is fulfilled.

Thus he calls the Galatians away from the teachers who had led them back again to the law and its works; like the Pope with his foolish laws, through bishops, priests, and monks, has now, yes long since, misled the people, and exterminated the Christain faith;—a thing which was foretold in the Scriptures concerning that Anti-christ. For this reason, whoever desires to be saved, should shun him and all his adherents, and all ecclesiastical orders, as he would Lucifer's own servants and apostles.

NEW YEAR'S DAY.

EPISTLE, GAL. 3, 23-29.

But before faith came, we were kept under the law, shut up unto the faith which should afterwards be revealed.

Wherefore the law was our schoolmaster to bring us unto Christ, that we might be justified by faith.

But after that faith is come, we are no longer under a school-master.

For ye are the children of God by faith in Christ Jesus.

For as many of you as have been baptized into Christ, have put on Christ.

There is neither Jew nor Greek, there is neither bond nor free, there is neither male nor female: for ye are all one in Christ Jesus.

And if ye be Christ's, then are ye Abraham's seed, and heirs according to the promise.

THIS, too, is really a Pauline epistle concerning faith, written in opposition to works, and, from the epistle next preceding, is easy to be understood. What is said there in reference to the servant, should be understood here, also, in reference to the pupil. For, these two illustrations, St. Paul introduces to teach us what the law does, and what it profits. We must, therefore, speak again of the law and its works; viz., that these works are twofold: some are extorted by punishment, or excited by the expectation of reward or gain; others are done freely and spontaneously, without the fear of punishment and the expectation of reward, from pure kindness, and a desire for that which is good. The *first* are the works of servants and pupils; the *second* are the works of a child and of free heirs.

For a youth under a tutor, does not what he desires, but, through fear of the rod, does what his master desires; and, whilst under the control of his master, no one can know his real character. But if he were free, his true character would appear; he would manifest the disposition of his nature, and the works which he would do, would be his own. The works, therefore, which he must perform through such restraint and coercion, are not really his own works, but rather the works of the tutor who extorts and forces them from him. For, were he not under the control of the tutor, he would not do any of these works, but the reverse.

In this plain, but well adapted example, St. Paul presents the province of the law, and the power of free will or nature together, so clearly that they could not be more clearly illustrated; and from this every one may learn the meaning, end, and operation of the law, as well as the power and conduct of nature.

For, in this youth we perceive a twofold effect: first, through this fear and constraint of his tutor, he is preserved from many evils into which he would otherwise fall, and indulge in a wicked and licentious life, becoming entirely dissolute; secondly, his heart is filled with more hatred towards his tutor who curbs his will; and his condition is as follows: the greater his external restraint from evil, the greater his internal hatred towards the one who restrains him; so that as, on the one hand, sin decreases externally, on the other, it increases internally. This we perceive also in experience, that youths who are most strenuously reared, are, when free, much worse than those whose rearing has not been so rigid. So impossible is it to help nature with commandments and punishments. Something else is required.

Thus too, as long as any one is in a state of nature, and destitute of grace, he does not what he desires, but he must do what the law, his tutor, requires. And all must confess that, were it not for hell, and the punishment of the law, no one would do good. Therefore, because such works are not the works of a free spirit, they are not his, but they are the works of the coercive and restraining law; so that the Apostle may well pronounce such works, not our works, but the *works of the law*, because that which we do contrary to our will, is not our work, but the work of him who constrains us.

Thus, if some one would take my hand by force, and with it slay any one, or give alms to an indigent person, this work would not be mine, although my hand did it, but that of him who forced it thereto; this work would, therefore, neither injure nor benefit me the least. Thus, also, the works of the law make no one pious, notwithstanding they are done by us. For our will performs them merely through fear of the punishment of the law; it would much rather do otherwise, if the coercive and menacing law did not constrain it; therefore, they are not our works. Now, every one must be saved through his own act.

If, moreover, any one, not through fear of punishment, as he might perhaps imagine, performs such works, he does them, nevertheless, on account of the promises and allurements of the law. This is as bad and wrong indeed, or worse than the other; just as if heaven were not promised; as if it were known that all must be done gratuitously, it would not be done at all. These works are, therefore, in like manner, not our own, but the works of the law and its allurements or incitations arising from the promise of favors and rewards. These works are more dangerous, and difficult to perceive, than the former, as they are more subtile and much more in conformity with free, spontaneous, genuine works.

But in tribulation, they will appear in their true character, when they are rejected, and a gratuitous performance of them is required, uninfluenced by the pursuit of reward, alone to the honor of God and for the benefit of our neighbor; here nature lies prostrate and impotent; here it will be found that she does no good work of her own, but merely extraneous works of the law; precisely as an irrational creature runs and labors, through fear of the lash, or for the sake of its food. How many pious people of honorable character, do you think, would now exist, if shame, punishment, hell, or heaven, were not before their eyes? Not one. Good order is preserved through fear of punishment or the expectation of gain. Hence these are all false and deceptive works, as the Scripture declares: "All men are liars and vain." Ps. 39, 7, Ps. 116, 11.

Thus, we perceive in all persons these two effects: First, by their tutor, the law, they are secured against a shameful and dissolute course of conduct, and, kept in the discipline of these works of the law, they sustain an honorable life externally; secondly, in their hearts, they really become enemies to the law and its punishments, and the more pressing the chastisement, the greater their hatred. Who is not an enemy to death and hell? But what else is this, but to be an enemy to the law which imposes such chastisement? But what else is it, to be an enemy to the law, but to be an enemy to righteousness? But what else is it, to be an enemy to righteousness, but to be an enemy to God himself? Is it not concluded here, that we are not only unjust, but also hate righteousness, love sin, and are enemies to God, from our whole heart, no matter how beautiful and honorable our external conduct may appear in our works.

Now, indeed, God desires to be loved with the whole heart, as the commandment, Deut. 6, 5, reads: "Thou shalt love the Lord thy God with all thine heart," &c., and that all our good works should really be our own, and those of the tutor, the law, of death or hell, or of heaven; that is, that we should not perform them through fear of death or hell, or for the sake of enjoying heaven, but through a free spirit, a desire and love for righteousness; for he that does a good work through fear of death or hell, does it not to the honor of God, but through fear of death and hell, and it is a work of death and hell; for these have extorted it from him, and on their account alone he does it, otherwise he would not have done it. He, therefore, remains a servant and slave of death and hell, with all such works; but if he remains a servant of death and hell, he must also die and be condemned, and the proverb, "He that fears hell, will go therein;" again, "Trembling will not deliver from death," applies to him.

But say you: "What will result from this? Who then can be saved? Who is without trembling and the fear of death and hell? Who does his works, or leads an honorable life, without such fear?" I answer: Aye! who then that is filled with such fear and a hatred of God's law and righteousness, loves God? Where then is nature? Where then is free will? Still you will not believe how necessary the grace of God is; still you will not admit that the conduct of all men is sinful, false, and deceptive; still you cannot be persuaded that works do not make any one pious.

Here you perceive indeed the necessity and advantage of the law, and God's design in it, namely, these two objects: *first*, to preserve discipline among us and to impel us to an honorable life externally, so that we may live among each other, and not devour one another; which would be the case, were there no law, no fear, no punishment, as it was formerly among certain heathens. For these reasons God did not abolish the secular sword, in the New Testament dispensation; nay, he established it, although he did not use it; and it is not necessary for his followers, but, to constrain impertinent and dissolute conduct, and to enable persons to live among each other in peace, to maintain themselves, and to rear their families. Otherwise, all countries would become dissolute, over-run with murderers and robbers; no woman or child would remain unviolated; but by the sword and the law, they are preserved in, and impelled to, a quiet, peaceable, and honorable life. Through these, however, they do not become pious,—their heart is not ameliorated. Their hands only, are constrained and bound, and these works, or this righteousness, are not their own, but those of the sword which extorts these works from them, and which through its punishment and the fear which it inspires, produces these results in them.

Thus, too, God's law urges and impels us, through fear of death and hell, to forsake many evils, and, like a tutor, keeps us in an honorable life externally. But by this, no one becomes pious before God,—the heart still remains an enemy to this tutor, hates his chastisements, and would rather be free.

Secondly, God's design in the law, is thus to enable man, through it, to know himself; to perceive how false and unjust his heart is; how far he is still from God; how entirely impotent his nature is; to disdain the honesty of his own conduct, and to perceive that it is nothing in comparison to that which belongs to the fulfillment of the law; and thus to be humbled; to come to the cross; to sigh after Christ; to long for his grace; to despair of himself; to place all his consolation in Christ, who will then give him another spirit, and change his heart; so that he will no longer fear death and hell, no longer look for life or heaven, being freely devoted to the law, will live in reference to it with a good, secure conscience, in the hour of death and during the whole course of his life, equally uninfluenced by the fear of death and the hope of heaven, or of any thing else. For thus says the Epistle, Heb. 2, 15: "And delivered them, who through fear of death, were all their lifetime subject to bondage." By this he shows clearly enough, indeed, that we must be without fear of death, and all who live in fear of death, are servants, and will not be saved. Now, neither nature nor law can liberate us from this fear. Nay, it increases that fear. Christ alone has liberated us from it: and if we believe in him, he will give us that free, undaunted spirit which fears neither death nor hell, which loves neither life nor heaven, but freely and joyfully serves God.

Hence, we perceive, first, how dangerous are the doctrines which, through commandments and laws, urge a person to believe that he must become pious through these. For in this way he is only separated further from God, from Christ, yea, from the law and all righteousness. These doctrines, thus inculcated, have no other effects, but that of rendering his conscience perpetually more fearful, timid, dispirited, and wretched, and of teaching him continually to fear death and hell alone, until ultimately his heart is filled with nothing but despair, so that in any aspect he must be the martyr of the devil.

Secondly, we see that there is a threefold use of the law, or that persons act in a threefold manner in reference to it. First, some disregard it wholly and entirely, and, in opposition to it, impudently lead a dissolute life. To these it is even as if it were not a law. Secondly, some, by means of the law, abstain from such a course of conduct, and are kept in an honorable life; thus they live externally within the discipline of the law, but internally they are enemies to the tutor,—all their actions proceed from fear of death and hell. Hence, they keep the law only externally; yea, the law keeps them externally; inwardly they do not keep it, nor are they kept by it. Thirdly, others keep it outwardly and inwardly; these are the tables of Moses in whom they are written outwardly and inwardly by the finger of God himself.

Now, as those of the first class are pious neither externally nor internally; so those of the second, are pious only externally and not in their hearts. But those of the third, are thoroughly pious. In reference to this, St. Paul, 1 Tim. 1, 8, 9, says: "But we know that the law is good, if a man use it lawfully." How then is it lawfully used? Answer: "The law is not made for the righteous man, but for the lawless." What is indicated by this? Nothing else but that whoever wishes to preach the law rightfully, must observe these three distinctions: he must not by any means preach the law to the third class, as if they should become pious through it; for this were perversion. But to the first class, it should be preached. For these it is instituted, that they may forsake their dissolute life, and permit themselves to be preserved under the tutor. But it is not enough for them to be thus preserved, and kept by the law; they must learn in return, to keep the law. Here, then, over and above the law, the Gospel must be preached, through which the grace of Christ, to keep the law, is given. Hence, there is quite a wide difference between observing or keeping the law, and being preserved or kept by it. The first neither keep it, nor are kept by it; the second are kept by it; the third keep it.

These three modes relative to the use of the law, are prefigured through Moses. First, when he broke the tables, when the Jews worshiped the golden calf, Exod. 32, 19. The breaking of these tables and their not reaching the people, point out the first class, who do not receive the law at all, but break it. Secondly, when he brought other tables which reached the people, but his face shone so bright, that Aaron and the people of Israel, could not endure the brightness and rays of his face; he had to hang a veil over it, when he wished to speak to them, Exod. 34, 30, 33. This indicates the second class, who receive the law, but keep it only externally: internally it is too bright for them, and they are afraid of it.

Therefore, hypocrites make for themselves a veil, as St. Paul explains it, 2 Cor. 3, 13, 14, 15, which is the arrogance of their works and external righteousness; they will not look the law right in the face, and perceive how futile such a righteousness is. Thus, as St. Paul says, "Even unto this day, * * * the veil is upon their heart."

Thus, too, Moses leads the people no further than to the Jordan, and slays two kings only, Sihon and Og, and divides the land to only two tribes and a half of the race of Israel. By this is indicated the half-righteousness, the little insignificant, outward righteousness. And yea, here, in the wilderness of Moab, Moses dies. No further can the law assist.

Joshua comes afterwards, and leads the whole multitude through the Jordan dry, into the country. Here there is no Moses, no law, but Joshua, Christ, who leads through faith, and fulfills all that was commanded by Moses. These are those to whom no law is given, as St. Paul says, and who become pious, not through works, but through grace; that is, those who do good, not through constraint of the law. Here there is no Moses. From all this, St. Paul, I think, should be easily understood in this Epistle; let us now take it into consideration.

"But before faith came, we were kept under the law, shut up unto the faith which should afterwards be revealed."

He does not say, before faith came, we were pious and kept the law; but on the contrary, the law kept us, and under it, we were locked up and preserved, so that we might not rush boldly and independently to the commission of our wickedness; yet this did not render us really pious. This locking-up and preservation however, were not designed to cause us to remain in this condition; but it was directed to the faith which was afterwards to be revealed, so that it might liberate and make us free; not in order to do evil, on account of which the law shut us up; but free in order to do good to which the law impelled us. Through this locking-up, we should learn to desire his faith, and to perceive our evil-disposed nature: for this liberation is spiritual, and liberates only the heart.

Thus if some one had you confined in a prison, in which you were very unwilling to remain, you might be released from it in two ways. First. physically, he might destroy the prison and make you personally free letting you go wherever you might desire. Secondly, he might render you mentally free, by many blessings upon you in this prison, lighting it up and making it roomy, and exceedingly pleasant, adorning it in the richest manner, so that no kingly palace, no kingdom, would be so desirable; and by so subduing and changing the disposition of your mind, that you would not for all the possessions of the world, be removed from it, but pray that it might be preserved, so that you might continue in it; which would no longer be a prison to you, but would have become a paradise. Tell me, which liberation would be the better? Would not the latter be preferable? For, by the former, you would remain a beggar as before; but here the disposition of your mind would be free, and you would be in possession of all that you might desire. Behold! thus Christ has in like manner liberated us from the law spiritually. He did not abrogate and destroy the law; but our heart, which was before unwillingly under it, he so changed, he did so much good, and rendered the law so lovely, that the heart delights and rejoices in nothing more than in the law. It would not willingly have one tittle of it fall from it. Now, as he in the prison renders for himself the prison narrow and oppressive, by his unwillingness; so, too, we are enemies to the law, and it is disagreeable to us, because, by it, in our unwillingness, we are shut up from evil, and are impelled to good.

In this manner, the Apostle beautifully comprises in these words, both the fruit and the use of the law. For, were I to ask: "For what purpose is the law good?" He answers: "It is true, it does not make us pious, but it increases our sins, and incites our nature by its commands and prohibitions; yet it has two offices. *First*, it locks us up and secures us, so that we may not break out with violence, and fall into the danger of an open, shameless life, as those do, who will not be locked up and secured by it; so that it is for this reason much better that there be a law, than that there be no law. For who could otherwise withstand the encroachments of others; Thus, too, St. Paul says, Rom. 13, 4, the secular sword is borne as a terror, not for the pious but for evil-doers.

Secondly, this locking-up conducts to a future faith, by its causing man to perceive his wickedness, and his distaste for that which is good, teaching him to know himself, and humbly confess his evil nature, acknowledge its guilt, and desire the grace of God, which does not abrogate the law,—which he, indeed, sees to be right and good and holy, but produces another heart in him, which loves this very good and holy law. Behold! this is the true meaning and best use of the law. It is, therefore, truly necessary that the law exist, to bring man thus to know himself and to implore the grace of God.

Here a contention arises, however, between true and false saints. False saints will not use the law any further than according to the first mode. Through this locking-up and preservation, they presume themselves already pious; nor will they learn from it, to perceive their wicked nature. They imagine that nature is good in itself, and that they naturally, indeed, can love the law. This, true saints deny; nor, indeed, is it true. According with the word of God, the experience of every one declares otherwise. And he that will not deny or dissemble, must confess that, naturally, he has no delight in the law of God, much less in the punishment of sins, in death and hell, presented by the law.

This great, this deep, and abominable filth of their hearts, they excuse, and cover with the fig-leaves of their own works in the law—even as Adam and Eve covered their shame—but by this covering it became nothing better in reality. Thus, too, by works and self-justification in the law, no one becomes better, but worse. On account of this filth, Christ rejected and dispersed the synagogues.

Thus it is clear, then, to whom Paul addresses these words; namely, to the self-righteous, who wish to become pious through the law and its works, and consider the first use of the law sufficient to render them pious. From this arises a class, who might be styled Absalom-ites. For, as Absalom remained hanging by his own head, between heaven and earth, in an oak tree, 2 Sam. 18, 9 ; so these also hang between heaven and earth. For, by this locking-up of the law, they do not touch the earth ; that is, they do not what their evil nature ardently desires. On the other hand, whilst the law does not make their nature any better, but only irritates and provokes it, so that they become enemies to the law, they are not pious, and likewise do not attain heaven.

Even as Zechariah, 5, 9, saw two women who carried an epha between heaven and earth, to Babylon, and a woman sat in the vessel, who is called *Impietas*, unbelief or ungodliness. This vessel or epha is the people of such holiness, vacillating between open vice and true piety. Therefore, Impietas, unbelief, is sitting in it.— The two women who carried it between heaven and earth, are *fear* and reward ; for, through the fear of punishment, or the quest of reward, they do

CONCERNING THE LAW AND ITS WORKS.

all their works. These two elevate, conduct, and keep them in their holiness; hence he also says these two women had wings like a stork or a vulture.

Wings, in the Scriptures, signify oral preaching, because speech flies and moves swiftly. Now, these saints preach about nothing but fear and reward; they wish to make people pious, merely through terror and allurement; they only make them worse; so that they really become greater enemies to the law, in consequence of its terrors; and, on account of its allurements, are only more desirous to accomplish their own designs, than they were before. Therefore, these false saints are really nothing else but the wings of the stork or vulture, which devour the chickens, and murder the souls. But, the true saints remain not in the middle between heaven and earth. They hear the terrors and enticements of the law, too, indeed, but they perceive in themselves that they regard the terror and enticement more than the law, and thus they see that, in truth, they are neither pure nor righteous; they fall down, confess, and exclaim, grace, grace, Lord God; to these Christ comes, and brings them true liberty through his Spirit, so that they become entirely heavenly.

Behold, this is being preserved and locked up under the law, unto the future faith. In this manner, prior to the faith, not only the Jews were locked up, but also those are locked up, who now and at any time, are endeavoring to become pious through the works, the threats, terrors, or rewards of the law. These, if not directed to the faith, or if the faith does not finally come, and is not made known to them, must render them worse, and they will ultimately fall into despair or obdurate presumption, beyond the reach of help. So dangerous is it, not to use the law correctly, so as to arrive at the faith by it.

"Wherefore the law was our schoolmaster, to bring us unto Christ, that we might be justified by faith."

Observe what is said here: No one is justified by the law and its works. For, if we could be justified by the law, faith would be unnecessary, and that which St. Paul says here, —"We are justified by faith,"—would be false. In justification, faith and works exclude each other entirely. If you ascribe justification to faith, you must not attribute it to works, to the law, and nature. If you ascribe it to works, you must not attribute it to faith. The one must be true and the other false; both cannot be true at the same time. Hence, the power and virtue of the law must be no other than that of making sinners, or of letting them remain sinners. That which does not justify, certainly makes sinners, or lets them remain sinners. But, since the law, moreover, is occupied with sins and sinners, it must do something more with them, than merely to let them remain sinners. What kind of an occupation would that be, which has no effect upon things, upon which it operates?

What, then, can the law accomplish, if it neither justifies us, nor makes us better, nor leaves us where it finds us? Its province must be wonderful, as it neither justifies nor leaves the sinner where it finds him. It necessarily follows, therefore, that it must magnify the sins, as St. Paul, Rom. 5, 20, says: "Moreover the law entered that the offence might abound." This, as already said, occurs in consequence of its locking up the sinner, and of its preserving his hands from a life of open wickedness, and of its awakening in his heart only a greater hatred and aversion to the law. Even as a pupil becomes more indignant, the more he is chastised, and the more his will is interdicted by his tutor; which hatred and aversion are nothing else than an increase of his evil will, which was forbidden; and they would never have arisen, had his will not met with opposition.

Thus, before the introduction of the law, man, or his evil nature, sins merely of himself, without thinking of the law. But, after the law is introduced, and constrains and threatens him, then his nature is irritated and becomes averse to the law, and begins not only to love sin, but also to hate righteousness. Behold, this is the province of the law in the sinner, and with sins. This, St. Paul calls increasing sins by the law, much less that any one should be justified by it. But happy is he that perceives and understands this; for the self-righteous do not understand it at all; they attribute no such wickedness or hatred of the law to nature; they find much good in it. Hence they understand not a syllable in St. Paul, who never speaks otherwise of the law; and if we would truly confess it, we find it thus in our hearts.

He also says, "unto Christ," or "until Christ," is the law our schoolmaster, so that no one may embrace any other faith than that in Christ. The law impels us to Abraham's seed, Christ, on whom all saints from the beginning have believed; as is stated in the preceding Epistle. Therefore it is not enough for the Jews and Turks, to believe in God who created heaven and earth: he that does not believe in Christ does likewise not believe in God. And were it even true that Christ is not God, (which is impossible,) yet those who do not believe in Christ, do not believe in God; for God has promised his grace in Abraham's seed. Now, this seed is Christ, as the Jews, the Turks, and all the world acknowledge. He, therefore, that does not believe Christ, does also not believe the promises of God; therefore he also does not believe in that God who created heaven and earth; since no other God has given the promise to Abraham, and since in no other seed of Abraham's name, but in that of Christ alone, are the blessing and faith gone forth and preached, in all the world.

Out of Christ, therefore, there is no blessing nor justification, in view either of the law, or of any belief. God will keep his promise made to Abraham, to bless all the world in his seed, and not in that of any other; he will, therefore, not establish the new and peculiar faith of any one, and yield or recall his promise. Therefore, faith in Christ justifies, as Paul, Rom. 10, 4, says: "For Christ is the end of the law for righteousness to every one that believeth." What does this imply? Nothing else but that all those who believe in Christ, are justified, and receive his spirit and grace through faith. Here will be the end of the law, because they are no longer under the law; and this is the ultimate meaning of the law, as follows: "But after that faith is come, we are no longer under a schoolmaster."

Although, from the preceding, it is easy enough to understand what is meant by being under the law or under a tutor; yet, since this doctrine and expression have gone entirely out of use, enough cannot be said about it. To be under a tutor or the law, is, briefly, to be a dissembler, to do many good works, and yet, not to be pious; to lead a good life, and never to be righteous; ever to teach and to preach, and never to learn or understand anything. The reason is, because all these are of such a character as not to do good from a free will and through love, or without fear of punishment or pursuit of reward. Therefore, they are servants, driven by the law, and the law ever continues to rule and to drive them, and thus they ever remain its debtors and subjects.

For the law demands a joyful, free, and cheerful will. This they have not; nor can they have it of themselves: faith in Christ alone produces it. Wherever this exists, there the law ceases its demands, it is satisfied, and fulfilled. The pupil is now able to accomplish what his tutor required him to do and know; he therefore dismisses him and demands nothing more; and is no longer his tutor, but his good friend and companion.

In this manner, faith liberates us from the law, not physically, so that we move in one direction and the law in another, and are so separated as no longer to be under it; but so that its demands are satisfied through us; so that we know and have what it desired us to know and have; namely, the Holy Spirit, who causes us to love the law. For, it did not desire works, nor would it be satisfied with them. It desired us to love it, and to satisfy it with love. Without love it would not release us, nor be remunerated; and destitute of love, with all our works, we must thus remain its debtors, and our conscience have no peace for it; it chastises us continually, as sinners and transgressors, and it threatens us with death and hell, until Christ come and give us his Spirit and love, through faith preached in the Gospel. Here, we are freed from the law, so that it no longer demands, no longer chastises, letting the conscience rest; no more terrifying with death and hell, but has become our kind friend and companion.

Now, as the withdrawal of the tutor from the pupil, is not such as would be effected by his death or departure; but it is a withdrawal of his controlling influence, because an effect has been produced in the pupil, by which he is enabled to accomplish what the father desired him to accomplish through the tutor; so, too, the law withdraws from us, not by ceasing to exist, or by being abrogated, but spiritually, because a change has been brought about in us, and we have what God desired us to have through the law.

Therefore, I have said that this figure concerning the pupil and tutor, is a beautiful, brilliant illustration, by which we may properly understand the law, and grace in us. For, the first use of the law, in which it locks up, and produces external piety, is so deeply established, and enforced by all teachers and writers, and conforms, besides, so nearly with human nature, that it is very difficult to understand its second use, in which it magnifies sins internally; hence, I may well compare it to a pair of scales, of which one scale is empty and the other is full.

In this manner, the law, when it causes external piety, increases sin internally; it imposes as much internally, through hatred and unwillingness, as it removes externally, in works, and much more; so that St. Paul, Rom. 7, 23, says, that, through the law sin becomes exceedingly sinful,— beyond measure. All of which the experience of every one must confess.

"For ye are all the children of God by faith in Christ Jesus."

Whoever is under the law, and works uncheerfully, is a servant, as the preceding Epistle declares; but, whoever has faith, and works cheerfully, is a child; for he has received the Spirit of God through Christ. But the Apostle refers to Christ, and indicates such a faith as believes and abides in Jesus Christ; so that no other faith is sufficient and right, let a person believe in God as he will.

There are some, especially among the modern, high Schoolmen, who say: "The forgiveness of sins and justification depend wholly and entirely upon the divine imputation of grace; that is, on God's imputation; so that it is sufficient. He to whom God imputes sins, or does not impute them, is thereby justified, or not justified from sin, as Ps. 82, 2, and Rom. 4, 7, 8, as they imagine, read, where it is said; "Blessed is the man to whom the Lord will not impute sin."

Were this true, the whole New Testament would be vain and futile;— Christ would have labored foolishly and uselessly, in suffering for sin;— and God himself would have performed a mere mockery and deception without any need; because he might well have forgiven, and not imputed sins, without the suffering of Christ; and thus, too, another faith, indeed, besides that in Christ, might have justified and saved: viz., that which would have relied on such gracious mercy of God, that sins would not be imputed.

Contrary to this abominable, dreadful opinion and error, the holy Apostle is accustomed always to refer to faith in Jesus Christ, and mentions Jesus Christ so frequently that it is astonishing to an individual who is unacquainted with this important matter. Indeed, every second word, (as it is said,) in the Epistles of St. Paul, is Jesus Christ; and these pagan doctors have so maliciously extirpated and silenced it for us, by their abominable and hellish dreams *of such perversion.*

Likewise, our learned doctors, therefore, in the universities, no longer know what Christ is, or the importance and necessity of him, and what the Gospel and the New Testament are. They imagine that Christ is only a Moses; that is, a teacher who institutes laws and commandments indicating how persons may be pious and lead a correct life. They then proceed with free-will and the operations of nature, and, with these, they wish to fit and prepare themselves for grace, based on storming heaven.

Now, if God confers his grace in view of these works, and through their diligent preparation, Christ must be of no importance. What need have they of him, if they can obtain grace in their own name and works? A doctrine which they not only teach openly, but also defend with the Pope's bulls and all their power, and condemn the opposite doctrine as the highest and worst heresy. I have, therefore, forewarned, and still warn every one, so that he may know that the Pope with the universities, has cast Christ and the entire New Testament further out of the world, than the Jews or Turks ever did. Hence the Pope is the true Antichrist, and his high-schools are the devil's own taverns and brothels. Of what importance is Christ, if through my own natural preparation, I can obtain the grace of God? Or, what more will I desire, if I have this grace?

Let us, therefore, guard against this hellish poison, and not lose Christ, the consoling Savior. Above all things, Christ must be retained. True it is, that, in Ps. 32, 8, and Rom. 4, 8, it is said: "Blessed is the man to whom the Lord will not impute sin." But, St. Paul introduces this to show that this divine imputation affects the believers in Christ alone, not the will or nature on account of its works. For, he introduces Abraham, inasmuch as his faith, when he believed the divine promise concerning his seed, was counted to him for righteousness. Now, although out of pure grace, God imputes not our sins to us, yet he would not do this, were his law and righteousness, not completely and amply satisfied before. This gracious imputation had first to be bought and obtained for us from his righteousness.

Since, therefore, this was impossible for us, he ordained for us, one in our stead, who took all the punishments which we deserved, upon himself, and fulfilled the law for us; and thus averted from us the judgment of God, and appeased his wrath. Thus, indeed, grace is given to us gratuitously, so as to cost us nothing; but yet, for us, it cost another much, and was obtained with an incalculable, an infinite treasure; namely, the Son of God himself. It is necessary, therefore, above all things, to be in possession of him, who has accomplished this for us; nor is it possible to obtain grace except alone through him.

Behold, from the time of Adam, therefore, to that of Abraham, no one was saved, except through faith in the woman's seed who should bruise the serpent's head; and, after Abraham, no one was saved except through faith in his seed. Nor, can any one be saved except through faith alone in this seed of Abraham, who is now come. O, it is not sufficient for you, without this Mediator, to attempt to come to God, through yourself, through your own energy; as the Jews, the Turks, and Papists, teach. Who will first reconcile you with God? He says, John 14, 6: "No man cometh unto the Father, but by me."

In the time of the famine, the Egyptians also wished to come to Pharaoh, the king himself, and complained; but he referred them to Joseph saying: "Go unto Joseph; what he saith to you, do;" Gen. 41, 55. Thus, in like manner, God hears no one, nor does he aid any one in obtaining salvation; but we all must come to Christ, who is placed Lord over all things, and with whom is the throne of grace; he obtained it for us. For this reason, it is vain to seek it elsewhere. Yes, if we were destitute of sin, as Adam was before the fall, we would have no need of Christ; we might come before God through ourselves. But, in the time of famine, since the fall, we must have a Joseph, who is without sins, and yet will receive us needy sinners, who come to him and desire it of him.

Hence, it follows, that the papists do not speak and believe otherwise concerning nature, than as if it were yet undefiled; as it was before the fall of Adam; they do not believe that it is entirely corrupted in sin, and that it is the enemy of God. For God is an enemy to sin; so sin is an enemy to God, as Paul teaches, Rom. 4 and 8; consequently they certainly do not believe what Moses, Gen. 3, writes in reference to the fall of Adam, or they regard that fall merely as a disgrace which has produced no effect in our nature, has not rendered it sinful, nor subjected it to the wrath of God. Since, then, they neither believe Moses, nor have any need for Christ, and, thus rejecting the Old and New Testaments, condemn the entire Scriptures; God in return has treated them right by permitting them to become the disciples of Aristotle, that dead and condemned heathen, and a retreat for the devil, who, through the laws of the Pope and the doctrines of men, fills them with his pollution till it runs over and over, and pollutes and contaminates the whole world; yet they ever remain in darkness, endeavoring to force themselves to God, without this faith in Christ, by their prayers, fasts, celebrations of Masses, their devotion and preaching.

And if they even mention and confess Christ, their meaning is nothing else but that, as a superfluity, God has constituted him such a lord as requires us to be obedient to God in this respect, and to regard him as a lord; that, otherwise, independent of this dominion of Christ, free-will might, by its natural energies, obtain the grace of God; and that, for them, the kingdom of Christ is unnecessary, and mere wantonness of God who desires him to be thus constituted a lord, and precisely as any other kingdom, to which any one is subject,—not because it is necessary to salvation, since independent of such kingdom, we may be saved,—but because it is God's will and commandment to be obedient to that king.

Consequently, then, with them, in the bottom of their hearts, Christ is no Saviour, but rather a tyrant and a task-master, of whom, nature, to obtain grace, has no need, but is only more burdened with him, as it must now have not only God, as before, but also Christ, as Lord, as well as his commandments.

In former days many persons prophesied that in the time of Antichrist all heretics would combine and exterminate the whole world. Now, under the Pope and the Turk, this has its full sway. For if Christ with the entire Scriptures, is rejected and condemned, so that nothing more than the mere name remains, it may be easily shown how all heresies, all errors, all darkness, that have existed from the beginning of the world, now reign; so that I often fear that all persons will now be condemned, except those who die in their cradles; and yet no one sees, deplores, or bewails that dreadful wrath of God, which hangs over us.

Behold, this is the indispensable reason why St. Paul always thus enforces faith in Christ, because he well foresaw this virulent doctrine which would presume to treat with God independent of Christ, as if God and our nature were on friendly terms, as if righteousness might love sin, and grant what sin desires.

Therefore, beloved friends, let us be wise, and learn to know Christ rightly; namely, that above all things, we must hear the Gospel, and thereby believe in Christ; not only for his sake, because he is Lord, but because he is the one who took the place of our sinful nature, and loaded upon himself all the wrath of God, which we had merited by all our works, and overcame it; and all this he did not reserve for himself, but assigned it to us as our own, so that all who believe this in and of him, shall certainly be redeemed from this wrath of God, and taken into grace, by him.

Hence, we learn how important and necessary Christ is to us, and that the position, that a person may, by his own natural powers, do so much that the grace of God will be given to him, is false, yes, a device of Satan himself. For, if nature can obtain grace, Christ is unnecessary as an intercessor and a mediator. But, if he is necessary, nature can obtain nothing but disgrace: it is inconsistent, to be a mediator for one's self and to have Christ as a mediator.

"For as many of you as have been baptized into Christ have put on Christ."

How beautiful is the order which the Apostle observes: "But after that faith is come, we are no longer under a schoolmaster." Why? "For ye are all the children of God by faith in Christ Jesus." But how does it come to pass that we become the children of God? "For as many of you as have been baptized into Christ, have put on Christ." Christ is the child of God. Whoever, therefore, clothes himself in the child of God, must also be the child of God; for he is clothed with divine adoption, which must undoubtedly constitute a child. If, then, he is a child, he is no longer under the law, where there is nothing but servants. And, if a child is under the law, like a child under a tutor, he is like a servant, as long as he is under it, as the text follows in St. Paul, and has been stated in the preceding Epistle.

But, what is meant by putting on Christ? The unbeliever* suddenly replies: "It is to follow after Christ, and to imitate his example." But, in this way, I might also put on St. Peter, Paul, or any saint, without any special reference to Christ; for this reason we shall let the faith which St. Paul so beautifully describes by the words *put on*, speak here. It is evident that those who are baptized, have never before followed Christ, but begin in baptism to follow after him; Christ must, therefore, first be put on, before he is followed. And there must be a marked difference between *putting on Christ*, and *following his example*.

It is a spiritual putting on in the conscience, and is effected by the soul's reception of Christ and all his righteousness, as its own, and by its confident reliance on these, as if it had accomplished and merited them itself; just as a person is accustomed to receive his apparel. This reception is, spiritually, to put on: this is the nature and character of true faith. Most assuredly is Christ so given to us that all his righteousness, all that he has and is, stands as our surety, as if it were our own. And, he that believes this, will enjoy the blessing, as indicated by St. Paul, Rom. 3, 32: "He that spared not his own son, but delivered him up for us all, how shall he not with him also freely give us all things?" Again, 1 Cor. 1, 30:— "Christ Jesus, who of God is made unto us wisdom, and righteousness, and sanctification, and redemption."

Behold, whoever thus believes in Christ, puts him on. Faith is, therefore, a thing so great that it justifies and saves a person; for, it affords him all the blessings of Christ, by which the conscience is consoled, and upon which it relies. Hence, the individual rejoices in Christ, and feels disposed to do all that is good, and to avoid all that is evil, no longer fearing either death or hell, or any evil, being so richly clothed in Christ.

This is satisfying the law, and being under it no longer. For, here, with the garment, the Holy Spirit is in the soul, and here is an entirely different person; here the soul is clothed in the adoption of God. It must, therefore, be a child. Behold, in this manner, no saint can be put on before God. Because, it is necessary for every one to put on Christ for himself, and he has nothing that he might give to another to put on.

After the reception and putting on of this garment, the example and imitation of Christ follow; then, in return, the person acts towards his neighbor, as Christ acted towards him; he grants his neighbor all the good that he has, and does for him all that he can; he also permits himself to be put on, and clothes his neighbor with what he possesses. But, the garment with which he himself is clothed in Christ, he cannot give to him; for no one can confer his faith upon another, or give him a similar

---

* B. The faithless.

faith. Though he may, indeed, pray for him, that he may in like manner be thus clothed with Christ; but every one must believe for himself, and Christ alone must clothe us all with himself.

Now, whoever is not in possession of this faith, that Christ with all his blessings, is his, does not yet believe right. Neither is he a Christian, nor is his heart cheerful and happy. For this faith, only, renders Christians cheerful, joyful, secure, happy, and children of God: here the Holy Spirit must dwell. O, what a beautiful, variegated, and precious garment is this, in which decorations, jewels, and ornaments so noble and profuse, associate all virtue, grace, wisdom, truth, righteousness, and whatever is in Christ; so that St. Paul might well exclaim: "I thank God for his unspeakable gifts;" and St. Peter, 2 Epistle, 1, 4: "Through Christ great and precious gifts are given to us." This is the variegated coat of Joseph, which his father Jacob made for him, in preference to his other children, Gen. 37, 3; for Christ alone is full of grace and truth. Again, this is the precious garment of Aaron, the High Priest, in which he served God; concerning which much might be said. For, St. Paul in these words refers us to these histories.

As we, moreover, put on Christ and receive him, so he also puts us on and receives us, and all that is ours, as if it were his own. Now he finds nothing good in us, but he finds sins only in us. These he assumes, and removes from us, as from his glorious garment. He intercedes, moreover, for us, and bears our sins, before God, so that they are not eternally punished, as St. Paul, Rom. 8, 34, says that Christ makes intercessions for us before God; in Ps. 41, 5, it is said: "I said, O Lord be merciful unto me; heal my soul; for I have sinned against thee;" and Ps. 69, 5: "O God, thou knowest my foolishness; and my sins are not hid from thee." All this is said in allusion to us personally, as St. Paul, Rom. 15, 3, explains it from this same Psalm, stating how Christ bore our sins, and neither rejected us, nor regarded his holiness too good for us; but as it is written; "The reproaches of them that reproach thee fell on me."

Now, it affords us pleasure to hear that he is our garment, and that he mediates for us, as his garment; but it is with great reluctance that we suffer him to purify his garment. If we desire to be his garment, we must certainly suffer him to purify it; for he neither can nor will appear in an impure garment. In the days of the martyrs, when he had newly assumed this garment, he began with earnestness to purify it with death and various sufferings; then he sat, as Malachi, 3, 3, says, and purified the sons of Levi, as a fuller who purifies garments. Therefore, where he effects much suffering, the indication is favorable; and wherever his garment exists, he continues to purify it with various kinds of suffering; nor will he cease: but wherever this is not the case, his garment does not exist.

"There is neither Jew nor Greek, there is neither bond nor free, there is neither male nor female: for ye are all one in Christ Jesus."

It is sufficiently clear that Paul does not mean that there is no Jew, nor Greek, no man, nor woman, in a a natural or a physical point of view; but in that respect, of which he speaks. But concerning what does he speak? Not concerning body and nature, but concerning faith, justification, and Christ, how in him we become the children of God, through faith; all of which is effected in the soul and conscience of a person, not through his flesh and blood; not through his hand or foot, but through the word and Gospel.

In this sense and in this respect, there is no difference between persons, whether they be Jews or Greeks, bond or free, male or female. In the view of the people and in physical transactions, the Jew has a different law, and mode of living from the Greek, the bond from the free, the male from the female. The Jew is circumcised, the Greek is not, the male does not cover his hair, the female puts on a veil. Besides this, moreover, every one has his mode for serving God; and hence the saying, Many countries, many customs. These, however, and every thing that is external, and not faith, render no one just and pious before God; nor do they hinder justification; for faith may exist equally in and with all these customs, persons, and distinctions, without any difference.

But the misfortune occurs that a person falls into these habits or customs, and perseveres in them for the purpose of becoming pious and just by them, and of aiding his soul in putting off its sins, and in securing salvation; there all is perverted—Christ is denied, God is lost, faith and the Gospel are abandoned; there works and the law rule again; there the conscience is already misled, thinking that if it observe not these customs, it is already externally lost, but if it observe them it might be saved by them. This is the most pernicious error on earth; against which the Apostle strives so vehemently. For it is impossible for Christian faith to exist with such an imagination or conscience. That person neither will nor can be justified and saved by anything in heaven or on earth, except in Christ alone. All other modes, laws, works, customs, persons, should be employed for the exercise of this life on earth, and for the benefit of our neighbors.

What defect, then, is there with the Jews, that prevents them from being saved? St. Paul, Rom. 9, 32, answers, that they wish to be saved by works, and not by faith. They wish none but Jews to be admitted into heaven; but God designs that none but Christians, whether Jews or Greeks, male or female, shall be admitted there. They think that if they observe the law, they will be saved, if not, they will be condemned; God, on the other hand, intends that he that believeth in Christ, shall be saved; he that believeth not, shall be damned, Mark 16, 16. Without faith, moreover, no one can keep the law, as stated above, and as St. Paul testifies, Gal. 6, 13, where he writes: "Neither they themselves who are circumcised keep the law." Why? Because they do not observe it willingly, but merely through fear and the incitations of the law. Now, since they think that they must be Jews, and enter upon the observance of the law, not otherwise than the Jews, thus cleaving to Jewdaism and laws, with their conscience fettered, they must perish eternally; for it is concluded that there is neither Jew nor Greek, as St. Paul says, but Christ and Christians.

Now, if they would first believe in Christ, and then, if they felt disposed, continue to be Jews, circumcise themselves, or permit it to be done, and keep their laws as they might see fit, without presuming to become pious and to be saved by these, but through the grace of Christ alone,—as all their fathers and the patriarchs did, as St. Peter, Acts 15, 11, declares;—it would be no detriment to them. This, however they will not do; they cleave so firmly to the works, the terrors, and allurements of the law, that even on account of these, they condemn and persecute all who teach otherwise, and preach faith. For this same reason, their predecessors also persecuted and killed all the prophets, and then said that, for the sake of God and his law, they exterminated the deceivers of the people and blasphemers of the law, and the services of God, as Moses commanded them.

But let us also notice the Jews of our day, who act still more rudely and improperly. Those Jews had, at least, a plausible indication, that they were bound by the law of God: our Jews, the Pope and his papists, drive us to their own inventions, and to laws merely human, which God has forbidden. They cry out very much in reference to the noble virtue, *obedience*, that without it no one can be saved, but with it every one may be. This obedience, however, they refer, not to the law of God, but to their own laws and inventions.

By observing their course of conduct, we clearly perceive that they expect to become pious and to be saved, not through faith as Christians, but by their works and laws, as Carthasians, Preachers, Franciscans, Augustinians, Prebendaries, Vicars, &c. They themselves acknowledge that they regard these orders and conditions as the right way to become pious and to be saved; so that it is clear, how their consciences cleave to works, and not to the grace of Christ. Although they read the words of St. Paul: "There is neither Jew nor Greek," yet they say there is, nevertheless, Carthusians, Franciscans, Preachers, Benedictines, Augustinians, this state and that state.

But when faith in Christ is mentioned, they exclaim: "We know indeed that we must believe in Christ, but that we must become pious and be saved through him alone, we do not believe. For what then," they demand, "would good works be useful? These orders and states would be vain. Thou desirest to abolish good works and the services of God. Away, away with that accursed heretic! Fire, fire, fire, here! Heretic, heretic, heretic! Shall St. Francis, Dominic, Benedict, Augustine, Bernard, Anthony, have thus erred?—What dost thou think? Whence comest thou with this diabolical faith?"

Behold, is it not true that our saints and Jews thus proceed? What then must we do with them? We must do as St. Paul did with the Gallatians; he exclaimed twice: "Though we, or an angel from heaven, preach any other gospel unto you than that which we have preached unto you, let him be accursed;" Gal. 1, 8, 9. Thus, too, we say, our preaching and the foundation of our faith, are that by faith alone, independent of law and works, justification and salvation stand.—Now, if the world were nothing but Carthusians, and would teach otherwise, let it be accursed. If all the world were nothing but barefooted friars, preachers, Augustines, Benedicts, and would teach otherwise, let it be accursed. Say, moreover, if one world were nothing but holy Augustines, another, nothing but holy Franciscs, a third, nothing but holy Dominics, a fourth, nothing but holy Benedicts, a fifth, nothing but holy Anthonies, a sixth, nothing but St. Pauls, a seventh, nothing but angelic Gabriels, what then? If they teach otherwise, let them be accursed. Still the word of God must stand, and *Christ alone must remain.* What more do you want?

Matt. 24, 24. Christ said of these sects, that many false Christs and prophets should arise, who would say, lo, here is Christ, lo, there is Christ! These should not be believed. They will do signs, so as to deceive even the elect, if it were possible. Two reasons prevented me, for a long time, from understanding this passage in reference to these sects and orders. The first was that they were so numerous, filling all the world. Had their number been less, I would not have hesitated. I imagined that God would not let so many persons err. I did not perceive that the text clearly said, there shall be many of them, so that even the elect, the number of which is small, may err with them. The other reason was, that holy persons were among them; as, Benedict, Bernard, Augustine, Francis, Dominic, and many of their followers.— I imagined, no error could exist here, and I did not perceive that Christ said the elect should stumble, and be tempted with error; who, however, should not continue in it.

Gideon, too, Judges 8, 27, was a great man in faith, by which he did great things; yet he was misled when he made an ephod; that is when he instituted a peculiar kind of apparel designed to be used in serving God. From which many evils afterwards resulted; his whole race was exterminated, as the Scriptures declare. Why then should it be surprising, if St. Benedict, Francis, Dominic, erred? Who can assure us that they did not err?

It is possible that it occurred here, as it generally does with the legends of all saints, that the people passed by the best practices and proper system of the beloved saints, and fell upon that, in which they stumbled as men. Here, their infirmities are exalted as their strength, and their strength is suppressed; for every one is disposed to follow the weakest and most insignificant, yes, the worst and not the best.

Yet, if they would practice these, their states and orders, as free, not with a view to become pious and to be saved by them, but merely to exercise their bodies, to serve their neighbors, and to honor God, and if they would leave their piety and salvation to be secured through faith alone; these would not be intolerable, and injurious to them; they would still not, however, be inoffensive to the illiterate mass, who are led thereby to think that such a course of conduct is the right way, and thus their faith is disparaged, if not entirely destroyed. For, faith is very tender and precious; it is easily injured, especially by works and practices so brilliant and glittering.

There is no doubt that, so far as their disciples were concerned, the holy fathers used these orders with freedom and propriety, yea, with a view to increase their faith; otherwise they could not have been really holy. But, these blind people mimic and follow after them, losing sight of the kernel, retaining the shell, doing the works, and forgetting the faith of the holy fathers; and still they wish to boast, and appear as if they observed the position, the orders, and examples of these holy men when, at the same time, they have nothing more than the shadow; they are real apes, who mimic everything they see, and still remain apes, without exercising anything like Christian liberty. This they show by their declaration:— "Shall we not become pious and be saved, through our conditions, orders, and works? If it depends on faith only, which everybody has, what did we seek in the cloisters? Why did we become monks? Why, then, are we priests? What avail the masses, then, which we hold, and the prayers which we offer? We might as well have continued laymen.

Here you perceive, from their own words, that they are neither believers nor Christians, and are unwilling to be one with all Christians, as St. Paul says here, that all the baptized have put on Christ, and are all one in Christ. They seek ways peculiar to themselves, superior to all Christians; and Christ is neither good enough nor sufficient for them to put on, and to be justified and saved in him.

Thus, they pervert this declaration of Paul, and say: "All the baptized are not one in Christ; but there are not only Jews and Greeks, but also Carthusians, barefooted Friars, Preachers, Priests, and those of similar orders: these are right ways to salvation." Thus, they seek, first of all, in their own performances, the salvation and piety which they should have had before through Baptism, in faith, as other Christians have them; they forget their Christian duties and name, assume, instead of these, human duties and names; they are no longer called Christians, but Carthusians, Benedictines, barefooted Friars, &c.

St. Paul speaks here of the bond and the free according to the ancient custom, (which is not common in Germany now, as it was formerly,) according to which the servants were bondmen, whom their masters could sell, and in regard to whom they could deal as with their beasts. Now, those who are not such bondmen, the Apostle calls the free. Now, those occupying cloisters might well be called these servants and bondmen, since they give themselves into the possession of men; and would to God, they would take themselves in consideration, and let their spiritual existence be a willing incarceration, not to become pious and to be saved in it, but to exercise in it their piety and salvation received through faith.

Now, as little as it contributes to, or impedes your salvation, to be a man or woman; so little does it contribute to, or impede it, to be a Carthusian or a priest, to perform externally various duties or works, or to assume different orders or ranks. To be a female, renders you neither pious nor wicked, even if you perform all the works appropriate for a female; but faith in Christ, independent of your womanhood and female duties and works, renders you pious.

Thus, to be a nun, renders you neither spiritual nor pious, nor does it save you, even if you observe in the closest manner all the regulations, laws, and works of the order of nuns; nay, even if you alone should fulfill all the works and duties of all nuns; but faith in Christ secures to you these blessings; faith, which knows neither nuns nor monks, nor laymen nor priests, nor shoemakers nor tailors, nor fasts, nor prayers, more than it knows Jews and Greeks, male and female, bond and free. But it is in all, and above all, without any distinction of orders, ranks, persons, gestures, works, costumes, meats, days, places, occupations; in a word, upon none of these, depend piety and salvation.

But, again, Christians may indeed cleave to piety and salvation; that is, they may believe in Christ, and become one in him, no matter how different their external pursuits; as St. Paul says: "Ye are all one in Christ;" and *Ps. 133, 1: "Behold, how good and pleasant it is for brethren to dwell together in unity!" For faith is one and the same in all, and renders one pious like the other. This, however, is not the case with the sects and orders; but in these each one assumes a mode of his own; and hence, it is a by-path.§

He says: "Ye are all one," precisely as if he spoke of the person of one man. This he says in opposition to the idea of multitude, thus: "Ye are not many, but one. Even if ye are many and different, in externals, not

* A. In regard to this, it is said, Ps. 68, 6: "God setteth the solitary in families: he bringeth out those who are bound."

§ A. And where there are no prelates in cloisters, who teach this, it were better, not to leave a stock or a stone of these cloisters standing; they are nothing but gates to hell; it would be better to leave them at once, and learn faith elsewhere, than to remain in them a single hour. Continence can be preserved without these. O, the numberless snares and scandals! How many noble souls, who might so easily be ameliorated, must be ensnared and suffocated here, in a most miserable manner? Woe, woe, woe to you pontiffs, bishops, and all who are commanded to take the oversight of these masses! Here, the words of Christ, Matt. 24, 19. will apply:— "Woe unto them that are with child, and to them that give suck in those days."

all being of the same condition or occupation, upon which piety and salvation do not depend; yet, inwardly, where salvation and piety lie, ye are one. It is true, in the eyes of men, the layman differs somewhat from the priest, the monk from the nun, a man from a woman; but, before God, there is neither layman nor priest,† man nor woman. One is like the other in faith. This is the proverb of the Scriptures: *non est prosopolepsia*, which the Apostles generally employ, and it may be rendered thus; "There is no respect of persons."

Here the figure, Exod. 16, 18, is fulfilled, where it is said the children of Israel gathered the manna; one more, another less; and, afterwards when they measured it with the measure omer, which contained as much as one was allowed to eat in a day, they all received alike; each one, his omer: and as the text says, those who gathered much, received no more; those who gathered little, no less.‡ This should be the case also now, not only in regard to faith, in which we all alike receive one Christ in one omer of faith, even if one does hear more gospel than the other; but also in love, so that the advantages and blessings of all Christians might be common; as the Apostle, 2 Cor. 8, 15, explains this figure: "He that had gathered much had nothing over; and he that had gathered little had no lack." Thus the burdens would be equal as they were in the beginning among the Apostles.

For as Christ acts towards us in faith, manifesting his love, pouring out his blessing upon us, making us all like himself, and himself like us; so we must also act towards our neighbor in regard to our professions, if we wish to be Christians. If our faith is right, we will, undoubtedly, do this willingly from our hearts. Here, then, all things are one thing, and all Christians, one person. Here, then, the law is entirely fulfilled. But, if we are unwilling to do this, then we have neither faith nor Christ. Hence, it is

† A. Nun nor monk.
‡ B. Than an omer.

easy to perceive how faith is now prostrated in all the world, and that there are no more Christians; and yet every corner is full of masses and divine services. These are sheer idolatry.

You will say, then: "In this way you will disperse all the cloisters and institutions, and give occasion for every one to run out of them, and to forsake his order." I answer: These are not my words and doctrines, as you perceive. Ask St. Paul, yea, Christ and God, in reference to this matter, why they disperse such institutions and transactions. Among the children of Israel, too, there were a singular people, called the people of Baal and Moloch, until all the country and towns were full of their self-devised and singular modes of worship; so that Jeremiah 2, 28, and Hosea 10, 1, say, they have erected as many altars and gods as they have towns; and yet they all wished to serve God in this way. Therefore God permitted the country to be destroyed.

The holy king Josiah became dissatisfied, 2 Kings 23, 5, severed and destroyed all their modes of serving God, not fearing the Pope's ban, however, or that it might be said in regard to him, that he had destroyed the services of God; as Rab-shakeh censured the holy king Hezekiah, on a similar occasion, 2 Kings 18, 22.*

Mark the words of Paul, how he guards and secures both sides, so as to keep us right in the middle track. He says: "There is neither Jew nor Greek," &c. If from these words, a Jew should say: "If being a Jew avails nothing before God, well, then, I will let it pass, assume the opposite, and become a Greek." Here St. Paul meets him on the other side. "No," says he, "to be a Greek also avails nothing." If the Greek should say: "Why, I shall no longer be a Greek, but will become a Jew." "No," says St. Paul, "it avails nothing to be a Jew." If the female or the bond should say: "Why, were only I a male or free, since being a female or being bond avails nothing;". St. Paul meets her, and says: "No, to be a male or a female also avails nothing." What, then, does avail? Why, not to pass to either side, but over, above Jew, Greek, bond, free, male, female, into faith and in Christ. The former are earthly ways; the latter is a heavenly way.

Thus, too, 1 Cor. 7, 18, he says: "Is any man called being circumcised? let him not become uncircumcised. Is any called in uncircumcision? let him not be circumcised." What more is this, but that, on the one hand, a Jew should not say: "Since my circumcision avails nothing, then the uncircumcision avails, and in it I will now become pious; and, on the other, a Greek should not say: "Since my uncircumcision avails nothing, if I wish to be saved, I must be circumcised." No, says St. Paul, not either, and thus concludes: "Circumcision is nothing and uncircumcision is nothing, but the keeping of the commandments of God." This is equivalent to saying, first believe in Christ, in which faith the commandments of God will be kept, and be pious and saved first, then be circumcised or uncircumcised, a Jew or a Greek, a male or a female, bond or free, as you will, the efficacy is the same.†

Now let us draw a rough comparison: If a young boy should learn the art of shoemaking, and would engage with a master so foolish and knavish as to teach him, that this trade is a means, through which to become pious and to be saved, and if the boy would believe him, and prosecute

---

* A. Yet, this doctrine does not destroy the cloisters or institutions, but teaches how to use them in a proper and Christian manner.

† A. Neither should a nun, priest, or monk say: "If my condition in life avails nothing, then I will become a layman." No, says St. Paul, to be a layman also avails nothing. Again, if a layman should say: O, if I were a priest, a monk, or a nun, for my condition as a layman is worldly and unblissful: No, says St. Paul, the condition of monk, nun, or priest, avails nothing, and is as worldly and unblissful as that of a layman. What, then, avails? Beyond yourself, beyond laymen, beyond monks, beyond nuns, beyond ecclesiastics, beyond worldliness. Believe in Christ, do to your neighbor as you believe Christ has done to you; this is the only right way to become pious and happy, and there is no other.

this trade under the impression that he must be saved through it, and that without it he cannot be saved, forsaking all other means, faith and love; what would you do in this case? Should you not commiserate the boy? Should not the master incur your displeasure and disapprobation? Now, how would you relieve the boy? Would you say—"Beloved son, the art of shoemaking does not render you pious. It avails nothing in heaven, you must become a tailor." In this way, you would lead him from one hell into another; and you would be just about as pious as that master. So these act, who advise a priest to become a monk; a monk, to enter some other, more difficult order, and thus cast the souls and consciences from one frying pan into the other.—But in this way, you must relieve him: "Beloved son, here there is neither shoemaking nor tailoring; but you must believe in Christ, and then do to your neighbor, as you believe Christ has done to you; then you may continue to be a shoemaker, or a tailor, as you please."

Behold, here you have liberated his soul; here his consicence will be filled with joy and peace; he will thank God and you; and, yet, he will not need to forsake his trade; no, he may follow it more joyfully and freely than he did before. For Christ does not release our hands from labor, our persons from office, our bodies from their condition, or rank, but he redeems the soul from false impressions and the conscience from a false faith. He is a redeemer of the consciences and a bishop of souls, as St. Peter says, 1 Pet. 2, 25; yet he lets our hands continue their labors, our persons their offices, and our bodies their conditions.

Now, act thus too, thou priest, monk, nun. Believe not those teachers who teach you that your condition, or rank, is a means through which to become pious and to be saved. They are nothing but blind leaders of the blind, the messengers of the devil, and murderers of souls; but learn first that to believe in Christ and to serve your neighbor, is the right way.*

* A. Then remain where you are.

But you will say: "Yes, but I became clerical because I wished to become pious and to be saved in this state, or condition; otherwise I would not have taken this step; and I believe there is not one in a thousand, who entered this state with any other intention; and if people knew this, no one, indeed, would enter this clerical state, and in thirty years every cloister and institution would pass away of itself, so that no one would need to destroy them."

Here I answer: Do you suppose then, that Christ was intoxicated or a fool, when he said that these false Christs will deceive many, even, if it were possible, the elect, Matt. 24, 24. And St. Peter, 2 Epistle 2, 2, says that many shall follow these damnable sects. Is it astonishing, then, that Christ spoke the truth? Will you believe the figments of your own mind rather than the words of Christ? Observe, therefore, where this clerical state does not proceed in this way, in faith and love, as stated, I would not only that this my doctrine were a cause of destroying the cloisters and institutions, but that they already lay in ashes. If you can liberate your conscience and soul through this doctrine, and so live in your clerical state as not to think to become pious, and to be saved through it, but only to exercise your faith in it over your body, and to serve your neighbor; then continue in it, and you need not run from it. But if you cannot do this, and your conscience continues to be held captive; it will be better for you to tear your caps and pates, and to forsake your masses and prayers eternally, and become a swineherd, if you can do no better. For nothing in heaven or on earth should keep us from liberating our souls and consciences.

If any one reproaches you as an apostate, a turn-coat, a vagabond monk, suffer it, and think of the declaration of Christ, Matt. 7, 3, where the one who had a beam in his eye, rebuked him who had a mote in his eye. You are an apostate from men; they are apostates from God. You ran away from men, in order to get to

God; they ran away from God, in order to get to themselves and to men.

Be careful, however, not to deceive yourself so as to forsake your state from improper motives. For, our old Adamic nature is very ready to adorn itself, and will take an ell, if you allow it the breadth of a finger. You may deceive men; God you cannot deceive. If you leave your state merely for the purpose of living free, and of being liberated from your order, and not wholly for the purpose of seeking the liberation of your conscience, you have not followed me; nor have I thus advised you; this I wish you to understand.*

In a word, one of the two: you must either lay aside your opinion or meaning, or you must forsake your order. Faith will not allow the opinion that you are to become pious, and to be saved by your spiritual life or order.† The only aim is at the head of the serpent, the opinion. If this were dead, so that persons would not imagine that they will or may become pious, or be saved by works and orders, all danger and dread would be dissipated.

But, the serpent is so careful of her head, that Christ teaches us also to be thus careful of our heads, where he says: "Be ye wise as serpents, and harmless as doves," Matt. 10, 16. The serpent will expose her whole body and all that she has, to secure her head, in which is her life.

Thus, we should be careful of our head, faith, risking all else for it; let the consequence be what it may, for in it is our life. This, the evil spirit seeks to destroy by such brilliant orders and states. When, moreover, we bruise the head of the serpent, that is, our opinion, which is a false faith resting upon works, all else becomes harmless. Matt. 12, 34, Christ calls the Pharisees a generation of vipers, because they adhered so tenaciously to their works and opinions. If, however, we were to secure our heads, like serpents do, and were we as wise in our ways as the children of the world are in theirs, then the simplicity of the dove would follow of itself, so that we would embrace for ourselves no external works, states, performances.

Here the greatest fault, however, is not Pilate's, but Caiaphas' who delivered Christ into the hands of Pilate; that is, the Pope, bishops, and doctors in the high schools, who as shepherds should prevent these things, and, yet like wolves, they themselves devour the sheep. Whilst they should preserve the faith, they exterminate it; and they not only permit these orders and states to rise in the world, but institute them; they establish them and extol them, reposing the head of the serpent upon silken pillows, giving her milk enough to eat and to drink. They have introduced into the world two declarations, and impressed them so deeply into the hearts of all, that it was impossible for the Christian faith to continue. The one is this: "The clerical state is a state of perfection." In this way they effected such a disparity between themselves and common Christians, that they almost alone were regarded as Christians, and the others as unworthy, reprobate domestics. In this way they caused every one to gaze and to stare; every one came flocking in, and wished to be perfect, and scorned the common condition in life as worthless, until they attained the notion that no one could become pious and be saved unless he become clerical.

Behold, in this manner, faith has fallen to the ground, and works and orders have arisen, precisely as if not only our becoming pious and being saved, but, also, perfection depends on their performance; when, at the

---

* You can remain in your orders indeed, and sustain your conscience free according to this doctrine. Mark the example which I have given in regard to the boy engaged in the craft of shoe-making. But, if you are so weak as not to be able to keep your conscience thus free, it is better to be far from these states.

† Since faith, however, may allow the order, it is better to forsake the opinion than the order; otherwise it might happen that there would be such a remorse of conscience afterwards, in consequence of the forsaken order, (if the opinion were not dead,) as would be equivalent to remaining in the order.

same time, all depends on faith alone, both to become pious and perfect.— O, what a banner the infernal Satan hoisted here! When that declaration was introduced and took effect, he then, doubtless, scaled the metropolis of Christianity. Thus, the blind, frantic multitude proceeds, ever talking about perfection, and not knowing one tittle about what piety is, to say nothing about what perfection is, thinking it must be accomplished by works and states.

Yet, besides this, they effected for themselves a large air-hole, saying: "Perfection and state of perfection are two different things. A person may indeed be in a state of perfection, and yet not be perfect; that is, he may be a clergyman, and yet not be holy; as generally they all are in a state of perfection, and yet none of them are in perfection." They also have St. Thomas from Aquin, who teaches: "It is not necessary to be perfect, but it is enough to be in a state of perfection, and to expect to become perfect."

Hence, it is their custom now, that a person may be in a state of perfection, and yet not be perfect, and that it is not necessary to be perfect, but only to strive after perfection. Blind, blind, blind, frantic, frantic, frantic, foolish, foolish, foolish, and mad are that people. Who does not know that a monk may wear a cap and a pate, and yet be a rogue at heart? He is in a state of perfection, and yet he is not perfect. A state of perfection is now called monk, cap, and pates. Let them lead the blind; Christ says they are blind and leaders of the blind. If St. Thomas was holy, which I doubt, he surely become holy more extraordinarily than any one else; this conclusion follows from his pernicious and venomous doctrines.

The other declaration is this:— "The Gospel divides itself into two parts, in *Consilia et praecepta*, counsels and commandments." In the whole Gospel Christ has presented but one counsel, namely, Chastity, which may also be observed in the laical state, by an individual who has that grace. But they have instituted twelve counsels in it, and they act in regard to the Gospel as it suits them. In this way, however, they have now divided and separated the world; their lives they make to subsist in the counsels, the lives of the laity, in the commandments, pretending that their lives are higher than the commandments of God. Consequently the lives of common Christians, and faith became like sour, putrid beer; every one stared open his eyes, contemned the commandments, and ran after the counsels.

And when they had run almost out, they finally found human laws, in clothing, meats, singing, reading, pates, &c., and consequently the commandments of God followed after faith, and both were exterminated and forgotten, so that now to be perfect and to live in the counsels, is to put on black, white, grey, or speckled caps, to bawl in the churches, to shave the head, to eat no eggs, meat, butter, and yet to eat and to drink the best, and to live an idle, sumptuous life.

Behold, this Satan desired to accomplish through these two declarations. The first exterminates faith and the whole New Testament with Christ. The second, hunts down the commandments and the whole Old Testament with Moses. These are the people, concerning whom all the Scriptures say that, in the end of the world, they shall reign under Antichrist. Two declarations more pernicious and virulent have never been made upon earth, which so powerfully and rapidly drive out of the world the entire Scriptures of God, so that it is not known what commandment or Gospel is. The Gospel does not present commandments; but it shows how impossible it is to observe them, and teaches faith in Christ, through which they are kept.

I wish, moreover, that all the cloisters were supplied with ministers who preach the true doctrine of faith, or, that they were laid in ashes. For these there is no medium, like there is for the conditions of laymen; the layman does not attach to his laical works the opinion that he becomes pious and is saved by them. The former, however, can neither live nor exist without that opinion. Here there is no remedy. Right or wrong, they must place faith in their works. Now, let this suffice for once, in regard to the sects. Alas, they are so deeply corrupted as to cost many words; I scarcely know whether it will profit much to present again, the clear, lucid words of Paul.

"And if ye be Christ's, then are ye Abraham's seed, and heirs according to the promise."

How does it follow that all who put on Christ and are his, are also the seed and heirs of Abraham, when, at the same time, they are not of Jewish descent? That all who put on Christ through baptism and faith, are his, and that, on the other hand, he is also theirs, is clear enough from the preceding text and explanation; and being all one in Christ and one with him, spiritually, however, not bodily, they must also be and have all that Christ is and has. But Christ is Abraham's seed; therefore they must also be Abraham's spiritual seed through him. Precisely as they have Christ, so they are also seed. They have him, however, not bodily in flesh and blood, but spiritually in faith, and hence they are not bodily, but spiritually his seed.

But here it is to be observed that the Apostle attributes to Abraham three kinds of seed. First, those who are only physically his children, deriving from him only their flesh and blood; this is a mere consequence of nature. With these God has no more to do than with heathens. This he shows in the case of Ishmael who, although he was of Abraham's flesh and blood and his first son in this respect, was nevertheless not reckoned in the Scriptures among Abraham's children. Again, thus Esau too was naturally Isaac's son and Abraham's flesh and blood; afterwards there were many of Israel, all of whom were Abraham's children as to their flesh and blood, and yet they were destroyed in the wilderness; subsequently there have been many who were condemned; and the greater part of the Jews are still condemned.

Secondly, those who are both physically and spiritually Abraham's children, who bring with them not only the flesh and blood, but also the spirit and faith of Abraham; as, Isaac, Jacob, the patriarchs, prophets, and all the blessed among the people of Israel. These are the true seed, with whom God has to do. This seed he delivered out of Egypt, led into the land of Canaan, and favored with innumerable blessings, as the Scriptures show. For the sake of this seed, he tolerated among them also the merely physical seed, and allowed them to enjoy temporally similar blessings. Now as Abraham was their spiritual father through the faith of Christ, so they were all his spiritual children also, independent of their natural relationship.

Among this seed Christ is the head, in whom Abraham himself and all Abraham's seed, his brethren and joint-heirs, are blessed. Now, this is the text in which he speaks concerning this seed, Gen. 12, 3, and 22, 18: "In thy seed shall all the nations of the earth be blessed." This is fulfilled in Christ. For they are altogether with Christ and in Christ, and Christ is with them and in them, one seed. Christ is blessed of God; his joint-heirs are blessed through Christ; the heathens through the Apostles, and the Jews in Christ, who are also his joint seed.

Thirdly, those who do not derive their flesh and blood from Abraham, but possess his spiritual disposition, or character; that is, Abraham's faith in Christ, his seed. Now, these are we and all Gentiles who are Christians in true faith. For precisely as unbelief is so strong as to separate even natural children, flesh and blood from Abraham's relationship, so that in the Scriptures they are not called Abraham's seed and the children of God, so, on the other hand, faith is so much more powerful as to constitute even those the true seed of Abraham, who are not of his flesh and blood, but merely bring with them the faith of Abraham, from his spir-

DR. LUTHER'S CHURCH-POSTIL.

SERMONS ON THE EPISTLES.

GAL. 3, 23-29.

itual disposition. Of this St. Paul speaks, Rom. 4, 13, Rom. 9, 8, and Gal. 3. This seed is indicated in the promise, in which God says to Abraham: "In thy seed shall all the nations of the earth be blessed."

If this blessing is to result to the nations, they must become like the seed of Abraham. For Abraham and his seed have nothing else, but this blessing. If, then, the inheritance, the chief good, the blessing is one and the same to Abraham's seed and to all nations on earth, they all must likewise be reckoned equal heirs, seed, and children of Abraham, whether they derive their flesh from him or not; so that it is concluded that Abraham has no seed except those only who believe. For in the Scriptures these are accounted to him as seed. To this conclusion we are forced by the promise of God, which says Abraham's seed shall be blessed, and shall bless others. All that are seed and heirs of Abraham, must be blessed, according to the force of the words of the promise.

Now, no one is blessed unless he believe. He that believes not, remains under the curse; so that, Rom. 4, 13, and 9, 8, St. Paul may well call such seed of Abraham, the seed of the promise; that is, not the seed of the flesh, but of faith, as designated in the promise, as he says, Rom. 9, 8: "They which are the children of the flesh, these are not the children of God: but the children of the promise are counted for seed." With this, also, the declaration, John 1, 13, "Which were born, not of blood, nor of the will of the flesh, nor of the will of man, but of God," accords.

Now you perceive what the Apostle means, when he says here: "If ye be Christ's, then are ye also Abraham's seed, and heirs according to the promise." As if he should say: "Ye are not the natural seed of Abraham,—which would profit you nothing at all, as it profits no one else,—but ye are his promised seed, upon which too the efficacy entirely depends." For Abraham has no other seed but the promised, blessed seed, God grant, whether they derive their flesh and blood from him or not. We must understand Abraham's seed according to the Scriptures, not according to nature. Now the Scriptures do not regard the nature, recognizing alike all who are blessed and believe, whether they are natural seed or not. Although God foresaw that there would undoubtedly be children of the blessing from the natural seed also; yet not in consequence of their nature, but for the sake of election through grace.

Now, you must properly comprehend the phrase, "Abraham's seed" and heirs, as already stated in the preceding Epistle in opposition to the self-righteous, that righteousness is not obtained through works, but it must precede them and accomplish them. For he that is an heir, does not work for the inheritance, or for a reward of the inheritance, but he already occupies the inheritance, and uses it with his works; so, he that believes is already pious and just, and saved, besides, without any works, through grace thus conferred. The works which he subsequently performs, are works of exercise in this inheritance.

If, moreover, you believe, you must

F

feel that you are an heir, and regard yourself as a child of God, without any doubt. If you doubt this, you are neither a child nor an heir; nor do you believe correctly. This you must not doubt either in life or in death. But, what is a Christian life but a commencement of eternal life? If, however, you merely intimate that you are a child of God, and acknowledge this faith, Caiaphas, as a great service to God, will rend his garments, and exclaim over you: *Blasphemavit,* and all the rest with him will say: *Reus est mortis;.* "We have a law, and according to this law he shall die; for he has made himself a child of God; 'crucify him, crucify him,' he is a heretic and a deceiver," &c., John 19, 7, 15. Let this be said in regard to you, and prepare for it; so it must be.

DAY OF THE HOLY THREE KINGS. [EPIPHANY.]

EPISTLE, Isaiah 60, 1-6.

ARISE, shine; for thy light is come, and the glory of the LORD is risen upon thee.

For, behold, the darkness shall cover the earth, and gross darkness the people: but the LORD shall arise upon thee, and his glory shall be seen upon thee.

And the Gentiles shall come to thy light, and kings to the brightness of thy rising.

Lift up thine eyes round about, and see: all they gather themselves together, they come to thee: thy sons shall come from afar, and thy daughters shall be nursed at thy side.

Then thou shalt see, and flow together, and thine heart shall fear, and be enlarged; because the abundance of the sea shall be converted unto thee, the forces of the Gentiles shall come unto thee.

The multitude of camels shall cover thee, the dromedaries of Midian and Ephah; all they from Sheba shall come: they shall bring gold and incense; and they shall show forth the praises of the LORD.

THIS Epistle or lesson is an admonition to faith, and a proclamation that the Gospel is to be preached in all the world, and that Christians shall be gathered from all nations. The prophecy is clear and easy and, hence, it requires but little explanation.

The fact that the Gospel is styled a light, glory, brightness, and a rising of the Lord, indicates that a distinction is to be made between the light of the Gospel and that of the law. This distinction should be carefully marked, so as not to confound the Gospel and the law, calling that Gospel, which is law, and that law, which is Gospel. In Advent, and in the preceding epistle, we heard that the Gospel is a declaration of life, a doctrine of grace, a light of joy, which promises, brings, and presents Christ, with all his blessings. But the law is a declaration of death, a doctrine of wrath, a light of sadness, which reveals our sins and demands a righteousness, which we cannot render; and, hence, our conscience perceives and feels, that it deserves death and eternal wrath, and consequently it becomes sad and restless. This prophecy of Isaiah falls upon a conscience in this wretched condition, in a manner so joyful, as to reanimate it again, to fill it with joy, and liberate it from the law and from sin.

For this reason, we may designate these two lights as follows: The one as the light of the Lord, and the other as the light of the servant, 2 Cor. 3, 13. The light of the Lord arose through Christ, and the light of the servant through Moses. Aaron and the Children of Israel could not endure the light and the brightness in the face of Moses; he had to hang a veil over it. But, on Mount Tabor, the face of Christ, when he was transfigured, was not intolerable; no, it was so lovely and delightful, that St. Peter, transported with joy, exclaimed: "Lord, it is good for us to be here: if thou wilt, let us make here three tabernacles,; one for thee, and one for Moses, and one for Elias." Nor was the light of Moses intolerable, but lovely; the Gospel renders the law, the tutor, which was before repulsive and intolerable to nature, agreeable, as we have already heard. Thus says Isaiah:

"Arise, shine."*

This rising, no doubt, has reference to one who has not yet risen, that is, to one who lies and sleeps, or is dead. This, it seems to me, is the passage, to which St. Paul refers, when he says, Eph. 5, 14: "Wherefore he saith, Awake, thou that sleepest, and arise from the dead, and Christ shall give thee light." Doubtless, Christ is this light, concerning which Isaiah here speaks, and which shines through the Gospel in all the world, and enlightens all who rise and desire him.†

Now, who are the sleepers and the dead? Doubtless, *all who are under the law*. These are all dead in consequence of sin. But especially are those dead, who disregard the law, and live independent of all restraint. The self-righteous who do not feel their wants and defects, are the sleepers. Both these classes have very little regard for the Gospel; they sleep and die continually. For this reason the Spirit must wake them up, so that they may see and perceive this. But the third class, who feel the law, and whose conscience torments them, thirst after grace, and sigh for the Gospel; they rest not till it comes and is given to them; they proclaim it for ever." In this respect, it is not also. Isaiah is one of these. Thus these sleepers and dead awake and receive this light.

For this reason he says, Permit yourself to be enlightened, or to shine. Permit this light to fall upon you. Crawl, thou dead, not into the grave of your filthy life; that is, quit loving and following your evil course of conduct, so that the light of the Gospel may fall upon you and find room in you. And thou sleeper, wake up, crawl not under the bed of your careless and drowsy security and presumptuous reliance on your own self-right-

* A. "For thy light is come, and the glory of the Lord is risen upon thee."

† A. But that Jerusalem is mentioned here, and not in St. Paul, matters nothing. Jerusalem does not occur in the text of Isaiah. It was introduced into the Epistle by some one else, because the prophet addresses Jerusalem or the children of Israel.

eousness, so that the true light may have some claim upon you also. Thus it is necessary frequently to admonish both these classes. A life uninfluenced by proper restraints is a great hindrance to the dead, and a secure self-righteousness will scarcely allow the sleeper to perceive and accept this blissful light.

"Thy light is come."—Why does he say, *Thy light*, when at the same time it is God's light?—as will appear hereafter. Answer: It is God's light and the light of all of us.* It is God's, because he gives it; it is ours, because it enlightens us and we enjoy its rays. In like manner, Christ says, Matt. 5, 45, in regard to the sun, that it is the Father's: "He maketh his sun to rise on the evil and on the good;" and still he says, John 11, 9: "If any man walk in the day, he stumbleth not, because he seeth the light of this world;" that is, this sun of God enlightens the world; and, in reference to himself, John 8, 12: "I am the light of the world." Besides all this, it is the special light of Jerusalem and the Children of Israel,† on account of the promise; for, it was promised only to Abraham and his seed, as Mary sings in the *Magnificat*, Luke 1, 55: "As he spake to our fathers, to Abraham, and to his seed the light of the Heathen, to whom nothing was promised, and yet it is said, they will receive it; as the words of the promise imply, and Isaiah here indicates.

There is no doubt that nearly all the prophecies of Isaiah, and of all the prophets, concerning Christ, arise and are drawn from the promise of God, made to Abraham, Gen. 22, 18: "In thy seed shall all the nations of the earth be blessed."

From these words it is clear, that Christ, the seed of Abraham, was to be made known throughout the world. This could not be accomplished in his own person; and hence it had to be accomplished by preaching; and it was necessary, not only thus to preach and proclaim, but also to show the char-

* A. And Jerusalem's.

† B. To whom the Prophet here speaks.

acter of the preaching, namely, that it is a proclamation of blessings and grace, by which all the world might be blessed.

And hence, too, the conclusion, that the seed of Abraham is true man as well as God; that he must be born of a virgin; that his kingdom cannot be temporal and earthly, and that he must die and soon rise again from the dead, and be Lord over all creatures. All this seems to be included in this divine promise, in brief, but clear and explicit terms; and it were easy to show, if time would admit, in a manner that any one might see and comprehend, how these prophecies spring up and flow from this promise, as from a fountain. For this reason, too, Abraham laughed in his heart, Gen. 17, 17, when that promise was made to him. For he understood it; as Christ himself indicates, where he says, concerning this laughing in his heart, John 8, 56: "Your father Abraham rejoiced to see my day: and he saw it, and was glad."

"And the glory of the Lord is risen upon thee."

We have frequently spoken of the little word *Gloria*. It means honor, brightness, splendor. It is nothing else but a great, a splendid report or cry, arising from a glorious reality, not from a mere empty proclamation. A glorious person must be regarded like a sun or a light, so that, precisely as the sun is a fountain full of light, and its lustre is the glory of its light, its diffusion and honor; (lustre is like a natural report of the sun, by which it is known and recognized in all the world, and is in no other way diffused and revealed,) the glory of an individual is the fountain, sun, and foundation of his glorious report, and this report is the lustre of this glory, by which he is proclaimed, extolled, recognized, and regarded as glorious. This, you will observe, is properly implied by *Gloria*, honor, renown, brilliancy.

Thus, the Gospel is *God's glory and our light*. It is our light, because through it we ourselves see and know God and all things; it is God's glory, because through it his work and all his glorious operations are preached, proclaimed, extolled, recognized, and highly esteemed in all the world.

But to speak more particularly in regard to this matter, it might be necessary to say that the Gospel is not the brightness itself, nor is it the light itself; but it is the *rising of that brightness* and *the approach of that light;* it is nothing else but a manifestation of that light and brightness; for the light and the brightness existed from eternity, as it is said, John 1, 4, 5: "In him was life; and the life was the light of men;" but it neither arose, nor was openly manifested, except through the Gospel alone. Hence, the Gospel is also a report, a cry, of Divine brightness and glory, so that the Scriptures call it the voice of God in Ps. 29, 3, Ps. 68, 34, and in many other places.

For this reason it is also called Gospel, that is, "a good message," because it reveals and proclaims divine blessings, divine glory, and divine honor or brightness, as it is said, Ps. 19, 1: "The heavens declare the glory of God; and the firmament showeth his handiwork." What else is proclaiming and revealing, but the preaching and proclaiming of the Gospel through the heavens, that is, the Apostles? What is the brightness and work of God, but the great, the glorious riches of his goodness and grace, poured out upon us?

Thus says St. Paul, Tit. 2, 11:— "The grace of God that bringeth salvation hath appeared to all men." How did it appear? Through the preaching of the Gospel. This seems to be the import of the words of Isaiah, where he says: "Thy light is come, and the glory of the Lord is risen upon thee." That is, the light and glory of God are preached and revealed to you. And that Christ himself is the light and the glory, appears from the following: "And the glory of the Lord is risen upon thee;" that is, is revealed. Again, it is said in this chapter, verse 20, "The Lord shall be thine everlasting light."

Now, the light and the glory are God himself, as Christ, John 8, 12, says: "I am the light." We have already heard in the Epistle for Christmas, that Christ is the brightness of divine glory. Hence, it is clear that Isaiah does not speak here of the coming or rising of Christ's birth, but the rising of the Gospel after the ascension of Christ, through which Christ is spiritually and happily risen, and glorified in the hearts of all believers in the world. The Scriptures speak more frequently concerning this rising, than they do concerning the birth of Christ. There lies the importance; on account of it he was born; upon it St. Paul bases himself, and says: *God promised the Gospel "afore by his prophets in the holy scriptures, concerning his Son,"* &c.

From this we may also learn what the Gospel is, and of what it speaks. It is a coming of light and a rising of glory. It speaks only of divine glory, honor, and fame; that is, extols nothing but the work, the grace, the goodness of God towards us; it shows that we should and must have his work, grace, and goodness, and God himself, if we wish to secure salvation. In this way it produces a twofold effect in us.

In the first place, it rejects our natural reason and light; it shows conclusively that they are nothing but darkness. Were there light instead of darkness in us, it would be unnecessary for God to let this light rise upon us. Light enlightens nothing but darkness. Hence this epistle or lesson severely censures and condemns all natural wisdom, all human reason, all heathen arts, all human doctrines and laws; it is conclusive that all these are sheer darkness, since the rising of this light is necessary. For this reason, we should guard against all human doctrines, and all the conceits of reason, as against darkness rejected and condemned by God, and only wake up and rise to behold this light and to follow it alone.

In the second place, it casts down all the glory and pride of our own works, our efforts, and free-will, so that we cannot draw consolation, or derive honor from any of these; they contribute rather to our shame and scandal in the sight of God. For if there is anything in us worthy of honor and glory, this divine honor and glory would rise upon us in vain. But, as they rise upon us, it is clear that there is nothing in us, which does not contribute to our shame and scandal. Concerning this St. Paul, Rom. 3, 23, says: "All have sinned, and come short of the glory of God." As if he should say: They may, it is true, have nature and the self-righteousness of men, and derive from these honor, praise, and glory temporally before men on earth, like those who are not sinners; but before God they are sinners, destitute of his glory, and unable to boast of him and his blessings.

Now, no one can be saved, unless the glory of God be in him, so that he may console himself with God alone and his blessings, and glory in these, as it is said, Jer. 9, 24 and 2 Cor. 10, 17: "But he that glorieth, let him glory in the Lord." This is the rising of divine glory. The Gospel in like manner condemns all our efforts, and extols only the goodness and grace of God, that is, God himself, so that we may console ourselves with him alone and glory in him only, as it is said, Ps. 144, 15: "Happy is that people, whose God is the Lord," and no one else. For this reason, it also follows in Isaiah: "For, behold, the darkness shall cover the earth, and gross darkness the people: but the Lord shall arise upon thee, and his glory shall be seen upon thee."

Here the prophet clearly indicates that *wherever Christ is not, there darkness exists*, no matter how brilliant it may appear; nor does he allow the medium devised by the high schools, when they say: Between darkness and Christ, the light of nature and human reason exists. They attribute darkness only to gross, wicked persons and fools. This middle light they regard as excellent, saying it may readily adapt itself to the light of Christ, and although it may be darkness when compared to the light of Christ, yet in itself it is a light. They do not perceive how highly enlightened they imagine themselves, since usually the very worst are the most rational: "The children of this world are in their generation wiser than the children of light," as Christ says, Luke 16, 8; and yet they are not better adapted, but much less adapted, to the true light, than others. This could not be the case, if such light were any advantage in securing the true light.

Devils, too, are wiser, more artful, and crafty than men, and still they are not the better for that. No, that kind of light is always at enmity with the true light, as Paul, Rom. 8, 7, says: "The carnal mind is enmity against God: for it is not subject to the law of God, neither indeed can be." Therefore, God knew no better way to deal with the pernicious light, than to condemn and obscure it entirely; as St. Paul says: 1 Cor. 1, 19, 20: "For it is written, I will destroy the wisdom of the wise, and will bring to nothing the understanding of the prudent. * * * Hath not God made foolish the wisdom of this world?"

It is also said in this same chapter of Isaiah, verse 19: "The sun shall be no more thy light by day; neither for brightness shall the moon give light unto thee: but the Lord shall be unto thee an everlasting light, and thy God thy glory." What else is this, but a rejection of all temporal wisdom? Away, therefore, with this babbling about natural light; adhere closely to the words of Isaiah and the Scriptures, which teach us to flee from such light as from darkness, and an enemy of the true light. For that is the light, which teaches the Jews and all tyrants to persecute and torture Christ and all his saints, and which cannot even to this day endure the true light; it always claims to be in the right and to be light, when at the same time it is darkness, and condemned by the true light; and hence it rages and instigates all kinds of evil.

Here, however, a simpleton may ask, How can all that natural reason teaches us, be darkness? Is it not clear enough that three and two are five? Again, if any one wishes to make a coat, is he not wise if he takes cloth for it, and foolish, if he takes paper? Is not a man who marries a pious woman, wise, and one that marries an impious one, foolish? Are there not innumerable instances in the affairs of human life, similar to these? You cannot, by any means, persuade us, that all this is darkness. Even Christ himself, Matt. 7, 24, 26, indicates that this is light, where he says: "Whosoever heareth these sayings of mine, and doeth them, I will liken him unto a wise man, which built his house upon a rock. * * * And every one that heareth these sayings of mine, and doeth them not, shall be likened unto a foolish man, which built his house upon the sand." Now, if the man who built his house upon a rock, is in darkness, who then builds wisely? Again, Luke 16, 8, Christ, speaking of the unjust steward, who had wasted his lord's goods, says, that he had acted wisely in pursuing the course which he took in regard to his lord's debtors. And St. Paul also says to the Corinthians, 1 Cor. 11, 5, 14: Nature itself teaches that a woman should not pray in the church, with her head uncovered.

Answer: This is all true; but here it is necessary to make a distinction between God and men, or between spiritual and temporal things. In temporal things and things which pertain to men, man is sufficiently rational. For these he needs no other light, but reason. Therefore, God does not teach us in the Scriptures how to build houses, to make clothing, to marry, to wage wars, to sail upon the seas, &c. For these, our natural light is sufficient. But in divine things, that is, things which pertain to God, and which must be so performed as to be acceptable to him, and secure happiness for us, our nature is so entirely blind, as to be unable to recognize them in the slightest degree.

It is so presumptuous as to plunge into these things, like a blind horse; but all its determinations and conclusions are, as certainly as God lives, false and erroneous. Here it acts like a man who builds on sand, like one who takes cobwebs for a garment, as Isaiah says, Isaiah 59, 6. Here it takes sand in the place of meal, do make bread. Here it sows wind, and reaps the whirlwind, as Hosea 8, 7, says. Here it measures the air with a spoon, carries light into the cellar in a tray, and weighs flames in a balance, performing all kinds of nonsense, that ever happened, or that can ever be devised. For all its efforts or designs are intended as services to God, when at the same time they are not.

But if you inquire of nature, what must be done to please God and to be saved, it replies: Ay, you must build churches, cast bells, institute masses, observe vigils, make chalices, pyxes, images, and ornaments, burn candles, pray a certain length of time, fast in honor of St. Catharine, become a priest or a monk, go to Rome and to St. Jacob, wear shirts made out of hairs, torture yourself, &c. These are good works, and proper ways to salvation. But if you ask how it knows that these things are acceptable to God, it is unable to give any other answer, but that it thinks they are. This is sheer imagination; yes, it is gloom and darkness besides. This is what Isaiah calls darkness and gross darkness, into which all who do not accept that divine light, must fall, and it is impossible for them to do anything that is right in the sight of God.

Nothing is more offensive to God, than to regard such gross darkness as light, instead of darkness, to reject the true light, and to persecute or put to death all who defend the truth in regard to this important matter. From that source arises all idolatry. The Jews had their Baal, Moloch, Ashtaroth, Camon Peor, and similar idols without number; so that Jeremiah, 2, 28, says: "According to the number of thy cities, are thy gods;" and Hosea, 10, 1: "According to the the multitude of his fruit he hath increased the altars;" and again, Isaiah 2, 8: "Their land is also full of idols."

Now, all this was nothing but divine service, by which they presumed to serve the true God. For this reason, the Prophets, who censured these things, were slain by them, as destroyers of the divine service and as blasphemers against God. But it was a service of God, instituted according to the dictates of nature, and not according to the commandment of God. In the service of God, he is the light himself, and will accept nothing else but that which he has commanded and instituted. We read, Lev. 10, 2, that Nadab and Abihu, sons of Aaron, were consumed before the altar by fire, when at the same time they were priests called of God, and had done nothing more than put strange, unconsecrated fire into the censer,—a thing which was not in accordance with the commandment of God; so little will he tolerate us to recognize and style that divine service, which he has not so styled. What else does an individual do, who presumes to do this, but make an idol out of God? He imagines that God entertains the same opinion that he does, and forms, at will, in his own mind, a God for himself, presuming that God must and will be delighted with anything which he may devise. This is nothing else but changing and perverting the will and intention of God to suit our will and intention. This is mocking God, and regarding him as a spectre, a wooden image, which we may change and fashion at pleasure; a thing which he will not allow by any means. For he will not permit us to make an image of him, or an idol, as is evident from the first commandment; nor will he allow us to misuse his name, as is clear from the second commandment. Both of these commandments are just and right. Hence it is impossible for the dictates of nature to please God in that way. No, it is the highest presumption on earth, and of all things the most offensive to him.

In view of this distinction between God and man, there can be no difficulty in distinguishing the true light from the false. Whatever is not commanded of God, should be avoided in the most careful manner, although angels or saints order and institute it. The greater portion of all the laws of the Pope and the orders of the ecclesiastics must be false. For the greater part of them are nothing but human devices, in regard to external works, which God has not commanded; and idolatry prevails more in the world now than it did in the days of the Jews; and yet persons presume to serve God in this way, when at the same time it is wrong in every respect.

Divine light teaches us to trust and believe in God, to leave all things to him, freely to submit to his workings and operations, to accept, perform, and bear all that may present itself, in his providence, and to serve our neighbor during the whole course of our lives. In such faith there is no difference in works; all are alike. In this state of mind we may well serve God, by erecting buildings, by planting, threshing, and performing all manner of external works. For all these proceed properly in divine light, in faith. This, God himself regards as his service and as a divine course of conduct.

In regard to this, however, nature and reason know so little, that they proceed to condemn such faith as error and heresy, accepting the works which they discover in the beloved saints and their orders, unwilling and unable to perceive that the saints did these works under the influence of divine light and faith which they condemn. Thus they make for themselves an idol out of the examples of the saints, persisting continually and irrevocably in their blindness and idolatry.

Hence the wholesome instruction of Solomon, Prov. 3, 5: "Lean not unto thine own understanding;" again, Prov. 3, 7: "Be not wise in thine own eyes;" which St. Paul, Rom. 12, 16, introduces: "Be not wise in your own conceits."

In their commencement, the papal laws also inculcate this principle, but for the purpose of terrifying all the world by these declarations of the Scriptures, so that no one may reject his foolish laws, in consequence of this doctrine,—a thing which would be just and necessary. His object is to captivate all persons, so that they may regard him alone as wise, and follow him, regardless of the wisdom of God. His laws consist of mere human devices, directly in opposition to this doctrine of Solomon and St. Paul. He forbids every one to think for himself; and yet he enforces in an abominable manner his own opinions throughout the world. But Solomon does not intend that we should be taught by ourselves, or by any human reason and devices, but of God alone, our Lord. Whatever is not taught or inculcated by him, we should avoid as darkness. For he neither can nor will allow in divine things an assistant master or teacher: he himself intends to be the light and teacher, so that our faith may be pure and clear in divine matters.

In temporal things, however, in which you may learn from a carpenter to construct a building, you may act otherwise: You may learn to paint from a painter, from a shoemaker, to make shoes; from a scribe, to write: but to serve God and to know how this and all other works become good, you learn not from man, but from God alone; for God teaches you to believe in him and to love your neighbor in all your works. Men teach you to work without faith, and to love yourself only, so as to forget God and your neighbor.

This, you will perceive, is the meaning of Isaiah, where he says: "Behold, the darkness shall cover the earth, and gross darkness the people." He cannot be understood as speaking of literal darkness,—the sun with its light continued as it was,—but of darkness which is opposed to the light, in regard to which he says: "Thy light is come," and * * * "the Lord shall arise upon thee." Now those upon whom the Lord does not rise and shine, are in darkness; so that darkness here is nothing else but unbelief and natural reason; precisely as the light is Christ, or faith in Christ, through which Christ dwells in the heart; as St. Paul says, Eph. 3, 17. Thus, too, earth here does not mean the natural earth,—this did not become darker through Christ,—but earthly men who neither believe, nor accept Christ through the Gospel, but rather continue in their earthly imaginations and natural light; as Isaiah explains himself, saying: "Gross darkness shall cover the people."

But what does this imply? Were not persons in darkness previous to the advent of Christ? If he brought the light through the Gospel, how does it happen that darkness then first appeared? We must bear in mind here, that Isaiah is speaking of the Jewish people only. These he divides into two classes. The one enjoys the light, and the other is overwhelmed in darkness; as was really the case. For this reason he says: "The earth * * and the people." So too David, Ps. 2, 1, says concerning them: "Why do the" people speak vainly "against the Lord, and against his anointed." Now the whole people of Israel awaited Christ, and from the shadows of the law through Christ, they enjoyed light. But matters seemed to be reversed. The greater portion of them fell, and merged deeper into darkness.

For, previous to the advent of Christ, there was a light, the law, in which Christ was promised to them. But when he came and fulfilled the law, they still continued to hang upon the law, and to await his approach, so that in this way, they seem to have lost the design and intention of the law, which they once had; and it happened with them, as it does with a person who leaves far behind him the light which he should have before him, or which he once had before him. He thus goes deeper into darkness, without light. A person who has his eyes fixed on a light before him, no matter how far it may be off from him, may see indeed whither he is going; but one who leaves it behind him and turns his back upon it, is overwhelmed in darkness.

In this way the Jews act, who have the law, which shines upon Christ who is already come, behind them; they reject its light which falls upon Christ, with the expectation, that it will shine for them upon another Christ who is yet to come. But here there is no light; this will amount to nothing; the law points to no other Christ.

For this reason he says: The earth is covered not only with darkness, but with gross darkness. In this way he indicates not only the blindness of this wretched people, but also their gross darkness; so that this light does not rise upon them. The Gospel is not preached to the Jews; they are unwilling to hear it. Therefore Christ, the light, does not rise upon them through the Gospel; and hence they remain covered in their unbelief without preaching and instruction; as God. Isaiah 5, 6, says in regard to this: "I will also command the clouds that they rain no more rain upon it;" that is, no preacher shall preach to them concerning Christ. This you perceive is not only being in darkness, in unbelief, but being covered with it; so as to hear no preaching, through which the light might rise upon them. O, terrible prophecy and example for all who reject the Gospel!

Yet, "Upon thee,' says he, "shall the Lord arise." The whole nation was not blinded. From it the better and greater portion of the Christian Church is derived; the Apostles, Evangelists, and numerous saints.— These are those who are neither in darkness nor covered with it. To them the Lord himself was preached, and so preached that his glory appears or is seen in them. He does not merely say: The glory of the Lord is risen upon thee, but that it shall be seen upon thee; so that it is not only revealed to them,—a thing which occurred also to the unbelieving portion, —but it appeared to them, and they know him and his glory. They persevered in these. Therefore, the rising of this light, that is, the Gospel, was not taken away from them.

This seems to be the meaning of Isaiah: This part of the text refers to the fruits of the preached Gospel, and the first, to the preaching of the Gospel. The Gospel arose, and admonished all to arise. But afterwards some became so hardened and overwhelmed in darkness, that the light did not arise upon them again, neither was it preached to them any more. Others were enlightened, and continued in that rising.

This always has been the case, even

to this day, in regard to the preaching of Christ and the Gospel. Some accept it, and are enlightened; others, the greater portion, condemn it as error, and turn away from it. For this reason it is, that they are overwhelmed in their unbelief; the Gospel is no longer proclaimed or preached to them, nor are they disposed to hear it: and hence they must, indeed, be covered up against the rising of this light.

No one should be astonished at this. The Scripture is unchangeable:—"Darkness shall cover the earth, and gross darkness the people." If this was the case with the chosen people, the Jews, the natural seed of Abraham; how much more may it be the case with us heathens, descendants from another blood and nature. We see even now, that no one is allowed to preach to them any thing that the Pope and the papists have condemned; they will not tolerate it. Therefore they remain covered up in their darkness; they have their own preaching, with which they protect and conceal their own blindness; and it happens to them as they wish, like it did to the Jews.

"And the Gentiles shall come to thy light, and Kings to the brightness of thy rising."

When the greater part of the Jews were unwilling to give place for the fruits of the Gospel, and continued in their blindness,—it could not exist without fruit,—it broke forth in all the world, and gathered in the Gentiles. This is what Isaiah says here, and it is clear in itself from the fulfillment. For the heathen nations embraced Christianity, and walked in Christ, the true light, through genuine faith. This fruit so increased that even kings, the most exalted on earth, humbled themselves under this faith. This circumstance was revealed, in order that preachers might not be puffed up when they convert kings or any one else, as if they had accomplished it themselves. God foresaw it all, caused it to be revealed, and promised the Gospel besides.

This declaration of Isaiah had a vigorous sway in former times, when many of noble rank and position among the Gentiles embraced Christianity. Now, however, they are so perverted by the Turks and the Pope, that this declaration seems to have little effect; and, strange to say, even other heathen nations have been perverted by them. But it is revealed, that Antichrist shall mislead all the world, that Christ restored.

But what is implied by the phrase, "To the brightness of thy rising." He styles Christ the glory or brightness of the rising, that is, of the Gospel, because the Gospel will be continually enforced and preached, so that it will always be rising up against human doctrines which are, in the highest degree, dangerous to kings and those in high places. Upon these the evil Spirit seizes first with his perversions and human doctrines, and having these, he can easily drag along with them the common, illiterate masses. In this way, the Pope first seized upon the kings and princes, and with them the masses. This he could not have accomplished, had the Gospel continued to rise; nor was any such thing effected, when it first arose. But now it is set, and human doctrines have arisen. Here, no one walks in God's light.

"Lift up thine eyes round about, and see: all they gather themselves together, they come to thee: thy sons shall come from afar, and thy daughters shall be nursed at thy side."

Here he begins to enumerate the countries, in which Gentiles are converted to the faith. And from the fact that he calls upon Jerusalem to lift up her eyes round about, and see, it is easy to perceive that he is speaking of spiritual sons and daughters, men and women who believe in Christ; and hence, too, their coming and assembling must be understood in a spiritual manner. They did not literally come to Jerusalem, but they believed in that light which had arisen upon her, and which was round about her, with their hearts and spirits. For no one can come to this light, by means of his feet; else, all those at Jerusalem would have been enlightened. The greater part of them, however, remained in blindness and darkness, as already stated.

Now, if the light is spiritual, the conclusion forces itself upon us, that the children, the coming and assembling are also spiritual. But for the force of this conclusion, we would have to understand the children and the assembling, not in a spiritual, but in a real, physical sense, as the words literally imply. But now, since the light is spiritual, the coming and the assembling must be spiritual; so, too, the children must be spiritual. For the natural children and seed of Abraham, did not, in consequence of the fact that they were of his flesh and blood, come to this light, but, because they were his spiritual children; as it is stated in the preceding Epistle.

The phrase, "Thy sons shall come from afar," also indicates that reference is had to spiritual children from among the heathens. The apostles, Peter and Paul, speak of the heathens as being far off, and of the Jews as being near. Eph. 2, 13: "Ye who sometimes were far off are made nigh by the blood of Christ;" again, v. 17: "Came and preached peace to you which were afar off, and to them that were nigh." The reason for such representation seems to be this: The Jews had the law and the promises of God concerning Christ, and the heathens did not have them. Now, since the heathens neither are nor can be the natural children of Abraham, or Jerusalem, and Isaiah still speaks of them here, he must certainly have reference to spiritual children.

In like manner, the Jerusalem,* which he admonishes to lift up her eyes and see, is not the material or natural Jerusalem,—the natural Jerusalem is not the mother of these children, but a murderess of the mother and children and father,—but, it is the spiritual mother; that is, the assembly of the Apostles and all holy Christians of the Jewish nation, which assembly is the Christian Church; and it is called Jerusalem, because it arose and assembled in that city, and thence extended throughout the world.

* B. Or the Jewish nation.

There had to be some special place or location in the world, for the beginning of the Gospel and Christianity. This took place in Jerusalem, in the midst of the worst enemies of the Gospel and Christianity.

Now, the design of Isaiah seems to be this: Look round about thee, upon the four quarters of the world; so great and broad will I make thee, that thou shalt be in all the world, and thy children shall dwell everywhere. All these words were designed to console the first Christians at Jerusalem, in consequence of the fact that their number was small and they were despised, as well as in the midst of their enemies, who should have been their best friends; as it follows in this same chapter of Isaiah. It seemed foolish for so small a band to undertake a matter so great and novel, and to raise itself up in opposition to such overwhelming masses.

The Jews thought they would soon exterminate them, and check their efforts; they commenced their work of slaughter, persecution, and expulsion, everywhere, presuming that it would be an easy matter to root out these poor, impotent people. Fool-like, they did not see that in this way they fanned the fire already enkindled, and scattered it throughout the world.— Their raging and raving only contributed the more to the fulfillment of this declaration of Isaiah and of the will of God, against themselves. By means of this persecution, Christians were driven into all the world, and the Gospel was extended, so that everywhere the sons and daughters of Jerusalem were gathered to this light.

It is in every respect characteristic of divine mastership to accomplish an object most successfully, through the instrumentality of an enemy. Even by their raging to exterminate the word and people of God, persons exterminate themselves, and only perpetuate the word and people of God; so that it is advantageous and profitable to have enemies and persecutors, for the sake of the faith and word of God. Incalculable consolations and advantages result from these. In regard to this, it is said, Ps. 2, 1: "Why do the heathen rage, and the people imagine a vain thing" against Christ? As if he should say, They strive and rage to exterminate him, without seeing that, in this way, they even strengthen him.

Thus too, here, Isaiah says to his beloved Jerusalem: Fear not, grieve not, cast not your eyes down, but lift them up joyfully, and look round about; be not misled by the fact that your nearest relatives are your worst enemies, that they seek to exterminate you, and regard you as too mean to dwell in their midst; let them rush on and go. Where they kill one of you, a thousand shall rise in his place. If they drive one of you away, he shall bring many thousands in return. If they extinguish the Gospel at one place, it will rise at ten other places, until, independent of their thanks and consent, you shall have sons and daughters everywhere in place of those who should be your sons and daughters, and who are your enemies; so that you shall ultimately be strengthened and multiplied, and they shall be diminished and exterminated; the evil designs which they wished to heap upon you, shall fall on them, and you shall enjoy what they begrudged you. We clearly perceive how all this was accomplished and fulfilled.

"Then thou shalt see, and flow together, and thine heart shall fear, and be enlarged; because the abundance of the sea shall be converted unto thee, the forces of the Gentiles shall come unto thee."

By "the abundance of the sea," we must understand here, not its natural water, but the country lying and the people dwelling along the sea; precisely as we might say in regard to the Rhine, that the whole Rhine has risen up, that is, the country and the people on the Rhine. It is customary in the Scriptures, although there are many and various seas, to call the Mediterranean sea, the Sea, without any surname; whilst the Red sea is designated by its surname.

Geographers call the Mediterranean sea by that name, because it lies in the middle of the country, rising from the West; on its left are Spain, France, Italy, Greece, and Asia, as far as Sicily; on the right, Africa and Egypt, as far as Palestine. Thus it is touched on both sides by great and powerful countries and nations, and it is full of islands, as Candia, Rhodes, Cyprus; now, for the most part, under the control of the Turks. The Mediterranean sea is called in the Scriptures the Sea; and the Jewish country lies on the West; Palestine at the end of the sea, and the Jewish country touches Palestine on the East.

Now the people on this sea, and especially those on the left side, are called by the general name, Gentiles, in the Scriptures. Those on the right side and towards the East are designated in the Scriptures by particular names. To these Gentiles we belong, and all who live towards the North, on the left side of the sea. Hence, St. Paul, 2 Tim. 1, 11, and in other places, calls himself, "A preacher and an apostle of the Gentiles." To this section of the country on the left side of the sea he preached and addressed all his Epistles, not having gone beyond the sea, on the right.

To these Gentiles Isaiah refers, when he says, "The abundance of the sea shall be converted unto thee, the forces of the Gentiles shall come unto thee." The abundance of the sea and the forces of the Gentiles are the same thing; and he shows himself, that we must not understand water by the abundance of the sea, but people.

Thus too, "Forces of the Gentiles" does not mean their strength or power. Of what advantage would these be in the Church? But it has reference to the great multitudes. We are in the habit of saying in regard to a great quantity of money, Here is a power of money; that is, a great pile of money. So here the forces of the Gentiles, that is, a great mass or multitude of Gentiles. We also call a lord mighty, when he has a great country, much land and many people.

This declaration of Isaiah was fulfilled for the most part through the instrumentality of St. Paul, our apostle. Through his preaching the abundance of the Sea was converted, and the forces of the Gentiles came to the faith. All this was said to show who the sons and daughters are, that were to come from afar, namely, the abundance of the Gentiles on the great Mediterranean, converted by St. Paul.

From this it appears again, that this coming is not to be understood in a strictly literal sense. How could such a mass and force of people assemble in the single town of Jerusalem, to say nothing of their dwelling and remaining there? He says the abundance of the sea shall be converted or turned around; precisely as when we walk and turn our faces or bodies around. This also shows that the Gentiles were not to come to Jerusalem physically, but their turning around is their coming. Previously they were turned to the world, but now they are changed, and turned to the Church.

In like manner does he call the abundance of the sea, in Hebrew, *Hamon*, which implies mass or abundance. To this, doubtless, the promise of God to Abraham, that he should be a father of many nations or Gentiles, refers. For thus God spoke to him, Gen. 17, 5: "Neither shall thy name any more be called Abram, but thy name shall be Abraham; for a father of many nations have I made thee."

Here God adds the first letter of the word Hamon to Abram, making out of it Abraham, and assigning his own reason for it, saying: He should be a father, *Hamon*, that is, of the abundance of the Gentiles; precisely as if he had said with Isaiah: He shall be a father, Hamon, of the Sea, a father of the abundance or multitude of the Gentiles. Hence St. Paul urges in his Epistles, that through faith the Gentiles are the children and seed of Abraham, according to the promise of God. To this Isaiah had reference, desiring to describe the fulfillment of this promise. At first he was called Abram, a father of the high, or high father, and afterwards he was called Abraham, a father of the abundance or multitude of the Gentiles, so that his highness and exaltation were completed in the Gentiles.

But why does he use such a multiplicity of words here: "Then thou shalt see, and flow* together, and thine heart shall fear [wonder,] and be enlarged?" What is implied by *see, break forth, wonder,* and *enlarged?* They are terms of consolatory promise. It is customary, in the Hebrew language, to use the word, *see*, to express the state of mind, when the will and desires of any one are accomplished, as Ps. 54, 7: "And mine eye hath seen his desire upon mine enemies;" that is, I shall see in them what I long since desired to see, namely, their suppression and the perpetuation of the truth. Again, Ps. 37, 34: "When the wicked are cut off, thou shalt see it;" that is, then thou shalt see what thou didst desire. Again, Ps. 35, 21: "Yea, they opened their mouth wide against me, and said, Aha, aha, our eye hath seen it;" that is, Aye, how pleasant this is; we long since desired to see it. Thus, here, too: "Then thou shalt see;" that is, thou art now a poor, little, impotent band; thine enemies see what they desire to see, and thou desirest to see thyself great and numerous. But this thou seest not yet; thou must see what thou desirest not, for a short time; then thou too shalt see, and they shall not see. When the multitude of the Sea shall be turned to thee, then shalt thou see what thou didst long desire to see; and they shall not see what they so ardently desired. Thou must have patience for a while, and not see; thou must endure apparent insignificance, and bear the cross.

This manner of speaking is consistent with the principles of nature. Our eyes naturally turn away from that which we do not wish to see, so as not to behold it. But, to that which we desire, they readily turn with admiration and pleasure. Hence, the proverb: "Where the heart is, the eyes also look." Thus, we may well say, He does not see, that is, it does not please him. For, of all the organs, the eyes are the most sig-

---

* B. Or, break forth.

nificant index of the pleasures or displeasures of the heart.

The word *flow*, also has reference to this pleasure and consolation. It is customary to say, in regard to a thing that is delightful and easily moved, It goes of itself. That which is soft, is pliable and yielding; but that which is dry, hard, and rough, is unyielding and inflexible, and is attended with difficulty and displeasure. Thus Isaiah wishes to say, Thou shalt see the pleasure of thy heart, in consequence of which, thou wilt be so delighted and filled with pleasure, as to flow, and do and endure everything with joy, pleasure, and alacrity, without trouble or displeasure. This is the fruit of the Spirit, resulting from the consolation of the divine promise. This renders persons mild, joyful, and flowing, with whom all things go well.

In the third place, how does the phrase, Thy heart shall fear, or be amazed, accord with the idea of pleasure? The real, the great pleasures which shall arise above our desires and expectations, will bring with them fear, or amazement, because they transcend all our expectations. When through the preaching of St. Peter, the Holy Spirit fell on the Gentiles, Cornelius and his, Luke, Acts 10, 45, says; "They were astonished, as many as came with Peter, because that on the Gentiles was also poured out the gift of the Holy Ghost;"—a thing which they did not in the least expect. Thus, too, Isaiah says, Jerusalem, in consequence of great joy, shall be amazed in her heart, or filled with fear, because such a large multitude of Gentiles shall unite with such a poor, little, persecuted flock.

In the fourth place, "Thy heart shall be enlarged." We may readily infer that this phrase has reference to true greatness, security, and freedom. These result from the consolation of the Spirit and the joy of the heart, which arise, when the operations of God upon us, transcend our expectations and desires. This is his manner of operating, as the text in Isaiah teaches, and as St. Paul also asserts, Eph. 3, 20. God always does "exceeding abundantly above all that we ask or think." Thus, too, he acted in regard to this, his little flock or band which he permitted to be persecuted and degraded, that it seemed to be destitute of life and influence; and yet, almost before any one could look around, it had spread throughout the world, and increased in strength and influence, surpassing all its enemies. This is astonishing in our eyes.

"The multitude of camels shall cover thee, the dromedaries of Midian and Ephah; and they from Sheba shall come: they shall bring gold and incense; and they shall show forth the praises of the Lord."

Isaiah having spoken of the Gentiles, who came from the abundance of the sea, West of Jerusalem, now speaks of the people or nations that come from the East. Midian, Ephah, Sheba, and the people who travel with camels, lie East of Jerusalem. We read, Gen. 25, 2-4, that Abraham had six sons by his third wife, Keturah,—Zimran, and Jokshan, and Medan, and Midian, and Ishbak, and Shuah. The fourth son, Midian, begat Ephah and Epher. Hence we have the two, Midian and Ephah, of whom Isaiah here speaks. Again, the second son, Jokshan, begat Sheba, and Dedan. Again, Gen. 10, 1, 6, 7, we read that Noah begat Shem, Ham, and Japheth. Ham begat Cush and his brethren. Cush begat Raamah. Raamah begat Sheba and Dedan, names similar to those of the sons of Abraham.

Now, it is and will remain doubtful whether Isaiah refers here to Sheba who sprang from Abraham, or Sheba who sprang from Ham. This, however, is of little importance. It happens on earth, that one nation drives another away, and occupies its country; like individual houses and lands in towns are changed and sold, and pass from one lord to another. I have already stated that the countries East of Jerusalem have various and particular names; they are not designated by the general name, Gentiles, like the countries on the Mediterranean sea. They have different names, Chedar, Midian, Ishmael, Nabajoth,

Ammon, Edom, Moab, Sheba, according to their primary lords. Moses, Gen. 25, 2, 3, 4, 6, says that Abraham separated his sons by his wife Keturah, from Isaac, and sent them towards the East. Hence, it is certain,* that they occupied many of those countries, and that Midian, Ephah, and Sheba became the chief countries.

According to Latin and Greek geographers, these nations or people are called Arabs, and they divide Arabia into three parts,—*Arabia deserta, Arabia petrea, Arabia felix;*—that is, desert Arabia, Arabia the stony, and fertile Arabia. Desert Arabia lies between Egypt and Judea, towards the East, through which the children of Israel were led by Moses; and this section only is called in the Hebrew language Arabia. For, in the Hebrew, Arabia means desert. Arabia the stony, touches Jordan towards the East; it is a large country. But Isaiah does not speak here of either of these.

The fertile and greater Arabia, lying far from Judea, on the other side of desert Arabia and stony Arabia, is called Sheba in the Hebrew; and it is a matter of no importance, whether it derives its name from the son of Abraham or from the son of Ham. Ephah is a part of this fertile Arabia. From this Arabia, or Sheba, the Turk Mohammed came, and his sepulchre is in the town Mecca, in that country. It is called rich, or fertile Arabia, because it abounds with precious gold and noble fruits; and, especially in frankincense, which is produced in no other portion of the world. This, with many other costly spices, the Queen of Sheba, in that country, brought to King Solomon. 1 Kings 10, 1.† Of this Sheba and Ephah Isaiah speaks here. These people used camels and the like. Midian, however, was their neighbor, and bordered with them on the Red sea, between Egypt and fertile Arabia.

Isaiah means that so many camels and dromedaries shall come out of that country, that the great multitude

---
* A. Credible.
† A. Now the Sultan occupies it, instead of the Turk.

will, even cover the country, as a great army covers the earth, where it moves and encamps. Not that the camels and dromedaries will come alone, but the people sitting and riding on them. He explains himself, when he says the multitude of camels and dromedaries shall come out of Midian and Ephah, by adding, and indicating people: "All they from Sheba shall come: they shall bring gold and incense; and they shall show forth the praises of the Lord;" as if he should say, The people from Midian and Ephah, shall come in such great numbers, that the great abundance and multitude of camels and dromedaries shall cover thy country. And why do I speak of Midian and Ephah only, parts and parcels of Arabia?—even all and every part of fertile Arabia shall come.

These questions may arise here:—Has this reference to natural camels and dromedaries? Did they really, literally bring gold and incense? Did all fertile Arabia really come? It is true, we do not read that any of these things really occurred in this way. Although, now, many explain this passage as having reference to the Magi, wise men, who came from that country after the birth of Christ, as the Gospel says; yet, their number was so small, that it cannot be said in regard to them, that their camels covered the country, on account of their great multitude. Nor were they the whole of the inhabitants of Sheba; they were only a small part of the people. We must not, however, resort to spiritual interpretation, unless necessity requires it.

But, since all this did not occur in a strictly literal sense; nor is it likely or credible that it ever will; since it is inconsistent with the principles of nature, that all they from Sheba shall come in a physical manner to Jerusalem,—a country of people so great and powerful come to one city;—since the preceding part of this chapter of Isaiah refers merely to spiritual light, the Gospel, faith, and to spiritual coming and assembling, and since the coming to the Church has no reference to the person of Christ, physically, we shall adhere to this view, and we feel satisfied that the causes and facts are sufficient to compel us to admit that this part of the chapter also refers to spiritual coming. Thus, the Christian Church shall see, flow together, be amazed, and filled with joy, when not only the abundance of the Sea, West, but also the richest and greatest people, or nation, Arabia, shall be gathered to her from the East.

Besides all this, the fact, that there are many things declared in this chapter that cannot be understood as referring to a literal coming, forces this conclusion upon us. As for instance, when it is said, v. 7: "All the flocks of Kedar shall be gathered together unto thee; the rams of Nebaioth shall minister unto thee: they shall come up with acceptance on mine altar."* Again, v. 10: "The sons of strangers shall build up thy walls, and their kings shall minister unto thee," &c. These things have not happened nor will they ever occur in a physical sense.

Therefore, this must be the meaning of Isaiah: The people of this country, Arabia, shall come in great numbers to the faith and the Gospel, and offer themselves up, with all they have, their camels, dromedaries, gold, incense, &c. For where there are true Christians, they will give themselves up, and all that they have, to the service of Christ and his followers; as we see even among ourselves, that large donations are made to the Church, and every one gives himself up, with all that he has, freely and willingly, to Christ and his followers; as St. Paul also writes in regard to the Philippians and Corinthians, 2 Cor. 8, 1.

This Epistle includes the greatest, the most numerous, powerful, and richest nations or people on earth,— the abundance of the Sea and the forces of the Gentiles. This is almost the heart of the people on earth, in regard to numbers and power. Arabia is regarded [...] noblest nation. B[...] that all the world [...] to the faith. For th[...] the gold, the ince[...] could be understo[...] strictly literal sense, [...] bringing must still [...] regard to the spi[...] But what the spirit[...] shall leave for the Go[...]

The phrase, "All th[...] does not imply that [...] came believers, but [...] country became Chris[...] there were some in it t[...] lieve; precisely as we [...] to Germany, because t[...] ish customs no longer [...] whole country is now [...] though the smaller p[...] true Christians, yet fo[...] these, all are called Ch[...] too, the whole Jewish [...] called the people of [...] and yet many of the[...] idols.

Finally he says, "T[...] forth the praises of th[...] true, the special work o[...] is, to confess his sins a[...] to show forth the grace [...] God in him. For, no [...] not see the grace of [...] light, can show forth th[...] honor of God. But no [...] cleaves to, and apprec[...] light, works, efforts, a[...] perceive the grace of [...] and continues, in his ol[...] Adamic nature. He ri[...] this light; he prefers [...] his own praises. Isa[...] plauds those who come [...] because they are true C[...] show forth the praises [...] doubtless, was the ha[...] the influences of this [...] and the Gospel.

END OF VOLU[...]

---

* A. What kind of an altar and offering would this be?

www.ingramcontent.com/pod-product-compliance
Lightning Source LLC
Chambersburg PA
CBHW032156160426
43197CB00008B/945